RUSH

RUSH

The Autobiography

EBURY
PRESS

3 5 7 9 10 8 6 4

First published in 2008 by Ebury Press, an imprint of Ebury Publishing
A Random House Group company
This edition published 2009

The Random House Group Limited Reg. No. 954009

Addresses for companies within the Random House Group can be found at
www.randomhouse.co.uk

A CIP catalogue record for this book is available from the British Library

The Random House Group Limited supports The Forest Stewardship Council
(FSC), the leading international forest certification organisation. All our titles
that are printed on Greenpeace approved FSC certified paper carry the FSC
logo. Our paper procurement policy can be found at
www.rbooks.co.uk/environment

Printed in the UK by CPI Cox & Wyman, Reading, RG1 8EX

ISBN 9780091928063

To buy books by your favourite authors and register for offers visit
www.rbooks.co.uk

This book is dedicated to Tracy – the love of my life – and to our wonderful sons, Jonathan and Daniel. All you have given me is a large part of me forever.

Acknowledgements

I would like to express my sincere thanks to the following who, by way of expertise, friendship or recollection of events where my own memory was a little hazy have helped this book come in to being: Julian Alexander and all at Lucas Alexander Whitley; Ken Barlow, Andrew Goodfellow and all at Ebury Press; Ken and Jean Bolam, Phill Dann and Dean Statham; Liverpool FC; *Liverpool Echo*; Arthur Montford; Dave and Christine Scott; John Turnock; the Football Association of Wales.

When I decided to commit my story to book form I contacted my friend and football writer, Les Scott, to make sense of and bring to order my many typed and scribbled pages. Les has collaborated on the autobiographies of, amongst others, Sir Stanley Matthews, Jimmy Greaves, George Best, Gordon Banks, Tommy Docherty and Tommy Smith and is also author of *End To End Stuff – The Essential Football Book*. When it comes to football writing I put him up there with the very best there is and was delighted he was available to collaborate with me. Les and I met regularly to structure my story, add 'colour' to my notes and apply factual detail. He put up with me ringing him at unsociable hours from the Far East when I had just remembered an anecdote about a certain player or detail of a game I felt was of significance. He kept the 'lid' on everything and pulled it all together, forever saying, 'No problem, we'll get there in the end'. That we did is in no small way down to Les, to whom I convey my sincere thanks for a job superbly done.

For Jane, Lauren, Ruby and Charley.

Ian Rush
2008

Contents

CHAPTER ONE

Happy Days

They would tumble down the Kop, gripping the shoulders of the person in front, a sea of ecstatic faces. Those who had been evicted from their favourite spot by sheer force of numbers pressing behind them left gaps on the terrace, like holes in some gigantic pebble-dashed wall. When order was restored and everyone settled again it was strange to see how haphazardly they had been rearranged, like jigsaw pieces thrown back in the box.

There was not a replica shirt in sight. In 1983 scarves were the way the fans showed their support, and just about every one of them wore a Liverpool scarf. Before kick-off, or following a goal, those on the Kop would stretch their scarves above their heads and slowly and rhythmically wave them from side to side. From down on the pitch I felt as if I were watching some tribal South Seas ritual.

But when Liverpool scored the noise was deafening. I'd see the ball home, glance up, and it was as though I had just turned some street corner into the teeth of a howling gale. I could feel the invisible force slam into my face.

I didn't run towards the fans, gyrate my hips or perform a little celebratory dance. Nor did I sprint across the pitch and then fling myself prostrate across the turf awaiting the congratulations of my teammates. On seeing the ball hit the net I would carry on running for a few paces and raise the finger of one hand in acknowledgement of the cheers. Of course, I was always smiling, but not just because I was happy, though I certainly was. The smile was one of contentment because I was continuing to do the job I was paid to do and loved to do – scoring goals.

When the likes of Kenny Dalglish and Graeme Souness came running towards me I would often laugh. Laugh out of sheer amazement that after probing away at the opposition defence, how simple it had been in the end to breach them. Sometimes my amazement was the result of Kenny having threaded another simple but beautifully timed and weighted pass into space, that I had somehow anticipated this happening, got on the end of it, kept my cool and beaten the goalkeeper by passing the ball through the gap he had left between himself and the post. Occasionally I would think, 'Surely this level of football demands greater strategies to beat defences?' but, as the old saying goes, football is a simple game.

Of course, it is difficult to do the simple things because there are eleven players trying to prevent you and your team doing just that. The great players, like Kenny Dalglish, Graeme Souness or Stevie Gerrard, can produce the simple but highly effective play amidst the heat of battle. It's what makes them great.

At the time I never realised I was creating memories for people. Players in their twenties never think of such a thing. I only realise this now due to the sheer number of people, mostly strangers, who have since come up to me and recalled this or that goal with such fondness and relish, invariably recalling the event with more clarity and detail than I ever could.

The fact that I may have contributed to creating a golden memory for someone is a source of great satisfaction to me now. A goal scored against, say, Arsenal, was an important but fleeting moment in my life. At the time it never occurred to me a goal could also be a source of pleasure for years to come for someone watching that day from the stands or terraces. With the passing of time, this has come to be a bonus I never expected from having played football.

The coolness that possessed me when I bore down on goal stayed with me once the ball hit the net. Renowned goal-scorers such as Jimmy Greaves, Roger Hunt, Gary Lineker, Alan Shearer and Michael Owen – dare I say, myself – all have one thing in common as far as having scored a goal is concerned: moderation in celebration. There is, however, another common denominator and it is the key to explaining why I and those mentioned were never given to over-the-top goal celebrations – none of us was afraid to miss.

If I missed, then I knew another opportunity would present itself soon and, given my track record, chances were I would convert it. I worked to the law of averages. Because I was never wracked by fear and tension when confronted with an opportunity in front of goal, when I put the ball in the net I never felt the need to run, jump, dance or dive to relieve my body and mind of pent-up emotion. Scoring goals evoked in me contentment rather than uncontrollable ecstasy. I was happy in the knowledge I still had the knack, that my talent had not deserted me.

I firmly believe my ability to score goals was something I had been born with. I remember once playing for my school, St Mary's Primary, against our bitter rivals Gwynedd Primary. St Mary's had not beaten them for five years. We won 8–4 at their school and I scored all eight. Then we won the return match 6–4 and I scored all six.

No one had taught me how to put a ball in the net. I had no

advice, no coaching, I just seemed able to do it better than other lads. Though I have given the matter a lot of thought I just don't know where this goal-scoring ability came from. Stanley Matthews once said, 'Good coaches have an important role to play in the development of players. They can improve and refine, but they will never define a player, because even the best coach can't put in what God left out.' He would know.

As a striker you develop your ability to read play and to antici-pate when and where the ball is going to arrive. You refine your ability to come off your man, attack space, stay onside, make your-self available, size up the angle, the gap, remain cool and make the most of what time you have in front of goal with the ball at your feet, which, often, is more time than you think. But you have to possess a natural talent for all this in order to improve upon it.

On occasions I have been asked to sum up my career as a player. My initial response is always that I was lucky; lucky to have been born with a knack to score goals; lucky that all the hard graft and dedication was rewarded; lucky to have been given the opportu-nity to demonstrate the talent I possessed at the highest level; lucky that for all the 'close attention' afforded to me during games, I managed to steer clear of a major debilitating injury; lucky to have played in a great team alongside world-class players; and, above all, lucky to have the support of a loving wife and family. That is not to say my career did not have its dark moments. I have grim memories of Hillsborough and Heysel, in particular, tragedies that affected me greatly at the time, and still do.

When you are in your early and mid-twenties you never give a thought to the day when your career will be over. You live for the moment. You are out to prove those who rate you as being right, and the doubters as wrong. You want to carve a career in the game, to make some sort of name for yourself. You enjoy the lifestyle, the camaraderie and friendship of your teammates. Above all, you enjoy your football. It's only when you start approaching thirty you begin to think ahead, waking up to the reality of your situation, that you only have a few years left in the game as a player. You find yourself increasingly working on your strengths as it suddenly dawns you are now at an age whereby you will never acquire devastating new skills. You start to top up the pension fund, put money away, make investments and hope to God the advice you have been given is sound. And if you have anything about you, you begin to think what else you can do in life, because, God willing, in your mid-thirties you have a lot more life to live.

I was fortunate to earn a good living from football and be blessed with the common sense not to fritter it away. I often hear people justify the money footballers earn, particularly the sums earned by today's players, by saying, 'It's a short career. There is no security in football.' What job is secure these days? The days when people such as my dad went to work in the steelworks and stayed there until retirement are, like the steel industry itself, long gone. I had the sense to invest but I was also lucky the advice I was given was sound. Secure? I never felt secure of my place at Liverpool; nobody did, not even Dalglish. Every time I crossed the white line I was conscious of the fact I was playing for the team, the supporters, the club – and my place.

As a player I never gave too much thought to the opposition. At Liverpool we never did. We were supremely confident in our own ability as individuals and as a team. We let the opposition worry about us. I never gave too much thought to who might be marking me. Start doing that and you're on to a loser straight away. I was always of the mind I would be the one creating problems, that my marker or markers had to come up with the solutions, not me. I knew what I had to do – score goals.

When I first arrived at Liverpool I had it in my head that I wanted to be a good team-player. I soon had it drilled into me – by Bob Paisley and his assistants Joe Fagan and Ronnie Moran – that the best way I could contribute to the team was to be selfish in front of goal. So I soon forgot about looking to play teammates in all the time, became selfish and went for goal at every given opportunity.

Before the ball was played I would make my move into space. You have to do that, get going and quick, because Kenny Dalglish or Graeme Souness knew where they were going to play the ball before they received it. They never played the ball into my feet unless they wanted me to hold it up. To carve up a defence the ball has to be played into space. I had to be constantly looking for those spaces and time my runs so that when I received the ball I was OK and not offside.

Some players, like Steve McMahon or Ronnie Whelan, could hurtle around the pitch for ninety minutes, a constant buzz and blur covering every blade of grass at speed. I was never a 'Stamina Sam' nor did I need to be. My job necessitated speed over the first two or three yards and, as Bob Paisley once said, 'That first two or three yards is in your head.'

In my mind's eye I can still see the Kop tumbling forward, hear the roaring noise. What I didn't realise then was that I was not only creating memories for many supporters but for myself, too. Great memories.

I was born in the local hospital in St Asaph in North Wales on 20 October 1961. That's what all the record books and my birth certificate say, but I grew up in nearby Flint. My mum, Doris, and my dad, Francis, were loving parents who worked hard and were good Catholics. I was the second youngest of ten children, and the youngest of my five brothers. I remember in my first few days after joining Liverpool, Ronnie Moran quipped, 'You've joined the best club in the world, son. Players, management, directors and our ten of thousands of supporters, we're all just one big happy family. Like yours, only smaller.'

My dad worked at the nearby Shotton steelworks. With such a large family to provide for he worked impossibly long hours to ensure there was food on the table and heat in the hearth. Mum too worked long and hard. With ten children, her daily life seemed to consist of little more than cooking, cleaning, washing and ironing. We lived in a three-bedroom council house in Woodfield Avenue in which I shared a bedroom with my five brothers. It was one of a street of comfortable homes, council-built in the 1950s, each with a useful strip of garden at the back and rectangle of garden at the front that was for decorative purposes only.

A sign of the times perhaps, but I knew every family in Woodfield Avenue and its surrounding streets, not least because few, if any, families seemed to move house. Plentiful work in the form of the steelworks was on the 'doorstep'; if not in the actual steelworks then in the ancillary industries that depended on them, such as the railways, maintenance or catering supply. Everyone knew one another and the fact that few moved home offered Woodfield Avenue and its neighbouring streets a strong sense of community and stability. And in this stability, we all found security. People felt safe, and even elderly folk had no worries about walking the streets late at night.

With three bedrooms and ten children, bunk beds were the order of the day. With six boys sharing a bedroom, privacy was impossible. Given we were such a large family and we had, as all families do, occasional differences, we had no major bust-ups, which, I would like to think, says much about us as people and is testimony to the fact we were a loving family. Looking back now, I consider my childhood to have been a very happy one.

Sharing a bedroom with my five brothers, however, posed problems. Not least of which was where to put personal belongings, like pencil cases, books and toys, but somehow we managed. When my older brothers started work, the problems of us all sharing the same bedroom were of a different nature.

My two eldest brothers followed Dad to work at Shotton Steelworks. At night, for all they tried to be as quiet as possible, I would be awoken by one of my brothers getting ready for bed after a night out with his mates or girlfriend, and awoken again at five in the morning by another brother getting up to work the 6am till 2pm shift. Once he had departed I would fall back to sleep, only to be soon awoken again by another brother arriving home after having worked the night shift. One of my abiding memories of childhood is that of interrupted sleep.

At the age of five I contracted meningitis. I was immediately admitted to Flint Cottage Hospital where I spent two weeks in a coma in an oxygen tent. Obviously, my recollection of this traumatic event in my life is very vague. Mum told me at one point it was touch and go whether I would survive or not. I spent over a month in hospital. Seemingly, while on the road to recovery, doctors feared I might suffer permanent brain damage. Fortunately that never happened, though try telling Kenny Dalglish that.

Ironically there was a positive result from my being close to death's door. Before my illness I was a small but chubby lad. Having spent over a month in the Cottage Hospital, during which time I hardly ate a thing, I lost a lot of weight. When I was discharged I was very lithe and though I regained my appetite in no time and settled back to eating Mum's regular meals, I never did put the lost weight back on again, which was to serve me well later in life.

When I was growing up in Flint there wasn't much in the way of leisure facilities for young people, so we kids made our own entertainment and for me that meant playing football at every given opportunity. Everyone, I am sure, has at one time or another thought back to their formative years and come up with what they believe to be their earliest memory. My first recollection in life is of kicking a football around in the back garden with my brothers. I was no more than a toddler but this image has remained with me, and my family has confirmed it to be true. Even when my brothers were not around I would go out into the garden on my own and kick a plastic football around.

I was taken with football before I even learned the names of any teams, let alone star players. The first team I ever heard of was Liverpool because my dad was a keen Liverpool supporter, but in early childhood the team that won my support was Everton. Everton won the FA Cup in 1966 and it was around this time, when I was five years of age, that I first learned the names of Everton players such as Alex Young, Derek Temple, Alex Scott, Brian Labone, Gordon West and later, following his transfer from Blackpool, Alan Ball.

Everton became my team because, along with Liverpool, they were the nearest big club to my home. The club often featured on television and, at such a tender age, I liked the colour of their shirts in the photographs I had seen of team line-ups in *Charles Buchan's Football Monthly*. For such tenuous reasons does a small boy lend his support to one club or another. Later in life I would become the player to score the most goals against Everton in Merseyside derbies.

Mum and Dad really did make sacrifices on our behalf. They often went without themselves to ensure their ten children had life's essentials. With so many children to feed and clothe there was literally no money for luxuries. Even as a small boy I understood this, as did all my bothers and sisters. What we were also acutely aware of was the love that we shared as a family. Even as a lad I knew this to be the greatest thing our parents could ever give us.

I can't ever remember having brand-new clothes. Every item I wore was passed-down, having been previously worn by at least two of my brothers. The 'make-do-and-mend' policy of my parents was both necessary and essential. I may not have had new clothes but those I wore were always washed, ironed and pristine. Much later in life, when I was earning a good wage with Liverpool, I was never reckless with money, and I think this had much to do with the respect and appreciation I had for everything I was given when a boy, be it clothing, toys or books.

I was six years old when I was given my first pair of football boots and they were older than I was. Three of my brothers had worn them before me, but that didn't matter. I was so thrilled to have a real pair of boots I wouldn't have minded if all my brothers – and sisters – had worn them. I never had a new pair of football boots until I joined Chester. It never bothered me. As my dad used to say, 'It's not the boots, it's the player wearing them that counts.'

There was a large open field near our house, and it was on this field that I spent countless hours as a boy playing football with friends. I was six years old when I first began to participate in these games. Quite often they were twenty-a-side with jumpers for goalposts. Looking back, these kick-abouts played an important role in the development of us youngsters. There was no referee but we adhered to the rules of the game as we knew them at that time. If there was a foul, a free-kick would be taken. If the foul was committed within what we considered reasonable shooting distance from the goal, there would be a penalty. Nobody ever argued. We knew if we didn't play to the laws of football the game would be spoiled for everyone.

Another advantage to these kick-abouts was our parents always knew where we were. Many was the time I would see dad or an older brother approaching across the field to tell me it was time for tea or bed. The fact parents knew where we boys always were, and that we were in such a large group, I suppose lessened anxieties and fears of their children being outside and out of sight. I consider myself fortunate to have grown up in an era when parents felt comfortable about allowing their children to play outside unsupervised. Though I often wonder if the 1960s really was any safer for children than now. Perhaps back then we didn't hear of unsavoury incidents involving children as there was no 24/7 nationwide media coverage. That said, in all my formative years in Flint I never heard of any child being accosted. Which was just as well. Growing up in such a large family and loving football as I did, I yearned to be outside with my friends, particularly on that field playing football.

I must have had something about me as a footballer because I was only seven years old when I was picked to play for my school team, St Mary's Roman Catholic Primary School, in a Flint schools five-a-side tournament. The tournament was for under-11s which meant I found myself playing against lads who were ten years of age. I was, however, never over-awed playing against lads who were older, bigger and stronger than me because the games I had played on the back field had made me used to that.

Playing for the school team meant I got to wear what I considered to be a proper football strip for the first time. In truth this was only the school shirt, as we lads provided our own shorts and socks. Nevertheless, the notion that I was part of a proper team thrilled and excited me. I scored two goals in the tournament, but the happiness I felt was soon crushed when a teacher informed me I wouldn't be playing again as I was too young. He explained he felt it wasn't fair to leave any of the older boys out for me and that I should not be too disappointed as my 'time would come'. Of course I was bitterly disappointed and for all I received sympathetic words from my parents, brothers and sisters I was still in the dumps about the situation days later. Though it was to be two years before I was selected again for my school team, my love of football never waned. On the contrary it became an obsession.

I was still a year younger than my teammates when I was finally selected again for St Mary's Primary, by which time the combination of my physical development and football skills learned on the back field instilled in me a confidence that I could more than hold my own against older lads.

I helped St Mary's win the Deeside Primary League, and was a regular goal-scorer in the team though I was playing in midfield. We also reached the final of the North Wales Junior Shield and my performances earned me a trial for Deeside School's representative side, though I didn't make it into the final eleven.

The following year was my last in primary school and the first when I really started to score goals on a regular basis. The highlight of my week was playing on a Saturday morning for St Mary's. At the time the Flint Schools Football Association issued an annual handbook to all teachers and pupils. The handbook listed all the school teams in their various leagues, together with the name and contact details of the supervising teacher, the team colours of each school and so on. I used to read this handbook religiously in bed every Friday night, looking up the section on the team I was to be playing against the following morning, noting their team colours, seeing where they had finished in the league the previous season, and the name of their teacher, who, to my mind, was their manager. When it was time for the light to be put out, I would lie in bed and conjure up images of past games against our opponents and dreams of what I might do in the following day's game. Of course, what I envisaged never happened, but many was the time I drifted off to sleep nurturing a dream of scoring with a shot from outside the penalty area, or putting the ball in the net after a solo run.

In my final year at primary school I found goals plentiful. There was hardly a game when I didn't feature on the score-sheet. I loved my football and the highlight came when I eventually won a place in our district representative team, Deeside Schools.

Deeside Schools played against representative teams from other local education authorities in North Wales, and participated in the Welsh Yeoman's Shield in which primary school representative teams from all over Wales competed. For me, playing in the Shield was like being a professional footballer because we travelled to other towns in Wales by coach. When I played for my school team I either made my own way to games, or else walked there and back with some teammates. Travelling, and by some distance, to a game on a coach was a great thrill because I knew that was how my heroes at Everton journeyed to away games.

Deeside became the first team from North Wales to win the Welsh Yeoman's Shield when we beat Newport Primary Schools 3–1 in south Wales and 7–1 at home. I managed to score three times in the two-legged final which, needless to say, delighted me. Far and away the best thing about winning the shield, however, was when I was told we would receive our medals at a special presentation ceremony, and that these would be awarded by Liverpool's John Toshack.

I shall never forget the day I was presented to John Toshack and received my Welsh Yeoman's Shield winners' medal. Not only was John idolised because of the partnership he had forged with Kevin Keegan at Liverpool, he was a national football hero due to his exploits with Wales.

I was very shy as a boy and was totally awestruck when meeting John. It was, up to that point, the greatest moment in my life. I had never met anyone famous before and felt totally tongue-tied in his presence. John offered me his congratulations. I said thank you when presented with my medal and that was it. I turned to rejoin my team-mates with my legs shaking. I had seen John Toshack on television and photographs of him in books and magazines but it seemed inconceivable to me that the world of a famous footballer should ever cross mine. Many years later, when I was coming towards the end of my playing career, I was invited to present medals at an international youth tournament in Aberystwyth that carried my name. One of my tasks was to select the player who impressed me most. It was a young Ukrainian boy called Andrei Shevchenko.

My performances for St Richard Gwyn High School, in particular for the Deeside and Flintshire County schoolboy representative teams, brought me to the attention of a number of scouts from League clubs. I was playing as a striker and scoring lots of goals. My dad tried to see me play as often as his work allowed, and when I was thirteen, after one game for Flintshire schoolboys, he was approached by a man who introduced himself as a scout for Liverpool.

The scout told my dad he had watched me play a few times and had been impressed on each occasion. He asked for his name and address, which Dad duly gave, and he left promising that he would be in touch very soon. Whether it was the fact I was only thirteen, or whether the scout had a change of mind about my worth as a footballer, I don't know, but Dad never heard from him again.

I was a keen all-round sportsman at school. In addition to playing football I also played for the school rugby and hockey teams. One would have thought my involvement in school sport and the discipline this gave me would be enough to occupy me and keep me out of trouble. By and large it did, but there was one incident when I came close to going off the rails.

When I was fourteen I fell in with a group of older lads who were totally uninterested in school, to the extent they often didn't bother going. This group numbered eight or nine lads who were disaffected with their lot, with their life in Flint and their future prospects. Most were sixteen years of age and had already started to drink in pubs, seeking out the run-down pubs in the town whose business was so bad the landlord wasn't too bothered about what sort people drank there, or how old they were.

I fell in with this group of lads because I found them funny. I had plenty of friends of my own age, but I felt that being popular with older lads gave me kudos. It was 1975 and in Flint at that time there was no question of disaffected young people turning to drugs. The only joint I knew was the one mum served for Sunday lunch, grass was what we played football on, and Coke was something we drank out of cans.

When this group of lads started skipping school I joined them. We would take towels and our swimming trunks and go to what was then called the local baths (swimming pool or leisure centre being too grand a description for the old council swimming baths). When not swimming we would roam the fields and countryside on the outskirts of town, keeping away from the town itself where the truant officer might come across us. For a time I became selective of the days I attended school, turning up just enough times to qualify for a place in the school football team.

On one occasion we took off for the day and went to Rhyl where we wandered into a souvenir shop which sold badges, posters, cards, spoons and ashtrays bearing the town crest – the usual things one finds in a seaside souvenir shop. Badges were all the rage at the time, both the pin-on type and the cloth sew-on variety – Led Zeppelin, Bay City Rollers, T-Rex, that sort of thing. We had the idea of spending the afternoon playing cards and, as no one had any cards, some bright spark suggested we should pinch some from the souvenir shop as well as helping ourselves to some of the badges on display.

We were pretty hopeless as thieves. When it became apparent our behaviour had aroused the suspicions of the shop assistants we made a run for it. The shop assistants were shouting for us to be stopped and stopped we were. On running out of the shop we turned straight into the path of a patrolling policeman who collared us all. I suppose we can't have been too bad because, having been ordered to stop, none of us continued running. The game was up and we knew it. To have run away would only have made matters worse.

I spent nine hours in Rhyl police station where we were all charged with the theft of badges and packs of playing cards. Eventually, at two in the morning, all our parents arrived at the police station to take us home. I was scared stiff and ashamed for having let my family down. On the journey home I felt the lowest I have ever felt. I was well aware that Mum and Dad had sacrificed so much on behalf of their children, that although money was very tight and the family budget did not allow for luxuries, none of my brothers or sisters had ever taken anything that had not belonged to them.

'Disgusted with you,' were the only words Dad said as we embarked upon the long and strained journey home. He didn't have to say any more. He was physically strong so could have belted me, and he could have given me a right ear-bashing, but the fact he remained silent, as did my mother, for the entire trip home spoke volumes.

My brothers and sisters were equally appalled.

'You bloody idiot. Wise up, before it's too late,' was all my oldest brother had to say.

I was already a shy lad, and in the immediate aftermath of this incident I said even less, but I made up my mind. I would never again go off the rails and bring such shame upon myself and my family.

I had to go to court, which again, proved a very frightening experience. The other lads received fines, but because this was my first offence and also because I was the youngest, I was given a two-year conditional discharge. In justifying his decision the magistrate made reference to the fact I had not been a problem pupil at school, that I had excelled in sport and done well in subjects such as maths and English. He concluded by saying he was going to give me a 'chance to prove my worth'. This came as a great relief to me because I had feared I would be sent to a young offenders' institution. My dad also consented to give me chance.

'Just about everyone goes off the rails once in life,' he told me. 'That's yours. Don't let it happen again because there won't be a second chance – not from me.'

The whole affair taught me an invaluable lesson, one which I have never forgotten. I wasn't a heartless, uncaring and insensitive teenager. The fact I had been involved in shoplifting was a source of shame in itself to me, but nothing compared to the shame I felt for having let down my mum and dad, brothers and sisters.

They were all hard-working, law-abiding people. I felt I had tarnished the name of our family and I felt really saddened by this. I resolved never to do such a thing again and to do something in life to instil in our family a source of pride and achievement. I knew I had a lot of work to do to put this incident behind me, but I was determined to buckle down and do just that. I had not been an academic high-flyer at school, but I resolved never to play truant again and to do my best in all subjects. Eventually I improved enough to gain five GCEs.

Because I was out playing football at every given opportunity I never spent countless hours glued in front of the television, though I did have certain favourite TV programmes. Particular favourites were *Happy Days* and *A Question of Sport*, then introduced by David Vine and with Bill Beaumont and Brendan Foster as captains. At the time the furthest thing from my mind was that I would one day appear on this programme. There were never family arguments over which programme we should watch. When I hit my teens my older brothers and sisters had left home, and other brothers were working shifts, so were coming in and out of the house at different times.

The most difficult aspect to growing up in a large family was finding space to do my own thing when I was a small boy. Every room seemed to be occupied by older brothers and sisters doing something, which is why I tended to spend so much time outside playing football.

Of course I inherited my love of music from my older brothers and sisters, in particular my brother Stephen. We had a record-player in the lounge, which was considered state of the art as it had two separate speakers. Whenever I could I would play my older brother and sisters' LPs . If the band was unknown to me I would skip through the tracks to get a feel for the style of the music and to see if there were any songs that appealed. In this way I would be introduced to a band or singer whose music I had never heard on the radio, such as John Martyn, Van Morrison, Alice Cooper or Billy Preston.

Throughout the 1970s my great musical hero was David Bowie. On first hearing *The Rise and Fall of Ziggy Stardust and the Spiders from Mars* in 1972, I was hooked. Like many people I had grown tired of leather-clad moodiness and what had become formulaic rock. With his orange hair, eyes of many colours and amazing Lurex costumes Bowie was totally different, a breath of fresh air. What I also liked about Bowie was the way he created a character for himself with every album he released. He retired Ziggy only to become Aladdin Sane and, I have to say, I followed suit. At one stage I too dyed my hair orange, then followed Aladdin Sane by changing it to purple. On occasions I even sported the Aladdin Sane lightning flash across my face. The only thing I didn't try to adopt was Bowie's bisexuality!

As the 1970s progressed, though I still loved Bowie's music, I no longer tried to ape his characters and images. When he released *Heroes* in 1977 the overtones of hedonism and drugs clashed with the lifestyle I was hoping to create for myself as a footballer. Though the Flint boys kept swinging, I was now happy within myself and no longer felt a need to project a manufactured image.

In 1977 I was about to leave school. I had done reasonably well in my final exams, and my teachers and career officer felt I would have no problem taking up a trade, such as painter and decorator, or electrician. I, however, had different ideas. I can remember the wide-eyed look on the face of the careers officer when I told him I had my heart set on being a footballer.

'Are you good enough?' he asked.

'I don't know, but I mean to find out,' I told him.

To his credit, he didn't attempt to dissuade me from pursuing my dream, but he did make a point of explaining the reality of the situation, telling me professional football is a harsh world, that of the few lucky enough to be taken on by a club the vast majority fall by the wayside. He and my teachers wanted me to embark upon a tradesman's apprenticeship so I would have something to fall back on should my ambition to be a footballer not work out. I did listen to this advice, but I was sixteen, and had the combination of stars in my eyes and the absolute desire to follow my dream.

Fuelling my ambition was the fact that, in my final year at school, my performances on the pitch had attracted the attention of a number of League scouts. A scout from Manchester United contacted my dad and invited us to have lunch at Old Trafford, see the set-up at the club and meet some of the players. As I had begun to apply myself to my studies in my final year of school, Dad wasn't keen on me going to Old Trafford during term-time. The scout understood and suggested he make the necessary arrangements during one of the school holidays. I was on tenterhooks. We waited and we waited – but heard nothing more.

I was very disappointed, but took heart from the fact that three clubs – Chester, Burnley and Wrexham – had invited me to trials. Of these three Burnley was by far the biggest club with a long-standing reputation for nurturing home-grown talent.

Burnley's youth policy had been created by manager Harry Potts in the early 1960s and had produced players such as Ralph Coates, Ray Hankin, Davie Thomas and Martin Dobson to name but a few. Even in the late 1970s the Burnley youth policy was still productive. Goalkeeper Tony Norman, Billy Rodaway,

Billy Ingham, Derek Scott, Peter Robinson and Ian Brennan were all regular first-team players who had come through the ranks, whereas Steve Kindon and Leighton James were both youth products who had moved to other clubs only to have returned to Turf Moor. Harry Potts was still manager but I found the youth set-up at Turf Moor somewhat overbearing. It was well organised, but to me it seemed strict and regimented.

Even at fifteen I was of the mind I wanted to enjoy my football. I attended three training sessions at Burnley, played in a practice game and not once did I see anyone smile or laugh. Football is a serious business, but at Burnley it was very serious indeed. I felt I would be given more latitude had I been a young squaddie in the army.

Wrexham was exactly the opposite. I attended a trial on a Sunday morning. There were around forty youngsters present and for the first hour there was no supervision. We just kicked footballs around amongst ourselves. Eventually someone – I didn't know who because he didn't introduce himself – formed us into groups. We did a little training then played small-sided games. At the end I showered and took off for home. The trainer didn't comment on my performance or application, nor did he inform me of when the next trial would be. In fact, he never spoke to me.

My experiences at Burnley and Wrexham – coupled with the disappointment I felt at not having heard from Manchester United – brought home the warning words of my career officer. My enthusiasm and ambition knew no bounds, but even at this tender age I began to realise that the reality of professional football was far removed from my idealistic view.

Though I had attended trials no one appeared to take an interest in me, or even engage me in conversation. Just when I was beginning to think all League clubs might be of similar ilk, Chester invited me for trials.

At this point I was playing a lot of football, for my school and representative teams such as Wales schoolboys and the Great Britain Catholic Schools Under-18 team, and also for a team called Hawarden Rangers in a local Sunday league.

The Chester youth team manager was Cliff Sear. Cliff had enjoyed a top-flight career as a full-back with Manchester City, making over 250 appearances for the club between 1956 and 1967. He made his debut for Chester against York City in 1968 and scored. Curiously, for a man who was to have a great influence on me and my development, that goal Cliff scored against York doubled his career tally of goals. Then again, Cliff had spent his career at Manchester City confronting the likes of Jimmy Greaves, Denis Law, Geoff Hurst and Jeff Astle. He had learned a lot about the role of the forward from having observed quality goal-scorers at such close proximity.

I warmed to Cliff straight away. There were only three other schoolboys attending trials, so we joined in the training with the first and reserve team players, which was a great thrill for me. Cliff appeared to have the time to talk to me. He offered encouragement and advice during and after training sessions, passed on tips such as when to hold the ball up and when to release it, when to push on, when to drop back to help defenders, the best way to take a ball in your stride, and so on. He and manager Alan Oakes made me feel welcome at the club and, within a fortnight, I was playing for the Chester youth team.

After one match, Cliff took me to one side. He told me he and the club were so pleased with the way I had applied myself in training and in matches that they were going to offer me an apprenticeship. It was the summer of 1978 and his words were the news I had been longing to hear. I was overjoyed and excited beyond belief. I couldn't wait to tell Mum and Dad that I was about to embark upon my dream career as a footballer.

However, Cliff did add that he did not want this news to affect my school studies in any way and told me he wanted me to continue to work hard with a view to passing all my exams. Coming from him, this only served to make me even more determined to do well in my final year at school.

But I was soon faced with a dilemma. Just after I had agreed to join Chester the Manchester United scout came back with the news United wanted to offer me an apprenticeship at Old Trafford. Dad was having none of it.

'You've given your word to Cliff Sear and to Chester. Now you have to honour it,' he told me. 'Besides which, the club have been good to you. Even at this stage they have helped you develop and looked after you. You can't renege on a promise.'

I was in full agreement.

Even at this embryonic stage of my career I was very happy at Chester. I was almost sixteen, felt obligated to the club and wanted to take them up on their offer, but I didn't have the verbal where-withal or confidence to tell the United scout, 'Thanks but no thanks', so Dad did it for me.

I knew even then that it was the right decision. Ever since the shoplifting episode I had come to realise you have to have some moral code in life and I felt good about not letting Chester down. The club had shown loyalty to me and I felt duty-bound to return their loyalty.

That Dad adhered to a strong moral code was never more evident than when another club came in for my services. A matter of weeks after he had informed Manchester United that I would be keeping my promise to join Chester, a scout from another club knocked on our door.

Again Dad and I explained the situation and the scout left, only to return some days later. On this second visit, he offered Dad a four-figure sum of money if I would turn down Chester and sign for the club he represented. Such an offer was totally illegal and Dad told the scout in no uncertain terms what he could do with his money.

'I don't earn much. We are a large family, and heaven knows we could do with a windfall but not that way,' Dad told him. 'I haven't got much, but I have my pride and dignity and we have honour as a family. No amount of money will ever buy that. We made a promise to Chester and we're going to keep it – and you can keep your money.'

That was Dad. His principles were of much greater importance to him than money. The stance he took only served to make me admire him all the more. I too felt good about the fact money had not turned my head. All I wanted to do was play football. Chester was the first club to offer me the opportunity of realising my dream to be a professional footballer. The club had looked after me and by politely turning down overtures made to me by other clubs, I felt, in my own small way, I was reciprocating. So it was, in the summer of 1978, I signed a contract as an apprentice at Chester for what I considered to be the very healthy wage of £16 a week.

CHAPTER TWO

All the Young Dudes

The Chester manager was Alan Oakes, who had been a team-mate of Cliff Sear at Manchester City. A Manchester City legend, Alan played 669 games for the club and was a member of the City side that won the League Championship (1968), FA Cup (1969) and League Cup and European Cup Winners' Cup (both 1970). Alan had joined Chester in 1976, initially as a player-coach, and had been at Chester for less than a year when manager, Ken Roberts, was 'moved upstairs' and Alan was offered the job of player-manager. Given Alan's career as a player had begun eighteen years previously, it is amazing to think he continued to play for Chester for a further six years. It is testimony to the fitness, stamina and enthusiasm of the man. During my final year of school, while I was playing for the youth team, Chester had finished in mid-table respectability in Division Three. Alan and the club appeared to be more than holding their own.

When I reported at Chester for my first day as a fully-fledged apprentice in June 1978, I saw myself as being a tough and fit sixteen-year-old. I had to reappraise that view of myself very quickly.

Having such a small playing staff, all the players trained together. The Chester first team squad included two goalkeepers, Grenville Millington and Brian Lloyd, the latter a full international with Wales; Bob Delgado, a tough, no-nonsense centre-back, who, for all he had been born in Cardiff, had joined Chester from Rotherham; Trevor Storton, who had begun his career at Tranmere and was signed by Bill Shankly for Liverpool for whom he had made five first-team appearances before arriving at Chester; Derek Jeffries and Ian Mellor, both former Manchester City players; Doug Livermore, who had seen service with Liverpool, Norwich and Cardiff; and Paul Raynor, Nigel Edwards, Bryn Jones, David Burns and Ian Howat, all products of the club's youth system.

The star of the team, however, was Ian Edwards. Alan Oakes had picked him up for a song from West Bromwich Albion and developed him into a fine striker, good enough to play for Wales and whose development and progress would, inadvertently, have a considerable impact on my blossoming career.

I was really up for it when I joined the rest of the players for the first close season training session. It was a very warm day in late June and it began with a four-mile run at some pace. I was still catching my breath from that when we were taken on to a practice pitch where there followed three-quarters of an hour of intense sprinting and shuttle-runs. That done, benches and weights were then produced and the rest of the morning was spent lifting weights to help build upper and lower body strength.

We then had a light lunch – salad, if my memory serves me well. I do, however, remember having trouble seeing the food on my plate because of the constant perspiration stinging my eyes.

After lunch we relaxed on the grass for half an hour before playing a full-scale practice match. The game lasted for about an hour. Just when I thought I had put in a good day's work for my first day, we were organised into small groups for another thirty minutes of sprints and shuttles.

I was exhausted but, as the senior pros took to the showers, Cliff Sear appeared with brooms, cloths, scrubbing brushes and buckets of water and detergent. When the senior pros left for home, I, along with the other three apprentices, set about scouring and cleaning the dressing-rooms in readiness for the following day.

When I eventually got home, Mum gave me my tea and I told the family all about my first day. I was so exhausted I went to bed at half past seven. Brothers coming and going from shifts didn't disturb me. I was so tired that, within minutes of my head hitting the pillow, I fell into a deep, relaxing sleep.

During my final year at school I had had it in my head that life as a young footballer was going to be glamorous. The reality proved somewhat different. Life at Chester didn't get any easier that summer. With every passing day, the training was stepped up. I thought I would be much fitter and faster than the pros in their late twenties and early thirties, and was totally taken aback to find this was not the case.

The senior pros were much, much stronger than me and, at this stage, much faster. I found the four-mile run a particular problem. It was taken at such a pace that it was purgatory for me. I would finish half a mile behind everybody else. Alan Oakes resorted to giving me a half-a-mile start, but I still finished last. When that happened, Alan and senior pros such as Trevor Storton and Bob Delgado would give me some stick, saying, 'You're slower than you look' and 'You gotta do better than that, son, or you'll die in a game. Douglas Bader could out-run you.' At first I felt they were being hard on a youngster, but soon came to realise they were trying to gee me up to work even harder.

I remember that after one particularly gruelling sprinting session I found that my legs turned to jelly. If anyone had played a ball to me then, I felt I wouldn't have had the strength to kick it, never mind go running off with it at my feet. Such hard training during the height of summer, rather than making me feel strong, often left me feeling weak. On one occasion, for all I was sweating buckets, I realised I was also shivering, and my limbs and muscles felt useless. Looking back, I was pushing my young body to the limit. However, I continued to buckle down and do what was asked of me. I kept at it, giving my all, and, as the days turned into weeks, I began to sense I was becoming stronger and fitter.

It's like looking into the bathroom mirror every day. You don't sense your face is changing, but should you see a photograph of yourself taken, say, a year ago, you then realise changes have taken place. It was much the same with the training at Chester. It was only after some six weeks that I saw I was capable of doing much more than I had in my first few days.

What I didn't realise at the time was that all the really hard work in training at a club was done pre-season. The intensity of the pre-season training was geared to having players achieve optimum fitness and strength for the start of the season. Once the season was underway, we would still train daily, but these sessions were less intense, geared to maintaining the level of fitness we had achieved. With matches on a Saturday and often mid-week as well, Alan and Cliff would give the players a tough and gruelling training session perhaps once a month, as a 'top-up'.

Not wanting to be on the receiving end of mickey-taking from

Alan Oakes and senior pros, I would grit my teeth and give it my all on the early morning four-miler. As the weeks passed, I became better at this. As the start of the season approached I was never going to be a serious threat to Seb Coe as a middle-distance runner, but found I was now able to keep up with the first team players.

I spent the 1977–8 season in the youth and reserve teams under the guidance and tutorship of Cliff Sear. Cliff taught me good habits. Not only in terms of applying myself to training and games, but also how to conduct myself off the pitch. He was full of good footballing advice, too. For example, on receiving the ball during a game, I would take off at top speed, hell-bent on outrunning opponents. Sometimes I did, sometimes I didn't. Instead Cliff told me to run at three-quarter pace when receiving the ball and moving forward. That way, when a defender came across to challenge, I had 'something left in the tank' to accelerate away from him. It's simple but, as I was to learn – and to be told on many occasions by Bob Paisley at Liverpool – football is a simple game.

Cliff also told me to attack space. For example, when we were on the attack and had possession of the ball out wide, I should aim to run into the space behind defenders. Of course, the run had to be timed so that I wasn't in an offside position when the ball was played. I was to learn that attacking space was one of the pre-requisites to any good striker. As a striker you like the ball played in early, the earlier the better, and if it that didn't happen you had to tell your teammates.

Another thing I learned from these early days was that once in space you had more time than you thought. You had to remain cool and calm, size up the situation, look for the gap the goalkeeper might have left and pass the ball through this gap. Lots of young lads presented with an opportunity on goal hit the ball as hard as they can in what they hope is a goal-bound direction, hoping sheer speed will beat a goalkeeper. In the pro game, it's different. A good goalkeeper will get his angles and positioning right, giving you little view of the goal. But what view you have you exploit, and you do this by staying calm and passing the ball through that gap. It's about looking up, sizing the situation in an instant and executing the three P's: not panicking, picking your spot, passing the ball through the channel (rather than blasting it).

I declined an offer from Manchester United because I had given my word to Chester that I would sign for the club on leaving school, but I was also hopeful that, by joining Chester, my development would be such I would be given a chance in the first team quicker than I would if I had joined a bigger club. At Manchester United I would have been just one of a large group of young players, every one of them a quality footballer with representative honours to their name at schoolboy international level. I had played for Wales schoolboys and under-18 teams but I reasoned that, by joining Chester, who only had four apprentices, my chances of playing League football were far better than they would have been had I have joined United.

Nowadays, with so many Premiership clubs buying foreign players, even recruiting youngsters from abroad for their academies, they tend not to recruit from the lower divisions of the League. In the 1977–8, it was very different. Should a young player make his mark in, say Divisions Three or Four, chances were a bigger club would come in for his services. But talented footballers are still there. For example, in May 2008, Peterborough United goalkeeper Joe Lewis was called up to the full England squad by Fabio Capello.

In 1975 Manchester United had bought Steve Coppell from

Tranmere Rovers and Gordon Hill from Millwall. During my first season with Chester, Liverpool bought Kenny Dalglish from Celtic but also goalkeeper Steve Ogrizovic from Chesterfield. Another goalkeeper, George Wood, joined Everton from Blackpool, Mark McGhee moved from Morton to Newcastle United, Colin Lee from Torquay to Spurs, and Derby County bought Gerry Ryan from Irish club Bohemians and Steve Buckley from Luton Town. Liverpool had previously bought Joey Jones from Wrexham, Alec Lindsay from Bury, Steve Heighway from non-League Skelmersdale, Ray Clemence from Scunthorpe United and, of course, Kevin Keegan from Scunthorpe. All these players established themselves in the First Division. I was very loyal to Chester but was hopeful that if I made my mark there a bigger club would come in and offer me the opportunity to play at a higher level.

I quickly established myself in the Chester reserve team which played in the Lancashire League. This was a league that comprised the youth teams of major north-west clubs such as Liverpool, Everton, Manchester United and City, Preston, Bolton, Blackpool and Bury as well as the reserve sides of Oldham Athletic, Southport, Crewe Alexandra and non-League Macclesfield Town. Thus began phase two of my football education.

The reserve teams that played in the Lancashire League contained a number of seasoned pros, players who didn't take too kindly to a sixteen-year-old trying to run rings around them and would give me a crafty knock when the ball was elsewhere. There were dangerous tackles that, once committed, would result in the perpetrator defusing the situation by immediately saying to the referee something along the lines of, 'Sorry, ref. Mistimed it. Not as quick as I used to be.' This would be said with a smile and the seasoned pro would then apologise to me, make as if he was concerned about my well-being by putting a comforting hand between my shoulder blades, in so doing pulling the short hair on my neck or pinching my skin. I, of course, would instinctively react to this. The old pro would then make out to the referee I was retaliating and being unnecessarily aggressive when offered a consoling hand and it would be me who received a ticking-off from the official.

Another ruse was for a defender to stand on my foot when Chester were taking a corner. I would just be ready to run and take off, only for a boot to land on one of mine. It would only be there for second, but it was enough to put me off my stride. Every time there was a corner some infringement would take place in the penalty area, but that's pro football. If a referee blew up every time he spotted a foul when a corner is being taken we'd have no game at all.

Unless you have played the game at pro level you will never know just how often arms are used without the referee taking action. I would be getting ready to meet a ball when the arm of a defender would come across my chest, just for a moment but, again, enough to put me off my stride and prevent me from making ground on my marker. Players running with the ball at their feet always kept opposing players at bay with an outstretched arm.

The arm was also used when a tackle had been made. Should a defender make a sliding tackle that resulted in both of us going to ground, he would then very quickly take to his feet, in so doing pressing down on me with one hand to keep me down while at the same time levering himself up. This was done so quickly officials never spotted it. It was all geared to quelling my speed and giving the defender an advantage.

It was light years away from the schoolboy and youth team football I had known, and the experience toughened me up. I quickly came to realise that pro football is not strictly played to the rulebook. I learned how to cope with this, to keep my temper under control and not to respond. Not reacting to these 'tricks' was a good way of dealing with defenders because it made them believe whatever they did was having no effect on me – even if, at times, it was.

I felt the best sort of retaliation was to score a goal. To my mind, doing that really rammed home the message that they had not got the better of me. Even when players almost twice my age were trying to kick lumps out of me, I would just give them a withering look and get on with the game.

As a striker I scored a few goals for Chester reserves that season, but nothing to get too excited about. I must have been doing something right, however, because Cliff Sear told me he was really pleased with my development and my contribution in games and training. Not only did Cliff tell me this, he made a point of mentioning it in an interview he gave for the *Chester Chronicle*: 'Ian Rush is the best prospect for his age this club has possessed in years.' Of course I was pleased to read this, but I didn't let it go to my head, and thought he might have said it for the benefit of the supporters. Throughout my career I never believed my own publicity, be it good, bad or indifferent. Even at sixteen I had my feet firmly planted on the ground, aware that I had a lot of hard work and learning ahead of me. Cliff's words, of course, cut no ice with senior pros such as Bob Delgado and Trevor Storton.

Part of my job was to clean the dressing-rooms and the boots of first team players, one of whom was Bob Delgado. Bob was arguably the strongest guy at Chester. He was of formidable build with a barrel chest and legs like bags of concrete. Football dressing-rooms are testosterone-driven places and every one will have its dominant characters. Bob was one of the 'leaders' of the Chester dressing-room, outgoing, sometimes brash, at other times crass, but generally kind-hearted and a good player to have on your side. Bob wanted to make sure Cliff's comments in the *Chester Chronicle* wouldn't go to my head and he took me to task in the dressing-room about the job I had made of cleaning his boots. 'Look at this . . . and this . . . and this!' he said, pointing to mud marks. 'In the bloody bath with you.'

At which point he picked me up as if I were a tailor's dummy, carried me over to the plunge bath and threw me in. I was grateful to be wearing my training gear and not my ordinary clothes. The senior pros were laughing and I laughed, too, although I didn't feel like it. To have taken umbrage or to have sulked would have resulted in more pranks. Besides which, I knew there was no malice in what Bob had done.

If you showed you could take a joke then you ticked the right boxes and were accepted by your teammates. What was more, dressing-room culture then allowed you, should you feel so inclined, to crack a joke or play a prank yourself. Throughout my career I never did throw anyone in a plunge bath, but having 'earned' my dressing-room colours, whether it be at Chester or Liverpool, I would make wise-cracks at the expense of other players, Kenny Dalglish included.

I enjoyed my first season with Chester reserves, I felt I had learned a lot about pro football, as well as my own game and character. I knew I had made the right choice in joining the club and that first season proved a very good one for Chester.

The first team finished in fifth place in Division Three, missing out on automatic promotion by only two points. I was really happy to be part of a club that had done so well but, being human, I also knew that the more the first team posted good form and results, the less chance there was of me being given an opportunity to show what I could do in League football.

In the summer the club gave me a wage rise to coincide with my seventeenth birthday, up from sixteen pounds a week to twenty. I gave half to my parents for board and lodging, and kept the other half for myself. I wasn't a frivolous spender of money. I bought my own clothes, spent some on records and allowed myself one night out a week. This was on a Saturday when I would either go for a drink in Flint with some pals, or, occasionally, with some teammates in Chester. Such is the influence of foreign coaches and managers on the culture of English football today that players going out to pubs is frowned upon. In 1978 it was different. I am not saying drinking was encouraged by managers, but players getting together for a drink never met with disapproval as it was thought it helped build team spirit and camaraderie. Many players went out on Saturday after a game when we had the Sunday to recover and get it out of our systems. Some clubs were also easy about players going out on a Thursday night as it was felt a moderate drink on this night would not affect performance on a Saturday.

Most of the grounds in the Lancashire League were the training grounds of League clubs so didn't have a players' lounges. On those occasions when we did play at ground that had a players' lounge, such as Oldham or Crewe Alexandra, or at non-League Macclesfield Town which had a social club, Chester reserves might have a quick drink with the opposition after the game. Supporters would be present, too, which is unthinkable today.

Throughout 1978–9 I continued to learn my trade with Chester reserves in the Lancashire League. The first team had not built on the relative success enjoyed during the previous season and were marooned in mid-table. Ian Edwards, however, was having a good season up front and scouts were beginning to take notice.

Peter Henderson was a new recruit. He had been spotted playing in midfield for Alsager College, a teacher training college aligned to Keele University, and also for Witton Albion in the Cheshire League. Peter's transition from non-League to League football proved seamless. Having joined the club in January he had already become a first team regular. Gary Felix, a young player from Manchester, had also been given a number of games. I felt I was knocking on the door of the first team, and the fact Alan Oakes had blooded Henderson and Felix gave me hope he might soon give me an opportunity.

By the last week in April Chester had three matches remaining, the first of which was at home to Sheffield Wednesday. The date is imprinted in my mind: 28 April 1979. There was no reserve team game so I arrived at Sealand Road at about one-thirty as I had been given the job of laying out the strips and kit in the home team dressing-room. I was in the process of doing this when Alan Oakes entered and asked me if I would follow him into his office. It sounded ominous. I had done nothing wrong so was at a loss as to why the manager would want a word with me.

'Ian, you're playing this afternoon,' he told me.

He may have said something else immediately after that but I didn't hear what because my mind was a whirl.

As I stood before his desk I felt suddenly gripped by excitement. This was the moment I had dreamed of, my debut for the first team.

My excitement must have registered on my face because he then said, 'I'm playing you in midfield. You've earned a chance. Just don't let excitement get the better of you. Focus your mind. I just want you to do the simple things. Don't try anything special.'

I took that to mean he didn't want me to try anything out of the ordinary. 'Special' for me would be scoring on my debut.

I thanked him for the opportunity and told him I would try not to let him or the team down.

'I'm sure you won't,' he said. 'You have ability, that's why you're in.'

With that he told me to return to the dressing-room.

'Just remember, Ian, keep it simple,' he reminded me, adding, 'Oh, and when passing the ball, just make sure it goes to a blue-and-white shirt.'

I am sure Alan Oakes had left it to the last minute to tell me I was going to make my League debut so as not have me wracked by nerves. I imagine he thought that if he had told me the news on the Friday, I would have been so excited I would have had trouble sleeping. (Little knowing, of course, that disrupted sleep was part and parcel of my childhood.) By not informing me of my debut until the last possible moment, I didn't have time to dwell on possibilities and feel nervous, or, conversely, become over-confident.

This was good management on the part of Alan. A young player given notice of his League debut can dwell on the day ahead, dupe himself into thinking he's now good enough for League football. When you are young you feel anything is possible and your personal limitations, if any, have yet to make themselves known. As with life, in football one of the drawbacks to growing older is that you become increasingly aware of the things which you are simply not equipped to excel at. The only downside to my great news was I didn't have time to call home and tell Mum and Dad.

It later transpired that I had been included in the team because Alan himself had sustained an injury. That didn't bother me because he could have chosen from several players. The fact I had been given the nod was a great boost to me.

When I joined the rest of the lads in the dressing-room, they already knew of my inclusion. Again I was told to keep it simple, to listen to what I was told out on the pitch. As we prepared to leave the dressing-room my teammates all wished me the best of luck.

I can still recall the entire Chester team that day: Brian Lloyd, Paul Raynor, Trevor Storton, Mark Nickeas, David Burns, me, Bryn Jones, Ron Phillips, Ian Mellor, Doug Livermore and Peter Henderson.

As it was my debut I would have been overjoyed to play against any team, but the fact that the opposition was Sheffield Wednesday gave the match an added edge. When I was a boy, Wednesday were one of the mainstays of the First Division. They had since fallen on hard times, dropped down to Division Three and were mid-table. But the club still commanded good support and quite a number had made the journey to Chester. Even though this was a fag end game to the season with nothing for either side to play for other than points and pride, a crowd of around 5,000 was inside Sealand Road when I proudly took to the pitch with my teammates.

In the Wednesday side that day were goalkeeper Bob Bolder; Peter Shirtliff; the former Arsenal player Brian Hornsby, Roger Wylde, Terry Curran and Ian Porterfield, Sunderland's goal-scoring hero of the 1973 FA Cup final against Leeds United. The game ended in a 2–2 draw with the Chester goals coming from Ian Mellor and Ron Phillips.

I didn't make a great impact on the game, but to get through it without making a telling error pleased me. When the final whistle blew my overriding feeling was one of relief I had not dropped a clanger that resulted in a goal against us, or had found myself totally out of my depth.

The likes of Ron Phillips, Ian Mellor, Paul Raynor and Trevor Storton were a great help to me, constantly talking, telling me when to push on, drop back, or release the ball. I was given encouragement from start to finish. Even a simple three-yard pass resulted in a 'well done'. One of the things I noticed was how much senior pros like Ian Mellor, Ron Phillips and Doug Livermore asked for the ball. To my eyes they seemed brimming with confidence. I too was confident but also wary of demanding the ball too often in case I didn't make good use of it or, heaven forbid, gave the ball away to the opposition. As I was later to discover, this was all a matter of self-confidence; assuming responsibility on the pitch came only with experience.

After the game Alan Oakes told me he was pleased with my effort and performance. 'No worries, Ian, you'll do for me,' he said.

I journeyed home as if on silver wings. I couldn't wait to tell Mum and Dad all about it. I had made my big breakthrough into League football and felt I was on my way to carving out a career for myself in the game.

My parents, of course, were delighted for me, though somewhat disappointed not to have been there. Dad was at pains to tell me this was just a start, that I should not get 'carried away' and think I had 'made it'. I later heard that at work on Monday all his workmates were congratulating him and asking him to convey messages of good luck to me. Some of his pals had been at the game and said I had done well.

The following week, Alan Oakes pronounced himself fit for the next game at Watford and told me I would be playing for the reserves. I was very disappointed to revert back to Lancashire League football but both Alan and Cliff assured me my time would come. I just had to keep working hard and be patient.

My progress had been such I knew I was on the fringe of the first team when 1979–80 got underway. Chester began with a fine 3–2 win at Wimbledon and followed this with a 3–1 success over Grimsby Town, then a creditable 1–1 draw against Sheffield United. The good start to the season seemed to put the kybosh on my hopes of being called up to the first team but I continued to give my all in the reserves, ever hopeful that, one day, I would again break through.

In mid-September Chester were due to play at Gillingham. In the previous match, at home to Millwall, Peter Henderson picked up an injury. Without ever wishing Peter any harm, I was hoping against hope he didn't recover in time. On the Thursday afternoon Alan called me into his office and told me I was to travel to Kent with the squad the following day and that, the way things were for Peter, in all probability I would be playing. It was music to my ears.

On the Friday, when the squad assembled at Sealand Road, Alan told me Peter Henderson had failed a fitness test. On being told this I tried to exude calm, but my emotions were riding a roller-coaster.

Gillingham were a decent Third Division side that played fluid, entertaining football. In midfield for Gillingham that day was Steve Bruce, whose no-nonsense tackling would become a trademark of his game in later years when he became centre-half for Manchester United. In Damien Richardson and Terry Nicholl, Gillingham possessed two very direct players whose running from deep caused us a few problems and it was those two players who, either side of halftime, set up two goals for centre-forward Terry Price.

Gillingham were leading 2–1 with five minutes of the match remaining. Again I thought I had done OK. We were on the attack looking to salvage something from the game. Ron Phillips played the ball down the left flank to John Ruggiero, who had come on as substitute for Ian Edwards. John pulled the ball back across the face of goal. I was coming up from deep and from eight yards side-footed the ball past the Gillingham goalkeeper Ron Hillyard. By no stretch of the imagination was it a spectacular goal, but the joy it gave me was almost overwhelming. All these years on, my first League goal at Gillingham remains one my most cherished memories. So often did I run that goal through my mind after the game, I doubt I shall ever forget it.

I was absolutely chuffed to bits to have scored, but though my effort had earned a point for us it didn't earn me a place in the next game at Swindon Town, and Chester came a cropper there, losing 3–1. Despite this being only our second defeat of the season, Alan Oakes was far from happy with the team performance and for the next game at home to Reading he rang the changes, one of which resulted in a recall for me.

The Reading game was not a good one for us. We lost 2–0 at home but I took great heart from the fact Alan said I was one of the few players to emerge with any credit that day. Having been told this I was doubly disappointed and somewhat perplexed to find myself back in the reserves the following Saturday when the first team travelled to Carlisle United.

Having drawn at Carlisle, Chester then beat Plymouth Argyle. The next game was at Grimsby Town and I was delighted to be named in the squad, though disappointed to be a substitute. Even so, I was more than happy to be involved in the first team and when Peter Sutcliffe sustained an injury during the second half I was called into action. We beat much-fancied Grimsby 2–0 and though I didn't manage to get on the score-sheet, felt I had done a job when coming on for the final twenty minutes. I was named as a substitute but never used for our next three matches, but then fate, or should I say financial necessity, intervened.

Near neighbours Wrexham were doing well in Division Two. For some weeks rumour had it Wrexham had been eyeing Ian Edwards, who was having another good season. One Friday in late October I turned up as usual for training only to hear Ian Edwards would not be with us. It transpired he was having talks with Wrexham and the word was they were about to offer £125,000 for him. Even by the standards of the day it was not a fantastic fee but, to a club the size of Chester, it was still a considerable amount of money.

The story of Edwards' pending transfer was not the only news. Alan Oakes told me he had included me in the team for the trip to Barnsley the following day. Against Barnsley I played behind a strike force of Peter Henderson and Ian Edwards. The game ended 1–1 with Ian Edwards, in what was to be his last game for Chester, scoring our goal.

A golden rule in football is never to say you have had a good game. It doesn't pay to boast, because if you blow your own trumpet chances are in the following game there will be an opponent out to prove you wrong. Though I didn't say as much, I felt my performance against Barnsley was my best to date in the first team. I had grown in confidence, strength and ability, and came off the pitch feeling I had made a positive contribution. Seemingly, I was not the only person to think this.

The transfer of Ian Edwards created a furore among Chester supporters who were angry that the club's star player had been sold. There were letters in the local paper saying that the sale of Edwards showed the club had no ambition, but the reality of Chester's financial situation left them with no choice. The club had to cash in on its prime asset.

Even though I had been given a few outings in the first team, I believed there were a couple of young players ahead of me in the queue to take Edwards' place upfront. I had, after all, spent much of my time at Chester playing in midfield, so what happened next came as a complete surprise to me.

I was still an apprentice and, although I had played in the first team, still had to fulfil my apprentice duties. I was tidying and cleaning the treatment room one day while Alan Oakes was receiving attention for a minor injury sustained against Barnsley. He was talking to the physio about our next game against Wimbledon, adding what a great loss Edwards was to the team, when, suddenly, he looked across to me.

'You know what, Ian?' he said. 'I think you're the player to take Edwards's place upfront.'

I didn't say anything at first. I was stunned.

'Well, are you up to the job or not?'

'I don't know,' I said, in part because I didn't really know if I could do a job as an out-and-out striker, also because I didn't want to come across as big-headed.

'Not the answer I'm looking for, Ian, son. Do you think you can do the job of leading the line?'

I didn't think he was going to give me another chance, so I took a deep breath before replying. 'I'll give it a go.'

That, thankfully, was enough of an answer for him.

Wimbledon were managed by Dario Gradi. They had yet to adopt the physical approach and long-ball game that later became their trademark. In keeping with Gradi's style and philosophy, Wimbledon played purist football with the ball passed across the ground. For my first League game as a striker I was grateful I was facing one of the footballing sides of Division Three.

Wimbledon took the lead when our full-back, Jim Walker, put

the ball through his own goal, and held that lead to halftime. During the interval, Alan encouraged Ron Phillips and Peter Sutcliffe to play the ball behind what he saw as a square Wimbledon back four, and told me to be on the alert to nip in behind them. Ten minutes into the second half this worked a treat. The ball was played into space behind Wimbledon's Tommy Cunningham, I latched on to it and, with their keeper Ray Goddard coming off his line to narrow the angle, kept my cool and stroked the ball wide of his left arm and into the far corner of the net. Further goals from Trevor Storton and Jim Walker, who made atonement for his own goal of the first half, gave us a 3–1 victory.

I felt instantly comfortable playing as a striker. The position suited me. I wasn't as actively involved in games with the ball at my feet as I had been when playing in midfield, but that is not to say I wasn't working hard for every second of a game. Over the course of ninety minutes even the busiest of midfield players will have the ball at his feet for a maximum of only three minutes in total. So, it stands to reason that what he does in the other eighty-seven minutes is as important as when he has the ball at his feet. Playing as a striker I spent a lot of time without the ball at my feet, and my back to the way I wanted to go. Much of my job was to run, check, then run off in another direction, always looking to make myself available to teammates. I was constantly on the look-out to move quickly into space in readiness to receive the ball.

I was also on steep learning curve. I quickly discovered that among the prize assets of a striker are sharpness and speed off the mark. From a standing position or a jog you have to suddenly explode to leave your marker in your wake, so I worked hard in training to ensure this aspect of my game improved. Whenever

Alan or Cliff had us sprinting in training, I was always first off the mark and out in front for the first six yards or so. Flyers like Peter Henderson or Peter Sutcliffe might overtake me but that was OK. I knew I was working to improve something that was important to the success of my personal game – those crucial first few yards.

Following the Wimbledon game we were beaten 2–0 at Blackburn Rovers but I soon settled into my new role as striker. I scored the only goal of the game at Oxford United after which I hit a purple patch. In the following thirteen League matches I scored nine goals, a return which pleased me as I was still very much untried as a striker at League level. The goals helped me grow in confidence. I no longer wanted to play in midfield. I saw myself as an out-and-out striker.

I am, essentially, a calm person. Good or bad, it takes a lot to get me worked up. This aspect of my character proved an asset to me as a striker when under pressure. I found I was never panicked into making a rash decision and snatching at a chance. I remained calm and cool-headed when presented with an opportunity on goal. What's more, I also found I had the ability assess a situation and process the necessary action to take in an instant.

Playing against Sheffield United at Bramall Lane we were trailing 1–0 when Bryn Jones played the ball behind the United centre-backs John McPhail and Tony Kenworthy. I cut in at an angle, latched on to the ball in what would be the old inside-right position and made for goal with McPhail breathing down my neck. The United keeper, Derek Richardson, came off his line to cut down my angle of vision, and I saw John Cutbush coming from the right to cover the goal-line. It's amazing what goes through your mind in an instant. There was only one gap, between Richardson and his left-hand post, so I went for it, side-footing the ball through the gap.

In such a situation I realised I was playing instinctively. If you start thinking about what you might do, it's too late because the opposition will have time to react and a defender will have the ball. When you're one-on-one with the goalkeeper you have to stay calm and, pardon the pun, don't rush yourself. Think too much and too many options go through your head, and the more options you give yourself the more chance there is you will make the wrong decision.

I was seventeen, still an apprentice, and the more experience I gained the more I realised there was to learn about football. I was very keen to keep on learning and it was to pay dividends. Not only did I keep my place in the first team for the remainder of 1979–80, I continued to score goals.

The further down the Football League you go the game is more physical, there are more tackles, the ball is given away more frequently, mistakes are made more often (and generally speaking, less punished). That's not to say entertaining football was at a premium. There was plenty of decent football played in Division Three, it was just that it was generously mixed with crunching tackles and more mistakes than you would get in Division Two and certainly Division One.

Grimsby Town, Blackburn Rovers, Sheffield Wednesday and Chesterfield were battling it out at the top for the three promotion places. Chester were a top ten team while Wimbledon and Mansfield Town looked doomed. As for the other two relegation places, with six weeks to go before the end of the season you could have chosen any two from nine.

I had played against most teams and what struck me most was there was not a lot of difference between top and bottom. You would think the top team had bags more ability than the bottom team, but I didn't find this to be the case. Generally speaking,

Wimbledon, who were glued to the foot of the table, were no less a footballing team than Grimsby, who were top. In fact, Wimbledon tried to play more football than Grimsby.

The differences between teams were small but significant. Earlier in the season I had come on as a substitute against Grimsby at Blundell Park, a lovely surface to play on. Grimsby were managed by George Kerr and though Chester beat them 2–0 and Grimsby were, at the time, mid-table, I sensed they would do well. Grimsby had ten outfield players who were snapping at our lads all the time, never giving us time on the ball. Every time I received the ball one of their lads would be breathing down my neck, putting a foot in, stopping me playing. When you have an entire team constantly doing that it tends to prevent the skilful players in the opposition doing their stuff. The more it goes on in a game, the more those skilful players get fed up. In an attempt to find some space they wander and the next thing you know the whole shape and form of your side has gone to pot. That happened to us at Chesterfield, another of the top sides.

Chesterfield played like Grimsby. They were at us all the time, with no let up. When that happens the playmakers can't function as normal. What's more, when a side like Chesterfield are on the attack, some of the opposition players are tempted not to go with them. They think, 'If I stay out of it and we break this attack down, I'll be in the space I need to do my stuff.' So one or two players don't track back as they should, and the next thing you know you're chasing the game, which happened to us that day at Chesterfield. Only we couldn't pull it back because they were snap, snap snapping at us again. It was frustrating and bloody annoying. With some players, even when they weren't being harassed to hell, they were expecting to be, so reacted as if they were and couldn't wait to get rid of the ball.

Football was like that in Division Three. A lot of teams set out to upset your shape and rhythm, and once they had done that they would have the lion's share of the ball. The sides that were most competent at this were the ones at the top. The ones who were not so efficient at this were near the bottom.

Once a team had disrupted the opposition, their success in a game depended on them having a slight edge when it came to ball-players and taking a chance in front of goal. Here just a marginal advantage proved crucial to success in a game, which is why, in terms of actual ability, there was not a great deal of difference between teams. How effective a team was at doing the little things would tip the balance of a game in their favour.

The highlight to Chester's season that year was a great run in the FA Cup. In round one we beat Workington Town 5–1 and I managed to score twice, my first FA cup goals. Victory over Barnsley in round two gave us a plum tie away at Newcastle United.

At the time Newcastle were challenging for promotion from Division Two and no one gave us much of a chance of achieving a result. I think many people saw the game as nothing more than a bumper pay day for the club, but we players were determined to enjoy the day and give a good account of ourselves. The Newcastle team included Peter Withe, Terry Hibbert, Tommy Cassidy, Stuart Boam, and John Connelly (a recent signing from Everton). There were about 30,000 inside St James's Park, by far the biggest crowd I had played in front of, and we stunned the home supporters after only two minutes.

The ball was played through to me. I managed to make progress into the Newcastle penalty area and pulled the ball across for Peter Henderson to rifle home past Steve Hardwick. It was a particularly bitter-sweet moment for Peter, who had been a Newcastle supporter from early childhood.

We were then under siege for the next hour or so as Newcastle proceeded to dominate the game. They threw everything at us in an attempt to get back on level terms but we executed the Third Division speciality. We harassed them to hell. Newcastle hit the bar, we made two goal-line clearances, and at times our defending was desperate stuff but we kept snapping away at them, got bodies behind the ball when we had to, and held firm. Twenty minutes from time we managed to break from defence. Ron Phillips made great progress down our left flank, crossed, and I met the ball with my left foot to make it 2–0. Suddenly I found myself engulfed by blue-and-white shirts. My teammates were so ecstatic you would have thought we'd won the FA Cup.

We held out to win 2–0. It was not only the shock result of round three but, arguably, of the entire competition that season. What I recall to this day was the generosity of the Newcastle supporters. As we made our way off the pitch we did so to generous applause. Those eternally let-down Newcastle fans must have been totally gutted but, appreciative of our efforts, they cheered us off the field.

We beat Millwall 2–0 in round four which led to an away tie at Ipswich Town in round five. Even before a ball was kicked this proved an achievement in itself, as it was the furthest Chester had gone in the FA Cup since 1891!

Sadly, Bobby Robson's Ipswich, who were near the top of Division One, had too much class for us, though I felt we made them work exceptionally hard for their 2–1 victory. We gave it all we had, but they were all top-quality players with the ability to ride-out the snapping challenges and keep possession of the ball. I noticed that no matter how quick we got to them, the Ipswich players always seemed to have enough time on the ball, a telling difference between the First and Third Division. Even so, the game was tight at times and our overall performance earned us plaudits. Chester made headlines in the sports pages of the national press and we felt pretty good about it, too.

As a result of our run in the FA Cup I received a bonus of £150 from the club and put it to good use by buying my first car, a second-hand Hillman Avenger. It wasn't exactly flash and its prime characteristics were some dodgy electrics and unreliable starting motor. That said, I was the proudest lad in Flint when driving from my home to Sealand Road to report for daily training.

Regular first team football resulted in my wages rising. I was by this time on a basic wage of fifty pounds a week. With bonuses I could earn eighty pounds a week, which, to my mind, was an extraordinary amount of money for a lad of my age to earn for doing something he truly loved. I was, however, very mindful of the fact I was very fortunate in this respect.

It was 1980, oil prices were rising (nothing new there then) and many industries were feeling the effects of this. In addition to which many of the traditional industries – mining, shipbuilding, fishing and steel – were beginning to contract. The gradual running-down of the steel industry hit Flint hard. The local steel-works began to shed labour and two of my brothers found themselves on the dole. I did my best to help the family financially, but was always aware of the effect on their pride that unemployment had brought.

Unemployment figures across Britain topped 1 million. Britain had a new government and Margaret Thatcher was a year into the job of Prime Minister, but things appeared to be getting worse. Before the general election the Conservatives ran a poster campaign showing people queuing at a dole office with the strapline 'Labour isn't working'. But any hopes the new government would get people back to work quickly evaporated. Interest rates rose. Redundancies and closures were widespread.

Unemployment was rife in the Flint area and many families I knew had to scrimp and save just to get by. I truly appreciated how fortunate I was in being paid well to play the game I loved. To be honest, at times it weighed on my conscience. I helped my own family as best I could, but I felt for my town's people. Harry Enfield's 'Loadsamoney' character is synonymous with the Thatcher era and may well have reflected the lives of a small percentage of people in the south-east but, believe me, for the majority, these were lean and very troubled times.

It was at this time that I met Tracy, who was to become my wife. Before meeting her I had been so dedicated to my football that I hadn't bothered with girls, but I was bowled over when first I saw Tracy in a Chester nightclub.

She was dancing with some friends and, being the shy type, it took me some time to gather the courage to ask her to dance. I dithered at the side of the dance-floor telling myself, 'This record isn't good to dance to,' only to tell myself the same thing when the next record was played. Eventually the DJ played 'Pop Muzic' by M. I have never considered myself to be a great dancer but felt I could make a passable attempt with this song and so nervously asked this beautiful girl if I could dance with her. I was delighted when she said yes. I tried to make conversation as we danced, but it was that awkward situation where you try to find some common ground, and, from my point of view, work out if you are going to be rejected as soon as the song finishes.

Having established our names I asked if she was local to Chester and was amazed when she told me she lived in Flint. It transpired Tracy was from what we called 'Upper Flint', which, as far as I was concerned, was the 'posh' part of town.

This was the catalyst to conversation. We did what people do in such circumstances, bandied names at one another to see if we knew the same people. After three dances, I suggested we have a drink and once again she accepted.

We talked about life in Flint which, for all we liked life in the town and the people, didn't take long. I had a mate who had started work as a reporter on a little magazine entitled, *What's On In Flint,* and told Tracy that every edition of the magazine consisted of a single page on which were written the words 'Bugger All'. This made her laugh and our conversation flowed from there.

It was on our first date that she asked me what I did for a living. When I told her I was footballer her reaction couldn't have been any different had I told her I was in insurance or worked as a painter and decorator. I gained the impression that she was attracted to me as a person, rather than my work or prospects.

We started to go out together regularly, for drinks, to the cinema, for meals, and saw the occasional band. Tracy was bright as well as beautiful, and had a good sense of humour. I enjoyed being in her company and found myself really looking forward to the nights when we had arranged to meet. A matter of weeks after having met her, I was head over heels in love, and, to my amazement, got the impression she quite liked me.

Life was great, but I was very much aware that my situation was in sharp contrast to many people I knew in the Flint area. At the time I had no ambitions other than to see my career out at Chester. I was very happy at the club and enjoying my football. I had forgotten about the idea I had as a fifteen-year old of perhaps making a name for myself at Chester and being spotted by a bigger club. There had been speculation in some of the newspapers that some First and Second Division clubs had been tracking my progress but I took this with pinch of salt. Until one day in late April 1980 when Alan Oakes asked me to step into his office.

Alan told me my goal-scoring exploits (I had seventeen to my name that season) had impressed Liverpool and the club wanted to sign me. He went on to say I should go home, discuss the matter with my parents, sleep on it and let him know my decision the next day. Seemingly, it was not so much a case of Chester wanting to cash in on me, though no doubt that had a certain appeal to the club, rather than Liverpool wanting a quick decision, as the transfer deadline was only a few days away.

I did talk the move over with my parents, but I didn't lose much sleep over it. I quickly came to the conclusion I would be making a fool of myself if I agreed to join Liverpool. They were one of the greatest clubs in the world. I just didn't think I possessed the class to hack it at Anfield.

The following morning found me in Alan's office again. I told him I wanted to stay at Chester. To be honest he seemed genuinely pleased, if not also a little surprised. He then went on to inform me that Manchester City had also made an enquiry about my services but he had, that morning, received a call to say they had pulled out, thinking me not ready for top-flight football, which, as far as I was concerned, confirmed my own view of myself.

On 26 April Chester enjoyed a 2–1 home win over Southend United. I didn't manage to score but felt I had played reasonably well. A couple of days later I received another request to report to the manager's office. Alan told me Liverpool were still keen on having me, so keen they had made a concrete offer, though at this stage he didn't tell me how much. Alan went on to say that should I join Liverpool I would be presented with an opportunity to develop as a player in a way that would be denied me should I remain at Chester.

'How much would you want to go there?' he asked.

I saw this as my opportunity to put the lid on the move, so came up with what I believed was a silly figure. 'A hundred pounds a week.'

Alan convulsed with laughter. 'You are joking?' he said eventually.

I felt my ploy of out-pricing myself had worked.

'Ian, I'd pay you more than that if you stay at Chester,' he said.

To be honest, at that time, I would have been quite happy to stay at Chester. The prospect of earning more than a hundred pounds a week, though appealing, was not the main issue for me. I enjoyed life at the club, I was playing League football regularly and felt that if I went to Liverpool I would be stuck in the reserves until they realised I didn't have what it took to play in the first team. Then I'd be discarded.

Later that day Alan collared me again.

'You really should think this all through,' he told me. 'I don't want you to go, but I also think that, as a player, it would be in your best interests.'

Not without some reservations I eventually agreed to go to Anfield with Alan and my dad for a meeting with Liverpool manager, Bob Paisley.

I had played at Melwood, Liverpool's training ground, for Chester 'A' team in the Lancashire League, and knew it was one of the best in the country. Apart from the pristine pitches and changing rooms, which were better than the majority I had experienced in the Third Division, Melwood boasted a restaurant and a players' lounge that wouldn't have been out of place in a top hotel. The pile on the carpet was so thick you almost needed snow shoes.

On first sight I would never have taken Bob Paisley for being one of the greatest managers in world football. He was dressed in a cardigan, a white shirt and a patterned tie of the knitted variety. His hair was swept back in a style that had never been in vogue in my lifetime and it seemed to be Brylcreemed. He looked like one of the old guys I used to see on the benches around the bowling green in my local park. Yet I knew behind the cheery smile and soft Durham voice was one of the most astute football brains in the game.

Bob showed us the set-up at Melwood, then took us back to Anfield. Even empty, the ground exuded an almost holy reverence with Archibald Leitch's curvaceous main stand gable drawing the eye. Above it was the board in red and white bearing the words 'Liverpool Football Club', as if anyone could be in any doubt as to whose ground this was.

I stood looking up at the deserted steps of the Kop, trying to imagine what it would be like to play when this famous terrace was full of supporters. On match days the swaying masses on the Kop (it had once had a capacity set at 28,000) sang their hearts out and chanted the names of their favourites. I did wonder if the day would ever come when they might chant my name and was immediately consumed by excitement at the mere thought.

I must have been one of the few players to whom Bob Paisley had to 'sell' Liverpool to as a club. He did a good job of it over lunch. I was very impressed by what I had seen. The facilities far out-stripped those of Chester. Bob himself, of course, I knew to be a great manager. I felt I would learn a lot from him and came to the conclusion this was a chance in a lifetime, that if I said no I might live to regret that decision. I decided to give it go. I think my dad was even more excited than me. Liverpool was his club, and here he was, chatting away to Bob Paisley over lunch at Anfield with the prospect of his son playing for the team he had supported since childhood.

Following lunch and my decision to sign for Liverpool we all assembled in Bob Paisley's office. I was too abashed to bring up the subject of money. Dad was unsure as how to approach the subject, so Alan Oakes did this on my behalf.

'Regarding wages, Bob, how much is the club willing to pay Ian?' he asked casually.

'Oh, er, say, three hundred a week,' was Bob's equally casual reply.

I felt as if someone had crept up behind me and hit me across the back of the head with a gold bar. I was speechless and struggled to retain some degree of composure. I looked at my dad. He was as wide-eyed as me. Dad reached into the inside pocket of his jacket, produced a pen, handed it to me and I signed the contract Bob Paisley had pushed across his desk towards me. Another date ingrained in my memory: 1 May 1980.

I returned to Chester to say goodbye to everybody, from my teammates to the tea lady. I found this difficult to do. Everyone had been so very good to me and had always been so supportive. I didn't consider the people at the club as work colleagues so much as friends. I knew I owed much to Alan Oakes and Cliff Sear, and it was Alan who offered a piece of telling advice as I thanked him for all he had done for me.

'Just remember this,' he said. 'Your first year at Liverpool will be the worst of your life. There'll be times you'll hate it so much you'll feel you want to come running back here, even pack the game in. Stick it out, tough it out, and you'll have a wonderful career. You have what it takes. Otherwise I wouldn't be letting you go. You've got to keep that same belief in yourself.'

To be perfectly frank I didn't fully comprehend the wisdom of Alan's words. I thought, 'OK, so it's going to be tough, but I can handle tough. No problem.' Liverpool had paid £300,000 for me, a British record fee for a teenager. I was going to earn what I considered to be a fortune and play for the best team in Europe, one of the best clubs in the world. Bring it on!

CHAPTER THREE

Don't You Want Me?

Having signed for Liverpool I continued to live at home with my parents. The Liverpool players reported first to Anfield for daily training, changing at the ground, then journeyed to Melwood by coach. When training was over, we would 'warm down' by jogging around the training ground before boarding the coach back to Anfield where we showered.

This routine had been instigated by Bill Shankly in the early 1960s and was to continue until Graeme Souness was appointed manager in 1991. I was told, by coach Ronnie Moran, that Shankly felt it unhealthy for players to shower immediately after training as they would still be sweating and the pores of their skin would be open, leading them to continue perspiring after having had a shower. I'm well aware this is not a major aspect to the daily life of players, but it proved correct and indicates just how forward-thinking Shankly and Bob Paisley (his then right-hand man) were and how much attention they paid to detail.

Shankly's legacy had been faithfully continued by Bob in many other ways. As he said, 'Why try and mend something that isn't broken?' True to Shankly's doctrine I was told that everything about Liverpool was the greatest: that they had the greatest players, supporters, trainers, scouts, training ground and facilities. According to Bob, even the tea ladies were great.

Bob had every right to be proud of what he and Shankly had achieved at the club. When the pair got together in 1960, Liverpool was a middling Second Division club with a ramshackle ground and a team not much better. Shankly's infectious drive, enthusiasm and total self-belief, coupled with Bob's practicality, technical nous and knowledge of players had seen Liverpool experience an unparalleled football renaissance. The club was now a giant of English and European football. I found the prospect of being part of such a dynasty a little daunting.

I certainly didn't expect to walk straight into the Liverpool team. They had just clinched their second successive League Championship, their fifth in seven years, and won the European Cup for the previous two years. As far as I was concerned I was about to embark upon another apprenticeship.

On my first day I looked around the dressing-room and couldn't quite believe I was in the company of the likes of Kenny Dalglish, Alan Hansen, Ray Clemence, Graeme Souness, Ray Kennedy and Terry McDermott. Every first-team player seemed to be an international and a household name. I was in awe of them and didn't have the confidence to engage them in conversation.

Three days after my transfer I made my debut for Liverpool reserves at, of all places, Manchester United. It was a time when the reserve teams of First Division clubs played at their home ground rather than the ground of lower or non-League clubs as is the case today. Even though there were only a few thousand supporters present, playing at Old Trafford for the first time was something of a thrill for me. Liverpool had a strong reserve team which included the likes of Steve Ogrizovic in goal, Kevin Sheedy,

David Fairclough, Alan Harper, Avi Cohen, Ronnie Whelan, Brian Kettle and Howard Gayle. Though painfully shy I didn't lack confidence in my ability as a player, but as we set about getting changed I realised just how difficult it was going to be for me to break into the first team at Liverpool. Even the reserves were formidable, containing players who would have walked into most other First Division clubs.

The game ended 1–1 with Howard Gayle scoring our goal. Given it was my first game and I didn't know any of my teammates, I thought I did OK. Reserve team boss, Roy Evans, seemed happy enough. After the game he said well done and offered me some encouraging words. I was still so tongue-tied I don't think I managed more than 'thanks' by way of reply.

Two days later, Liverpool reserves travelled to Bloomfield Road to play Blackpool for the final reserve match of the season. I can't recall the game in any detail, but it does have a place in my memory because I scored my first Liverpool goal, converting a cross from Alan Harper. The match ended 3–3 with Harper and Colin Russell scoring our other goals.

I had been at Liverpool for less than a week, played two games for the reserves and scored a goal. In my book, it was a satisfactory start to my career at Anfield.

The day after playing against Blackpool reserves I received a phone call at home. It was from Mike England, the Wales manager, informing me that he had included me in the Welsh squad for the Home International Championship. I couldn't quite believe it. I was both proud and excited as were my family, particularly Mum and Dad.

Mike England had just been appointed Wales's manager and this was his first squad. He had been out of British football for some years as he had been living in the USA where he had a number of business interests. It's unthinkable now that someone, even of Mike's pedigree, would be appointed as manager of one of our international teams in such circumstances. While in the USA, Mike had maintained a number of contacts in the game and, immediately following his appointment, spent much time on the telephone. Seemingly, it had been one of these contacts who had alerted Mike to my performances and progress at Chester, rather than it having anything to do with my being a Liverpool player.

I was struggling to come to terms with how my career and life had changed with such express speed. Less than a fortnight previously I had played for Chester against Southend United. Now I was a Liverpool player and on the verge of international football. It had all happened so quickly I couldn't put it into proper perspective.

Wales's first game in the Home International Championship was against England at Wrexham's racecourse ground. Four days before, England, under Ron Greenwood, had beaten world champions Argentina at Wembley, a game which marked the first appearance in the UK of Diego Maradona. Before this victory, England had enjoyed a 2–0 win against Spain in Barcelona. Mike England and I could not have wished for tougher debuts as international manager and player respectively.

In the event I didn't make the final eleven against England but was named amongst the five substitutes. On paper England were far and away the stronger team and included four of my new teammates from Liverpool: Ray Clemence, Phil Neal, Phil Thompson and Ray Kennedy with two others, Terry McDermott and David Johnson, amongst the substitutes. (I had still not plucked up the courage to talk to any of them.) Also included in the England side were Glen Hoddle, Trevor Brooking, Steve Coppell and Paul Mariner. It was a formidable line-up. Bryan Robson only made the bench.

England were without Kevin Keegan, however, while Wales were without Alan Curtis of Leeds United and Robbie James of Swansea City. All three were recovering from injuries. (Robbie's injury occurred when he was playing for Swansea against Cambridge United. He attempted a header near the post and, instead of connecting with the ball, headed the woodwork. He had to have ten stitches. The joke in the Wales dressing-room was the post had twelve.)

I still have the match programme from the England game. Under the heading 'Wales' Newcomers' there is a photograph of David Giles of Swansea and me. David is resplendent in a Wales under-21 shirt, while a very callow me is seen looking every inch the international player – in a dark, long-collared shirt and v-necked jumper from Burton's.

Before the game Mike England gave a rousing team-talk, telling us we were all players of true international class. Given I had yet to play for Wales at full international level I took it he was referring to everyone but me. Mike went on to say Wales were now respected and feared as a team throughout world football and we had it in us to beat any side. Whether this was true or not I don't know, but he said it with such conviction and emotion we believed him. What was more, the team carried this belief on to the pitch and enjoyed one of the most historic wins in our football history, beating England 4–1, this after having trailed to a goal from Paul Mariner.

It was a sensational start to the Home International Championship and to Mike England's career as manager of Wales. For the record our goals were scored by Mickey Thomas, Ian Walsh, Leighton James and an own goal from Phil Thompson. The star of the show was Leighton James, who led the England defence a merry dance. I was never called into action, but given the performance of the Welsh team that day, I didn't expect to be.

Though watching from the bench I felt very proud to be a part of the Wales squad that day. In later years, I remember a reporter from a broadsheet newspaper saying to me, 'Do you regret not having been born English?' I was incensed by this. I told him exactly how I felt about being Welsh and how proud I was of my roots and country.

Buoyed by what was a famous victory over England (only Wales's second in twenty-five years) we travelled in great spirits to Glasgow to meet Scotland four days later at Hampden Park. Again I was named as substitute and again I was confronted by another Liverpool teammate, this time Kenny Dalglish. For Wales it was very much a case of 'after the Lord Mayor's show'. The team never reproduced anything like the performance they had against England and trailed to a first-half goal from Willie Miller. Midway through the second half, Ian Walsh picked up an injury and Mike England told me to get warmed up. Four minutes later I made my international debut for Wales.

In my twenty-five minutes on the field a couple of chances did come my way but unfortunately I didn't manage to convert them. As a striker, I never believed there to be such a thing as a half-chance. Every opportunity at goal, no matter how difficult, was a chance as far as I was concerned.

Disappointingly, we never managed to equalise, and Miller's goal was the only one of the game. Though I was only on the field for some twenty minutes I was so very proud to have represented my country, a feeling which never left me whenever I pulled on the famous red shirt.

For our final game, against Northern Ireland at Ninian Park, I was a substitute again. On this occasion I was not called into action. Northern Ireland, who were also playing under a new manager in Billy Bingham, not only beat Wales 1–0 but secured the Home International Championship, their first outright Championship success since 1914!

Afterwards Tracy and I took off to Spain for a holiday. It was some holiday. Life was terrific. I had no doubt whatsoever I had met the girl with whom I wanted to spend the rest of my life, I was with one of the greatest clubs in the world and I had represented my country at full international level. Everything was going right for me, but I was soon to realise how fragile life can be.

I was really looking forward to putting down some sort of marker at Liverpool when I reported back for the 1980–1 season. As a player I wasn't lacking in self-confidence but could still hardly believe the club trumpeted as the best in Europe could be interested in me. That Liverpool had signed me for what was then a sizeable fee didn't bolster my confidence. To me, confidence comes from what a player does on the pitch, not the stature of the club he belongs to, or the size of the fee the club has paid for his services.

I knew I had a lot of hard work ahead of me if I was to break into the first team and set myself a goal of two years to do so. I reasoned that if, after two years, I had still not made the first team I would return to Chester and see out my career at Sealand Road. That was my thinking: simple, neat, all worked-out. I was some four months short of my nineteenth birthday. I recall once seeing a small-ad in the *Liverpool Echo* which read: 'For Sale Complete Set of Encyclopaedia Britannica. No longer needed. I have a nineteen-year-old son who knows everything.' I need say no more.

Having only had a couple of weeks' experience at Liverpool, when I reported back for pre-season training in July 1980 I still didn't know anybody or realise what the club and its culture was all about. Keen to make an impression, I was always first to arrive at Anfield for daily training. It was as the players changed into their training kit in readiness for the short trip to Melwood that I was first made aware of the differences in dressing-room culture between Liverpool and Chester.

In 1980 Blondie was riding high in the album charts with *Parallel Lines*, and all young people were listening to 'indie' rock. I was into this type of music, in particular the Sheffield band Human League, but I also liked 'two-tone' as performed by The Specials, Madness, The Beat and Selector. The first-team players at Liverpool, by contrast, listened to the likes of ELO, The Commodores, Diana Ross and Barry Manilow. With every musical movement comes a style of dress. At the time the fashion was skin-tight jeans or trousers and white socks. Along with all my mates back in Flint and Chester, I dressed this way. I would buy my white socks from Millets and my 'skinny' Levi jeans from an 'alternative' clothes shop. The likes of Kenny Dalglish and Graeme Souness would arrive wearing Ralph Lauren casual shirts and Pierre Cardin trousers purchased from the city's most exclusive and expensive clothes shops. When they saw what I was wearing they took great delight in taking the piss.

Every dressing-room has a culture and its ringleaders. Most of the time there is nothing sinister in this, just ebullient players confident of their own ability who like to create a dressing-room 'atmosphere'. Kenny Dalglish is often thought of as being quite a dour person, devoid of humour. Actually the opposite is the case.

Kenny was one of the prominent characters in that Liverpool dressing-room and would always lead the banter, making wise-cracks and quips about everybody and anything. I didn't know a

RUSH

single player and was still too shy to talk to them, but that didn't stop Kenny.

'Been repairing the car, have you?' he'd say to me. 'You know you're supposed to get changed out of old work clothes before coming here. Have you got bad credit or just bad taste?'

Then Graeme Souness and Alan Hansen would chime in.

'How many polyesters died to make that shirt?'

'What's it with you, Ian? Quieter you are, the louder your socks?'

I couldn't have felt more self-conscious.

Looking back, I must have appeared a bit of a scruff. I took to wearing a plain T-shirt and pair of jeans to go to training, thinking this would be 'neutral', but the mickey-taking continued unabated.

I didn't have the wherewithal or confidence to quip back. I took the stick and said nothing, but the more it went on the more I began to resent it and the players who were dishing it out.

At Chester, when Alan Oakes or Bob Delgado made a wisecrack at my expense, that was it for a few days. Besides which, the senior Chester players, along with Alan and Cliff, were always offering advice and tips on how I could improve my game. At this stage none of the Liverpool players did this. In those early days, as we prepared for 1980–1, I was the subject of mickey-taking in the dressing-room every morning. I would force a smile but inside I was squirming.

At one point I couldn't wait for training to be over, to get out of Anfield and back to Flint where my pals dressed the same as me, listened to the same music, shared the same interests and in whose company I felt comfortable and secure.

The one aspect of my life the dressing-room wags never passed comment on was my church attendance. (I was, and still am, a regular churchgoer.) There seemed to be an un-written rule that no one talked religion or politics at the club. I later learned that this 'rule' had come from Bill Shankly over twenty years previously. Seemingly, Shanks saw religion and politics as a matter of personal belief and didn't encourage discussion of either subject as he felt it could result in possible argument and thus be detrimental to team spirit.

I was a teenager who had been catapulted from a small, friendly Third Division club to the current League Champions whose players were all household names. I was finding the transition difficult, although actually playing against experienced top-class players held no fears for me.

At the time I wasn't aware that the constant mickey-taking was perceived as harmless banter geared to assessing character and, although this may not have been a conscious thought on the part of the players, to ingratiate me into the culture of the Liverpool dressing-room.

I often thought about the advice Alan Oakes had given me on leaving Chester, that my first year at Liverpool would be the worst of my life and that I must 'stick it out'. I was so unhappy I didn't feel like sticking it out. Life at Liverpool wasn't as I had expected it to be. I guess Alan knew this would be the case. For the first time in my life, I was being put through the mill in order to discover my true potential and I wasn't liking the journey, which I now see as a rite of passage.

As my schools career officer had told me, football is a ruthless, demanding business. It is demanding not only physically but mentally. The mental toughening-up process begins in the daily testosterone-driven atmosphere of the dressing-room where you have to swim rather than sink. If you can't handle mickey-taking from teammates, there is no way you are going to cope when your team and you are up against it before 80,000 frenzied supporters in the San Siro in Milan or the Nou Camp in Barcelona.

I began 1980–1 playing in the reserve team in the Central League which started with a rousing 4–0 win at Coventry City. I was more than happy that I managed a goal. The following four reserve team games, however, proved pretty unremarkable from my point of view as I worked to adjust to the level that was expected of me.

The Central League was of a very good standard of football. First Division clubs such as Liverpool, Everton, the two Manchester clubs and Leeds United would name thirteen players for the first-team game on a Saturday; those that didn't make the thirteen played in the Central League side, which often also included first-team players coming back from injury. I found I was coming up against international players on a weekly basis.

It wasn't a case of being out of my depth. I felt I was contributing to games, but I missed the guidance and advice I had been given at Chester and the warmth of that club. I wasn't expecting to be mollycoddled at Liverpool, far from it, but I felt very much left to my own devices. At Chester I would play for the first team on a Saturday and, at some point during training in the following week, Alan Oakes or Cliff Sear would take me to one side, highlight an aspect of my play from the previous game and work with me to improve upon it. This didn't happen at Liverpool. I was left to cope as best I could, and work things out for myself. As a teenager I was still very much at the learning stage in my career, and the lack of guidance along with being singled out for mickey-taking in the dressing-room made me feel isolated and, at times, unwanted.

Still too shy to talk to the likes of Dalglish and Hansen, the fact

I didn't say anything in response to their mickey-taking, of course, encouraged them all the more. Generally speaking I got on well with my fellow reserve-team players, but I did detect certain resentment towards me from other young players at the club. I felt some of them, those who had been at Anfield from schoolboys, were rather distant and cold towards me. Perhaps they resented the fact the club had paid such a substantial fee for me, and that, despite this, I wasn't exactly on fire.

In my teenage mind I felt all it would need for me to ask for a move back to Chester would be for the management to get on my back. Which, given I was not producing the goods in reserve games and not making an effort to endear myself to other players, I thought might happen any day. My disenchantment must have been evident to Roy Evans, who was in charge of the reserve team, because, one day after training, he took me to one side.

'You've got the ability to walk into the first team,' Roy told me. 'It's not down to me or the boss. It's all down to you, son, and how much you want it. Instead of focusing on other players, what they say to you and how they treat you, start focusing on you – your personal game, your attitude, your reaction to things. Start thinking about what you want from this club and your career, and, if it's what I think it is, be single-minded.'

Roy was aware of my unhappiness and his words were geared to lifting my spirits, but they also made me think about how I might not be making an effort to assimilate, and what I really wanted from my career. I suddenly realised I had to take a long, hard look at myself.

Following my chat with Roy I put the thought of returning to Chester out of my head. I came to the conclusion this was negative and defeatist. I knew I had potential and vowed to work hard to realise it.

My change of attitude was helped by a sudden flurry of goal-scoring for the reserves. Having not scored since the opening day of the season, in mid-September I notched a hat-trick in a 5–0 win over Preston and went on to score four in the following five reserve matches. I was playing in midfield and though the goals dried up in November, in early December I managed to score against both Wolves and Blackpool. Goals apart, I felt my overall displays were improving, though I knew I was still feeling my way. Then, in mid-December, I was given a fillip.

Kenny Dalglish sustained an injury in training and Bob Paisley collared me after Thursday morning training. He told me I was in the first-team squad for the game at Ipswich Town and, given that Kenny was unlikely to be fit, in all probability I would be taking his place.

This was the moment I had been waiting for. In truth my call-up took me by surprise. I felt there were reserve team players ahead of me in the pecking order. But Bob Paisley, it transpired, wanted a forward who could link up with striker David Johnson, and he was of the mind that I fitted the bill. I certainly wasn't going to argue.

Ipswich were joint top of Division One with Aston Villa, with Liverpool in fourth place. Bobby Robson had assembled a very good team which boasted an unbeaten home record. In players such as George Burley, Mick Mills, Frank Thijssen, Arnold Muhren, Terry Butcher, John Wark, Paul Mariner and Eric Gates, Ipswich had blended class with competitive strength. There were easier games in which to make my Liverpool debut but I never felt over-awed by the quality of the opposition.

Chester were always strapped for money so, when playing an away game, we only stayed over on a Friday night when it was absolutely necessary, for example at Gillingham or Exeter City.

For trips to Sheffield United, Carlisle or Oxford we would travel on the morning of the game and return immediately after the match. Liverpool, on the other hand, stayed overnight for home matches as well as away games, initially at the Lord Daresberry hotel in Warrington, later at the Holiday Inn on the outskirts of Liverpool.

For some players sharing a room, particularly with someone you hardly know, never comes easy. I was fortunate in this respect. Having shared a bedroom with my brothers, privacy was an alien concept to me.

We arrived at our hotel in Ipswich at around five on the Friday afternoon. Joe Fagan informed me I was to room with substitute Jimmy Case. This relaxed me. Jimmy was not one of those players who had indulged in the mickey-taking. He was friendly, chirpy, easy-going and, having been assigned a room together, he made me feel welcome.

All players are different. On away trips some turned the hotel room into a tip, with clothes scattered on the floor, glasses and water bottles littering every surface, toothpaste all over the sink, wet towels on the bathroom floor, soiled underpants hanging over the back of a chair, the loo not flushed after a pee. Others, like Alan Hansen for example, were meticulously neat and tidy. His shirts would be carefully folded like origami, shoes placed in line in the wardrobe, dirty clothing placed in a carrier bag inside the holdall, the little paper bags that the teabags come in always placed in the waste-bin after use. Everything had its place. I was not one of these players, but Jimmy Case didn't seem to mind my untidiness.

In the evening we assembled for a light meal in the dining room, then it was up to the rooms again to watch some TV before lights out at 10pm. I was too excited to sleep. While Jimmy dozed off, I lay there trying to imagine what the game would be like, conjuring up images of doing this or that until, eventually, everything became a blur.

The following morning I ate a light breakfast and thought there might be a team talk from Bob about Ipswich, but there wasn't. Apparently, this was normal. Bob paid very little attention to the opposition other than to refer to their formation. No one at Liverpool ever worried about the opposition. Every player was so confident in our ability as a team that they were happy to let the opposition do the worrying. We went for a short walk, bought some newspapers and read them on our return to the hotel. This was followed by a light lunch after which we packed our bags and boarded the coach for Portman Road.

As I changed I looked across to the likes of Ray Clemence, Alan Hansen, Phil Neal, Ray Kennedy, Graeme Souness, Terry Mac and Sammy Lee. Their very presence instilled me with confidence. I was glad Souness, Hansen and Clem were in our dressing-room rather than the one next door. I didn't think I was going to set the world on fire on my debut, but with such a team of class players around me I was confident I wouldn't disgrace myself.

The game against Ipswich was highly competitive, which I had expected, but, given the number of quality players on the pitch, not exactly a football classic. Alan Brazil gave Ipswich a first-half lead, which gave us some work to do. I found the pace of the game far quicker than I had been used to in the Central League, but at no point did I ever feel play was passing me by. On the contrary, I found I was involved from the start, though I was mindful to keep it simple and not take chances that might result in a mistake or, heaven forbid, an Ipswich goal.

As the second half progressed I felt I was well into the pace of the game and, as we began to assert ourselves, the equaliser came late in the half when Jimmy Case, who had come on as a substitute for David Johnson, fired home after I had linked up with Graeme Souness and Terry Mac.

A point at Ipswich was gratifying, though there was also dissatisfaction that we had not done enough to turn the single point into two, there only being two points for a win at the time. That's how it is in football. Lose and you rue the fact you didn't manage a draw. Draw away from home and it is never enough.

Having endured weeks of constant mickey-taking, the attitude of the first team players towards me suddenly changed. Both before and throughout the game, I received nothing but encouragement from my teammates, particularly Souness, Lee and Terry Mac. Irrespective of how brief my elevation the first team turned out to be I now sensed I was one of them. I had a role to play in the team and they needed me to do my bit for the cause. To help me do this, players constantly talked to me and encouraged me.

After the game Bob Paisley said, 'Well done,' but I wasn't deluding myself. The injury to Dalglish was not serious, and he was expected to be fit for the following game against Wolves. Though I hoped I would have some sort of involvement in that game, I expected to return to reserve team football. I wasn't wrong.

Until April I did my bit in helping Liverpool reserves win a second successive Central League title. I thought I was improving with every game, and this made me lose my inferiority complex. Roy Evans was delighted with my progress, and must have notified Bob Paisley, because I was called up once again to the first team, this time in dramatic fashion.

Liverpool had never won the League Cup. The nearest they had come to doing this was in 1977–8, when beaten in the final by Nottingham Forest after a replay. For a number of years, when the League Cup was a new concept to English football, Liverpool, with their eyes on bigger prizes, had not deigned to enter. In 1980–1, however, with the League title looking as if it was going to either Aston Villa or Ipswich Town, and having exited the FA Cup in January at the hands of Everton, Liverpool made a concerted effort to progress in the European Cup and, domestically, in the League Cup. They had succeeded in reaching the final of the latter and were due to play West Ham United at Wembley in March. Although I was in the squad I didn't expect to get a shirt, and so it proved. I watched the game as one of the reserves seated behind the Liverpool bench. A very tight game ended 1–1 after extra time. The replay was set for three and a half weeks later at Villa Park.

Then David Johnson sustained an injury. I had played my second game for the first team against Stoke City the previous Saturday which resulted in a comfortable 3–0 victory. Knowing this was only my second first-team match, and my home debut to boot, Liverpool supporters gave me a fantastic reception, which still lives with me now. They were right behind me from the start and applauded almost my every touch of the ball which spurred me to even greater effort. Again, I felt I had done reasonably well without making any great impact on the game. It was expected that the experienced Steve Heighway would recover from an injury he had picked up in time to replace Johnson for the League Cup final replay, but the winds of providence were blowing a gale that week.

On the morning of the replay Steve was subjected to a fitness test and failed it. Bob Paisley, never one to stand on ceremony, simply said to me, 'Ian, son, you're in.'

I couldn't believe it. I had only two first-team matches under my belt and now I was to play in a major cup final. After Bob had given this news to the media I was told by a reporter that I would create a record, being the first player to make his League Cup debut in a final. Needless to say, records were the furthest thing from my mind that day.

I can still recall the Liverpool team that faced West Ham on 6 April 1980: Ray Clemence, Phil Neal, Alan Kennedy, Phil Thompson, Alan Hansen, Ray Kennedy, Kenny Dalglish, Sammy Lee, me, Terry McDermott and Jimmy Case.

The West Ham team included Phil Parkes (whose ability as a goalkeeper was such that if he were playing today he'd walk into the England team), Frank Lampard senior, Billy Bonds, Trevor Brooking, Alvin Martin, David Cross and Paul Goddard.

Playing in a League Cup final was, up to this point, the most momentous moment of my life. Before the game, however, I didn't feel any more nervous than I had done in my previous two outings for the first team. I was never the sort of player so riddled with nerves I traipsed too and fro from the loo before match. I might feel a few butterflies in my stomach, and only then for a few moments, but that was about it. I reasoned that I was in the team because Bob Paisley and Joe Fagan believed I could do a job for Liverpool and, even at this embryonic stage of my Anfield career, it was a belief I too now shared.

My excitement was so great it over-rode any disappointment I felt that the game was to take place at Villa Park, not Wembley. The sense of occasion was not diminished in the least for me by the fact Liverpool approached the game as they would a normal League match. There was no special preparation on the training field, no protracted team meetings, no commemorative suits or blazers, or special hotel arrangements. It was simply a case of going down to Birmingham on the coach and doing the job. In contrast to the tight first meeting, the replay was full of open and entertaining football. Even when Paul Goddard gave West Ham an early lead, I was still confident we had enough to come back and overhaul them. I agonised when I had a shot at goal only to see the ball crash against the angle of post and bar. Minutes later Ray Kennedy headed the ball against the bar, but our constant pressure eventually paid off. Before the first half was out, goals from Dalglish and Hansen put us in the lead, a lead we were never to relinquish. Prompted by Trevor Brooking and Alan Devonshire, West Ham gave it a go in the second half, but such was our dominance, I felt the final score of 2–1 somewhat flattered our opponents.

When the final whistle blew I couldn't believe how quickly the game had appeared to pass. When I was presented with my winners' medal I blinked at it disbelievingly. It seemed so unreal, that in only my third game for the first team I now had a major domestic honour. Overjoyed I joined my teammates for the customary lap of honour. As we held the League Cup and the sponsors' Milk Cup aloft in front of our marvellous supporters, I felt my Liverpool career had finally taken off.

We celebrated victory in some style. Both cups were filled with champagne and passed about for all players and backroom staff to sip. There were smiles all round but I don't think there was a broader smile than mine. I felt very much a part of the celebrations and the team. I was expecting to wind down with a few beers at the club's post-final banquet, but Bob restricted each player to two small bottles of beer. As he reminded us, within a matter of days, we had an important European Cup tie.

I sensed my dad was quietly pleased and proud that I had made it into the first team at Anfield. He was never one to heap praise, as I think he didn't want my relative success to go to my head. Not that there was any danger of that. When I was a boy I saw my dad as being gifted with dazzling accomplishments. He could mend a puncture, paint the house, cut hair, fix the radio, make a gate for the railings at the front of the house and bowl a googly. I now began to sense that we might be on the verge of a role reversal.

My mum, brothers and sisters were also pleased for me. It made me think back to the time when I had brought shame on them all and vowed to do something with my life that would make them proud of me. I knew I still had much to prove at Anfield, but having won a League Cup winners' medal, I felt I had gone some way to keeping my boyhood promise to myself.

I never felt my mates in Flint were resentful of what I had achieved. On the contrary, every time I met them they wanted to talk of little else but life at Liverpool. I had shed my 'two-tone' style clothes, but so too had they. Time had moved on, people had changed and not just their style of clothes

Just as I had made new friends at Liverpool in Ronnie Whelan and Sammy Lee, my old mates had also made new friendships with the people they now worked with or at the clubs and pubs they now frequented. I was always really pleased to see one of my old mates but, as time went by, after the initial flurry of talk about what we were up to in our respective lives, the conversation would then tail off and there would be a slightly embarrassing silence, the way it is when old friends meet and realise they have gone very different ways. That said, I was always glad to see them and made a point of asking them lots of questions about their lives, in the main because I felt rather self-conscious about talking of life at Liverpool in case they might think I was boasting.

I wanted to be Ian Rush the Liverpool striker, wanted to play in front of 40,000 people every week, wanted the lifestyle my success on the field had brought me, but I also wanted people to see I was still the Ian they had known years ago and that none of this had changed me as a person. In essence I felt the core of my being was the same as it had always been, but there was no doubting I had changed, as everyone does with the passing of the years.

I was learning all the time, the League Cup final being no exception. Whenever I had the ball at my feet against West Ham, I was conscious of the fact I had to use it constructively, as possession was the name of the game at Liverpool. As in my two previous outings at Ipswich and Stoke, whenever a Liverpool player passed the ball I noticed he would run ten or so yards to offer an option to the teammate he had made the pass to. Likewise, whenever I had the ball with my back to goal I found I had ready options, which made things easier for me. I was, of course, always looking to exploit space in and around the West Ham penalty area because I knew that's where Dalglish, Terry McDermott, Sammy Lee and Jimmy Case were going to be playing the ball. They did this consistently, with imagination and variety, allowing me to make incisive runs, which, if not exactly pulling the West Ham defence all over the place, served to distract them, which, in turn, provided openings for my teammates.

In the wake of our League Cup success another realisation dawned on me: the better the players around me, the better I seemed to play. In addition to which, rather than being over-awed, I found I relished the big occasion.

Following the League Cup final replay I played in five of Liverpool's remaining seven league matches without ever featuring amongst the goals. For all I was enjoying an extended run, I never considered myself a fixture in the first team. No player at Liverpool ever did, Dalglish included.

David Johnson was still unfit and, human nature being what it is, I was far from unhappy when he was still sidelined for the first leg of the European Cup semi-final against Bayern Munich. At Liverpool prestigious games came thick and fast. Every game was a big one, and I was conscious that this would be yet another yard-stick by which I would be judged.

But I couldn't wait for the chance. While conscious I was on a steep learning curve I felt I was up to playing against the best, and at Bayern Munich there were three players deemed world-class: Uli Hoeness, Paul Breitner and Karl-Heinz Rummenigge. After my miserable start at Anfield I was now really enjoying life at the club and even duped myself into thinking every door would open up for me.

The first game against Bayern Munich at Anfield ended goalless. It was a frustrating night for me, the team and our supporters. We put Bayern under pressure for large parts of the game but they offered ample evidence of their quality by riding out the storm. When David Johnson recovered from his injury in time to play in the second leg in Munich, I feared the worst. Sure enough, for the return in Munich I was relegated to the bench. Though disappointed I was far from disillusioned. I had already reasoned that Bob would opt for David's experience.

Liverpool's never-say-die attitude and resilience was never so much in evidence as it was that night in Munich. Bayern gave it all they had – which was a considerable amount, believe me – but a Ray Kennedy goal cancelled out one from Rummenigge, and Liverpool won through on away goals. I wasn't called into action but, given the game was delicately balanced and, at 1–1, the tie had swung in Liverpool's favour, I knew I would not get my boots dirty. A European Cup final against Real Madrid now beckoned.

These were heady times for English clubs in Europe. Liverpool's European Cup final victories of 1977 and 1978 had been followed by successive victories for Nottingham Forest. Our victory on away goals over Bayern Munich meant an English club was to appear in a European Cup final for an unprecedented fifth successive year. (The following season Aston Villa made it six.)

English club football was admired and feared throughout Europe, though, to everyone's frustration, the success of English clubs in all three European competitions had not been mirrored by the national team. Throughout the 1970s England had failed to qualify for the finals of a major international tournament. England had automatically qualified for the 1970 World Cup finals as holders and the 1966 tournament as hosts, which meant it had been eighteen years since England had actually qualified for the finals of a World Cup by virtue of the group stage. The press and English supporters were becoming increasingly twitchy about this lack of success. Given the achievements of English clubs in European competitions it was a conundrum for which no one really came up with a plausible answer. So here goes . . .

When Liverpool played in Europe we adapted our style, playing a more patient game at a slower tempo than First Division matches, retaining possession until an opening presented itself. Should we find ourselves under pressure, we became expert at soaking it up then swiftly breaking. This style, and that of Nottingham Forest (which was, by comparison, more cautious), had proved highly effective against Continental opposition.

England's critics, who seemed to comprise the majority of the press, were of the mind the problem lay in the style of football played by the majority of First Division clubs which, compared to that of top-flight international football was blighted by inferior technique, imagination and skill. Little wonder, it was believed, given the shortcomings of our domestic football, England could not suddenly export style, artistry and enlightenment in international tournaments. The critics may have had a point but it still didn't explain why, given the perceived shortcomings of the international team, English clubs had been so successful in Europe. Looking back I think part of the problem for England was the national team's inability to reproduce the cohesive team performances that had become the trademark of Liverpool and Nottingham Forest.

Liverpool were consistent in combining hard graft and resolute play with a fluent passing game. The mantra was we should never give the ball away. The opposition might win the ball but rarely did Liverpool make a gift of it. Conversely, when the opposition had the ball, Liverpool worked extremely hard to deny them space and opportunity. We supported each other on and off the ball, and had the skill and the confidence to play adventurous, attacking football.

Since 1965 season after season of European football at Liverpool had been overseen by Bob Paisley and Joe Fagan. They continued to learn with every game, because you never stop learning in football, but I doubt there was a management team in the world which possessed the continuity, experience and knowledge of Bob and Joe. In six years since 1974, if you include caretaker boss Joe Mercer, England had had four managers and in that time underwent wholesale changes to the team. Often the changes in personnel were stark. For example, after losing to Spain at Wembley in March 1981, the England team showed six changes for the World Cup qualifying match against Romania a month later. Bob Paisley had changed the Liverpool team over the years but so gradual were these changes they appeared seamless.

Liverpool never underestimated the opposition but there was no fear factor, either. The same could not be said of England. The pressure on the national team to succeed was immense and, unlike Liverpool, their track record over the past decade had hardly been exemplary. By the late 1970s England had acquired baggage which, no matter how much they tried to ignore it, they carried on to the pitch.

While foreign players had yet to make an impact on our game, Liverpool and Nottingham Forest comprised players from the Home Countries and Ireland. At the time Liverpool had Kenny Dalglish, Graeme Souness and Alan Hansen, all Scots and obviously denied to England. That trio were the bedrock of the Liverpool team and one of the reasons for our success was that the team comprised others who complemented those great players. Arguably, the reason Scotland did not enjoy success in international tournaments either was they did not have sufficient players of calibre to bring the best out in Dalglish, Souness and Hansen.

After all my perceived trials and tribulations I was now enjoying life at Anfield. I received a bonus of £800 for having helped win the League Cup, in addition to which I was on a first-team win bonus of £250. I was sitting well financially, particularly for such a young lad, and traded my old banger for a new car. One day I found myself standing looking at the display window of one of the trendy city clothes shops frequented by my Liverpool teammates. I bought myself some shirts, trousers and shoes, and when I turned up at Anfield wearing my new outfit, no one passed comment. The days of being the subject of constant mickey-taking were over.

Regular involvement with the first team gave me confidence, not only as player but off the field as well. When it came to wisecracks and verbals, I began to assert myself.

'Hey, I'm fittest. I do sit-ups every night before I get into bed.

Timed myself the other week: sixty-two minutes!' Graeme Souness once boasted during dressing-room talk about fitness.

'Was that the night they put the clocks forward?' I quipped.

Laughter rippled around the dressing-room and Graeme's moustache literally bristled.

I was now joining in and enjoying the banter of my teammates. But although I also now dressed like them, I never bought a Commodores or Barry Manilow album. I felt I had to draw a line somewhere.

In my first months at Liverpool I had disliked Kenny Dalglish, who was such a dominant figure in the dressing-room. Now that I had had a decent run in the first team Kenny's attitude to me completely changed. He was forever giving me advice during games, making me aware of situations, pointing out weaknesses in opponents and the opposition defence, telling me when and how to make my runs off the ball and so on.

That I had made the first team and held my place helped me assimilate with other players, too. But as is often the case in life, just as you are duped into thinking you have turned a corner and everything is going your way, you are unceremoniously brought down to earth.

Bob named eighteen players for the trip to Paris for the European Cup final against Real Madrid. With five substitutes to be named, this meant that two players were going to be mighty disappointed. With David Johnson fit again I didn't expect to play in the final against Real Madrid in Paris. I did, however, expect to be on the bench as Bob Paisley had taken me to one side before we flew out from Liverpool, and told me I would 'definitely be involved'. But on the morning of the final, Bob called us to a team meeting in the hotel.

'I'm going to have to disappoint two of you,' he said.

So be it.

'Avi Cohen and Ian Rush.'

I can't remember what Bob then went on to say because I wasn't listening. The moment I heard my name I felt the adrenalin prickling my forehead. I was stunned. I would have been disappointed not to have been given a shirt if Bob have said nothing at all, but to be told I was going to be 'involved', only for him to go back on his word hit me hard. I was devastated.

Liverpool beat Real Madrid 1–0, courtesy of a super solo effort from full-back Alan Kennedy. I was genuinely pleased for my team-mates, the club and our supporters, but after the game felt totally out of it. So much so that I didn't attend the celebratory party at the hotel. Instead I joined two of my pals from the reserves, Kevin Sheedy and Ronnie Whelan, for a drink in another bar.

It is never good when players who have been left out get together. They brood, moan and tend to wallow in self-pity. In such circumstances a player will tell his mate, 'I think you should be in,' and give some sort of reason for his inclusion, in the hope his mate will return the compliment. In such a situation disappointment only festers.

Kevin, Ronnie and I were very disappointed, and, being human, we of course moaned about our respective situations. Kevin was of the mind he was never going to break into the first team on a regular basis, and said he felt the time had come for him to move on. Ronnie and I didn't go so far as saying we wanted out of Anfield, but we played Job's comforter to one another.

Again it was Roy Evans who lifted my spirits, just as he had done in those early months at the club.

'Get over your disappointment,' he advised me, 'because, believe me, no matter how good a career you might go on to have, there will be other disappointments. You've got to ride them, buckle down, be single-minded and not let them be obstacles to you achieving your goal.'

Bob Paisley might have looked like Walt Disney's idea of a grandfather – indeed he could often be seen walking around the corridors of Anfield wearing carpet slippers and a cardigan with leather elbow patches – but he was the most astute manager I ever played for, whose retiring demeanour masked a remarkable knowledge of players and tactics.

I had committed myself to a three-year contract when I signed for Liverpool, but I'd heard that making it into the first-team squad would entitle me to a £100 a week rise on top of my existing £300 a week. Before the start of the 1981–2 season, I went to see Bob to discuss this matter. Bob had a surprise in store for me, and it wasn't of the nice sort.

'I'll give you a ten per cent rise,' he told me.

I had no agent so dealt with such matters on my own. Though only nineteen, I was determined to obtain what I felt I was due.

'I think I've done well for you in my first season, so why are you not offering me a better rise?' I asked.

His reply took the wind out of my sails. 'Because you're not worth it.'

My surprise must have registered on my face because he then continued.

'You have to prove yourself first. You've done OK, but you've got to get into the side regularly. Ten per cent. Think it over.'

I didn't have to. The offer was unacceptable to me so we remained at loggerheads.

As our pre-season friendlies got underway I found myself playing with the reserves. Liverpool's summer signing from Brighton, Mark

Lawrenson, had gone straight into the first team, along with goal-keeper Bruce Grobbelaar, who had been signed during the previous season from Crewe Alexandra. The inclusion of these two players, who had arrived at Anfield after me, left me feeling unsure of my future, so before the new season got underway I went back to see Bob.

'What's happening? Why have you left me out of the side?' I asked.

His reply was pretty damning. 'You're not worth your place, simple as that,' he said. 'You're supposed to be a striker but you haven't scored any goals.'

'I keep being told here that football is a team game,' I informed him.

'It is, but that's part of your trouble. I've watched you in matches, and in training. All you look to do is lay the ball off to a teammate. I know you're only nineteen, but you're scared to take responsibility on your shoulders. I tell you, when I was your age I was in charge of a tank in a war.'

'I also keep being told here that the name of the game is posses-sion. That we should never give the ball away.'

'Think for yourself, son. Or are you too scared or incapable of doing that? As a striker you are our first line of defence. When an attack breaks down, part of your job is to close down, try and win the ball back, or hold up their defenders, playing it forward until we re-group.'

'I do that.'

'Yes, but as I say, it's only a part of your job. You main job is to score bloody goals and you're not doing it! You're not showing the instinct of a natural goal-scorer. All the great goal-scorers – Lofthouse, Greaves, Law, you name them – they were all selfish in front of goal. That's what you have to be. You're right, it IS a team game, but when you have the goal in your sights you have to think only of yourself.'

'I can score goals,' I said, feeling increasingly agitated.

'Then bloody well do it! We bought you to score goals. Stop being a whinger, get out there and prove you can do it.'

I took to my feet. 'I'll show you I can bloody well score goals,' I told him and headed for the door.

'Either that or you can go,' he told me matter-of-factly.

This rocked me. I felt my legs turn to jelly. As far as I was concerned his words were tantamount to placing me on the transfer list. I felt my world crumbling about me.

What I didn't know was this was Liverpool's way with young players. They would tell you a few home truths then leave you to sink or swim.

I felt my days at Anfield were numbered, that it would be better for me to move on. But to prove Bob wrong and to secure a move to a decent club, I was determined to score as many goals as I could for the reserves. I reasoned that the more goals I scored, the bigger the club would be who came after me. I vowed to myself that from now on I was going to be the most selfish, ruthless striker on the planet.

Liverpool reserves kicked off the season against Blackburn Rovers and did so in some style, winning 6–0. Mindful I had to be selfish I went for goal at every given opportunity and succeeded in scoring twice. I followed that with another two in a 4–1 win over Derby County and our goal in a 1–1 draw against Aston Villa reserves.

My sudden goal-scoring spree with the reserves prompted speculation in the press that the Crystal Palace manager, Terry Venables, was about to make a bid for me. South London was a long way from home, but Palace were being hailed as the 'Team of the 1980s' and seemed to have a lot going for them. It wasn't as if I didn't know anyone at Crystal Palace. The team there comprised two friends of mine, Peter Nicholas and Ian Walsh, from the Welsh squad. The thought of a move there was not unappealing, particularly as my goals for the reserves had still failed to win me a place in the first team, even though Liverpool had endured a poor start to the season, winning only two of the first eight League matches.

In October, Liverpool were drawn against Exeter City in our defence of the League Cup. Before the tie David Johnson once again succumbed to injury. I had scored seven goals in eight outings with the reserves. The day before the Exeter game, as we players were walking off the training ground at Melwood, Bob came alongside me.

'Johno's injured. I'm looking for a selfish bastard to play upfront,' he said.

'I'm your man,' I told him without hesitation.

'You know something, Ian, son?' said Bob, not looking at me. 'I think you might be right.'

CHAPTER FOUR

Once in a Lifetime

Before the League Cup tie against Exeter City I had been on the bench for the European Cup match at Anfield against OPS Oulu of Finland. Liverpool secured a 1–0 win in Oulu and few expected any problems in the return leg. So it proved, and with Liverpool five goals to the good, Bob gave me a run-out in front of the Anfield faithful.

There were only ten minutes remaining but it gave me enough time to register my first ever Liverpool goal. Meeting a low cross from Kenny Dalglish, I kept my head down to fire the ball past the Oulu goalkeeper, who didn't think it prudent to move. My goal was a simple tap-in and I should have been overjoyed, but at the time I was still entrenched in the reserves, and any joy I felt at scoring my first goal for the first team was tempered by my belief that, irrespective of how many goals I scored for the reserves, that was where I was going stay.

As with Oulu, no one believed Exeter City possessed the quality to cause a major shock at Anfield, particularly as top clubs paid due reverence to the League Cup by fielding full-strength sides, Liverpool being no exception.

On the night Exeter did a decent job of containing us initially but, after fifteen minutes, I was fortunate enough to break the deadlock, and in some style. I was never a scorer of spectacular goals; the vast majority of mine were scored inside the penalty box, a good many of them 'poacher's goals'. Having quelled a first attack from Exeter I was thirty yards from goal when I received a cross-field ball from Kenny. The ball sat up perfectly. I didn't have to think about it. I went for goal, and the ball flew past Exeter keeper Len Bond. It was still rising when it ballooned the roof of the net. It was exactly the start I had hoped for. I was always comfortable playing the ball with either foot, though the vast majority of my goals were scored with my right. This one I'd hit with my left. I wondered if Bob had noticed this.

The goal and the nature of it spurred me to even greater efforts and before the half was out I had helped myself to a second. Further goals from Terry Mac, Kenny and Ronnie Whelan rendered the second leg a formality.

The game was a watershed for me. While I appreciated Exeter were not the sternest of opposition, I felt I had gone some way to proving my claim to Bob Paisley that I could score goals. I knew the real test of my timbre as striker, however, was to score goals consistently at the highest level and, given an extended run in the team, I was confident I could do that. For all my inexperience at the highest level I had demonstrated the sort of selfishness in and around the penalty area that I had been producing with the reserves. The sort of single-mindedness Bob had told me I had to incorporate into my play.

Whenever I had the ball against Exeter, even when presented with the merest sniff, I had gone for goal. Having scored twice I found it disconcerting that, after the game, Bob didn't speak to me. Not even a 'well done'. From this I deduced my goals had not changed his view of me. He must have been re-evaluating, however, because, on the Friday morning, when he announced the team for the home game against Leeds United, I kept my place.

With all due respect to Exeter, I was aware that the game against Leeds would be a barometer for Bob to judge my worth as a striker. It was all very well notching up a couple of goals against Exeter in the League Cup, but Leeds, although they had not enjoyed the best of starts, contained quality players such as goalkeeper John Lukic, Frank and Eddie Gray, Paul Hart, Trevor Cherry and Peter Barnes. I relished the opportunity of pitting my wits against players who not so long before I had only read about or watched on television.

The atmosphere in the dressing-room before the Leeds game was very different from what it had been against Oulu and Exeter City. There was confidence but also a tension that had been absent in the two previous games. Since the mid-1960s, Leeds had been Liverpool's great northern rivals along with Manchester United. There was a rich history to past meetings between the clubs. In 1969 Leeds had clinched the First Division title courtesy of a draw at Anfield while Liverpool reversed the roles some years later at Elland Road. For seventeen years, ever since Leeds' return to Division One, the fixture had produced fiercely contested matches and the expectation was this meeting would only add to the combustible history between the two clubs.

Tradition had it that if the Liverpool captain won the toss he would choose to attack the Anfield Road end in the first half in order for the team to enjoy the vociferous support of the Kop in the second should the game be evenly balanced. Kenny lost the toss, however, and we began against Leeds by attacking the Kop.

Some seventeen minutes of enterprising but uneventful football had elapsed when I hurled myself at a bouncing cross and managed to steer the ball with my right foot past the on-rushing

John Lukic. I saw the ball home, glanced up in time to see the Kop jump in the air en masse before deliriously tumbling forward. I was as delirious as any of them. I took to my feet and jogged along the front of the Kop raising a finger in acknowledgement of the cheers before being swamped by a mass of red-shirted teammates. When I finally extracted myself from them Graeme Souness said, 'Tremendous stuff. Now get another.' That was typical Graeme. He was never satisfied. He would be forever urging me to greater achievement, always demanding more. I remember once scoring five against Luton Town only for Graeme to tell me to make it six.

Leeds were a quality side, but successive managers had made the mistake of allowing a number of players who had once formed the hub of a superb team to grow old together, a mistake that had never been perpetrated at Liverpool. A good team needs a balance of youth and experience. Leeds had too many players in excess of thirty and they struggled to cope with the pace and tempo of the game as dictated by us.

As the game progressed my darting runs off the ball increasingly resulted in me finding space. The Leeds defenders just couldn't keep up. I remember thinking, 'If this continues I fancy myself for another.' On the half-hour mark we put the issue and the game beyond doubt or, at least, Leeds' Trevor Cherry did when he couldn't get out of the way of an effort from Kenny and put it through his own net.

In the second half we picked up the same script, placing the Leeds defence under increasing bouts of pressure. Some five minutes from time Kenny and Sammy Lee exchanged passes on the right. I knew the ball would be arriving and, leaving Paul Hart and Trevor Cherry to their own devices, I sprinted into space at the near post. The ball duly arrived and from the tightest of angles I diverted it past John Lukic. For a second time that afternoon the Kop erupted and I found myself before the equally delirious Anfield Road end, arms aloft. As I jogged back to the halfway line for the re-start I suddenly became conscious that the Kop were chanting my name. When I eventually made it back into our half of the field I felt as if I were floating on air.

The dressing-room was buoyant. Kenny, who had talked me through the game, was the first to shake my hand. The rest of the lads, assistant manager Joe Fagan and coach, Ronnie Moran, added their congratulations, but there was not a word from Bob. The total absence of recognition from him left me feeling that my goals had done little more than fuel further interest in me from other clubs, to say nothing of putting a few thousand on a possible fee.

That is how I felt at the time, though experience was to teach me Bob never singled a player out for praise. As far as he was concerned, when Liverpool won, the team had won and not by virtue of the efforts of an individual player. He would, as he did in the aftermath of our victory over Leeds, say, 'Well done, lads,' but that was as far as he ever went in the way of plaudits.

I was brimming with brio when I left the dressing-room only for my feeling of well-being to be tempered when I was confronted with a crowd of reporters. In 1982 the press had more or less free access to players once a game was over. Unlike today, where the press are kept at bay from Premiership players and post-match interviews are selective and strictly monitored, back then there were no such restrictions. I found myself besieged by a gang of football reporters firing questions at me.

For me this was an ordeal, more so than facing Leeds, because I was still painfully shy. I mumbled a few insipid replies to their questions. It wasn't that I couldn't find the right words to describe how I really felt and place the game into some sort of perspective from my point of view. I just couldn't muster the necessary confidence to be so open with such a large group of football journalists. Though I had hit the back of the net twice, I suddenly felt devoid of confidence, as if my goals had been scored under false pretence.

In the following game at Brighton (something of a bogey side for Liverpool in the 1980s), things began well for us but then went somewhat pear-shaped. In the first half we raced into a two-goal lead courtesy of Kenny and Ray Kennedy only for Brighton, prompted by former Anfield favourite Jimmy Case, to come back in some style. The game ended 3–3. I never featured on the scoresheet and five minutes from time, suffering the effects of a knock on my right ankle, was substituted by Mark Lawrenson on his return to the Goldstone ground.

My injury kept me out of the following two games: a 2–2 draw in the European Cup at AZ Alkamaar and a 2–1 home defeat to Manchester United. Irrespective of how dedicated a player is to the shirt and the club, when sidelined he has mixed feelings when his team do well. A part of him wants to the team to win, but another part of him is quietly satisfied when they don't because it will improve his chances of a recall. It's human nature and I was no different when Liverpool failed to win two key matches in my absence. It encouraged me to think I might get the nod when I was pronounced match-fit, and so it proved.

At the time the first and second rounds of the League Cup were played over two legs. This was a highly contentious issue with clubs, players and supporters. By playing early rounds on a home and away basis the Football League hoped for an increase in match revenue for clubs but this rarely proved the case. Supporters understood the reason for two-legged ties in European competition, but when it came to the League Cup attendances invariably indicated fans preferred a one-off tie.

In particular, the two-legged ties found no favour with lower division clubs. When drawn against a top team, a lower division side would fancy their chances of creating an upset in a one-off, but the chances were lessened over two legs. At successive annual meetings of the Football League lower division clubs voiced their opposition to two-legged ties in the early stages of the League Cup. It was a stance that received support from top clubs concerned about fixture congestion, but in their wisdom the powers that be continued with this unpopular system.

Since its inception in 1960–1, the League Cup had grown in stature and importance. In those early days a number of top clubs did not even deign to enter the competition, believing the fixture list contained too many games as it was, and this at a time when clubs were more dependent on gate revenue than today. The League Cup came of age when the final was switched to Wembley in 1967 and the winners were afforded entry into the Fairs/UEFA cup, a move that made the big clubs re-evaluate their view of the competition. That top clubs paid due reverence to the League Cup can be evidenced by the fact Liverpool, for all we were 5–0 up on aggregate, fielded a full-strength team for the second leg at Exeter City: a situation I can not envisage happening these days.

Having been pronounced fit, I replaced David Johnson at centre-forward, the only other change being an enforced one. Graeme Souness was struggling with an injury, which led to a rare outing for Kevin Sheedy.

The 'have' and 'have not' situation of big and small clubs was brought home to me when the Liverpool team coach pulled up outside Exeter's ground. At the same time an old, battered Ford Escort drew alongside us and two Exeter players got out with their bags while the driver, another Exeter player, then drove off, presumably to look for somewhere to park in the neighbouring streets, as there didn't appear to be a club car park.

Even the most ardent Exeter supporter knew the tie was over, but Liverpool were such an attraction on the road and such rare visitors to the south-west that a crowd of just under 12,000 turned up to St James' Park. From the start the Exeter players seemed resigned to a damage limitation job. Should they have come away from Anfield with a draw or even a one-goal defeat it would have given them hope. But they began the game without edge and optimism.

We were 3–0 up at halftime, 8–0 on aggregate, and I had two more goals to my name. There was nothing left for Exeter supporters to enjoy but the rare and, in the circumstances, dubious treat of observing Liverpool at close quarters. Bruce Grobbelaar was one of those spectators. He had so little to do that when Lawro or Phil Thompson had the ball he was calling for it to be passed back so he could have a touch, which neither of them did. In the end we scored six to make it 11–0 on aggregate. Exeter's only consolation was that the club enjoyed a decent pay day from the large attendance.

Bob continued with me at centre-forward for the following twelve matches, eight in the League, three in the League Cup and the return European Cup tie against AZ Alkamaar of Holland. Our form proved better than at the start of the season but there was little doubt that we were stuttering and spluttering. Five of those eight League matches were won, but there were also home defeats to Southampton and Manchester City, which gave Bob much food for thought. Having already lost at home to Manchester United and drawn with Middlesbrough, Aston Villa and Swansea City, the notion of Anfield being an impregnable fortress was looking somewhat flaky. Even the 3–2 home victory over AZ Alkamaar (5–4 on aggregate) had been less than convincing. It had been some time since Liverpool had shipped four goals in a European tie and there were long discussions taking place in the Anfield boot-room.

I had scored three goals in those twelve matches, one of which was my first in a Merseyside derby (how my dad loved that one!) in a 3–1 win against Everton, our best performance to date. I celebrated my first goal against Everton with my usual quiet satisfaction. At the time I didn't feel a great deal of significance at having scored against Everton; a goal was a goal irrespective of the opposition. I just loved scoring and always felt a buzz when play re-started. The goal gave my game an extra edge and I would take to my toes, wanting the ball and challenging opposing defenders with gusto.

But this wasn't the strike rate I had hoped for and I was concerned about keeping my place in the team, though heartened by dressing-room talk that Bob appeared to be looking elsewhere for answers to our inconsistent form. If there was any saving grace, it was that every other team at the top of Division One was also experiencing topsy-turvy fortunes. Come autumn Ipswich sat at the top and Liverpool were tenth, but Ipswich's lead was such they could be caught.

That wasn't good enough for Bob or Liverpool. In the early 1960s Bill Shankly coined the phrase, 'First is first and second is nowhere,' and it had become a mantra at the club. Having missed out on the League title the previous season, Bob was hungry for Liverpool to win it again, for what would be a record thirteenth time.

As Christmas approached, the midway point in the season, those who knew Bob well – the likes of Kenny, Graeme, Alan Hansen and Phil Thompson – sensed the boss was not at all happy with results and performances. Bob wanted us to be consistent, which we hadn't been. He wanted us to be a force to be reckoned with at home, which we hadn't been. He felt we were conceding too many goals, which we had been. Seemingly, Bob also felt we were too slow in the build-up to our attacks, which allowed the opposition time to get back and re-form. The word amongst the senior pros was that Bob was about to make a significant change.

I use the word 'significant' deliberately. Apart from an enforced change due to a player being injured, lasting changes to the Liverpool line-up were rare and, by virtue of that fact, tended to be significant in that such a change usually meant the end of a career at Anfield for the player who lost his place.

I'd enjoyed a decent run in the first team but David Johnson was still sidelined and I was always conscious I could revert to the reserves once he was fit. I was determined to produce the sort of performances – and goals – to make such a decision very difficult on Bob's part. However, the fact remained that I had only got in the side by virtue of an injury to a regular player.

In keeping with many managers of the time, Bob felt he knew his best eleven and stuck to it, irrespective of whether Liverpool were playing a crucial league game or a 'tie-over' job as in the League Cup at Exeter.

On 8 December we played Arsenal in a fourth round League Cup replay at Anfield, the first tie having ended goalless at Highbury. Deep into the second half, the game was still deadlocked. Bob decided to change things, his idea being that a resolute Arsenal back four were never happy with players of pace running directly at them.

He replaced Sammy Lee with Craig Johnston and within minutes the change reaped dividends. Craig's direct running unsettled the Arsenal pairing of David O'Leary and Chris Whyte. Following an exchange of passes with Kenny, Craig fired past

George Wood to put us ahead. Arsenal had to come out of their shell if they were going to get something from the game and we set about exploiting the space this created. Terry McDermott scored from the spot and Kenny added a third. Not for the first time, Bob had demonstrated he was a master at quickly sizing up a situation and responding with the right decision.

Following the Arsenal game we set off for Tokyo where we were due to play Flamengo of Brazil in the World Club Championship, then simply the meeting of the European and South American Champions. Having arrived in Tokyo we had a day of preparation before meeting Flamengo, who had already been in Japan for five days. Apart from the long-haul journey and lack of preparation, we also had a twelve-hour time difference to contend with. There had been some discussion as to whether to re-adjust and adapt to the new time zone or simply stick to GMT. When Nottingham Forest had taken part the previous season they never changed their watches, stuck to GMT, sleeping by day and training at night. Such a decision resulted in the bizarre situation of the Forest party taking breakfast in their hotel dining room while other residents were having their evening meal and vice versa.

We decided to re-adjust, but the time differential still proved problematic as we were only in Tokyo for a few days and never truly rid our system of jetlag. As a consequence we weren't at our best when facing Flamengo, and lost 3–0.

To be honest, we weren't too despondent. I sensed all everyone wanted to do was fulfil our obligation and get back to England as soon as possible.

When we arrived back in England there was a surprise awaiting us: it was snowing. The bad weather caused many games to be postponed and we enjoyed the bonus of some rest and recovery time before Manchester City were due at Anfield on Boxing Day.

When Bob announced the team to play Manchester City he told us Terry Mac was to be replaced in midfield by Craig Johnston, but there was another change. Ronnie Whelan who, like me, was enjoying an extended run in the team was switched to the left of midfield in place of Ray Kennedy with Ronnie's place in the centre given to a recalled Sammy Lee.

It was a white Christmas for many, and only eight Boxing Day games survived the weather. Unfortunately, from Liverpool's point of view, our game against Manchester City was one of them. Without taking anything away from City, we were dreadful. At halftime we were a goal down and in the second half conceded a penalty. Ronnie Whelan gave us some hope of salvaging something from a bad afternoon, only for Kevin Reeves to press home the cold voice of reason.

Bob said nothing after the game, though we were all aware he was fuming. That's how it was with Bob, as with Bill Shankly. On the rare occasion of a bad performance by Liverpool, nothing was said after the game for fear people, high on adrenalin and emotion, would say something in the heat of the moment they would later regret. After Monday training at Melwood, Bob held a meeting in the lounge. He began by holding up a page from a newspaper showing the First Division League table.

'In case any of you haven't realised, it says here we're twelfth, and you know these things, they don't lie,' said Bob. 'Bloody Swansea top of the League. When I see the likes of Brighton and Southampton above this club, it tells me something's wrong here.'

It was as if someone had placed a coffin in the room. I sat in an armchair, terrified to move for fear of being the one who cut through the icy silence.

'Now to the problem,' announced Bob. 'Everything here, off the pitch, is being done right. The problem is it's you lads who aren't doing things right – out there on the pitch. We're better than any side in this League, and you had better set about proving that or there will be others on their way. You can start at Swansea in the FA Cup on Saturday and carry on from there. That's all, lads. It's up to you lot. If you don't buck up your ideas, THEN it will be up to me.'

That, more or less, was all Bob said. He was a quiet, undemonstrative man, not given to ranting and raving, and fair in his dealings with players. We weren't playing well and the onus was on us to change that. In giving every player an opportunity to put matters right he had issued a veiled threat and we all knew what that meant: someone was already on their way out. A couple of days later Ray Kennedy joined Swansea.

Bob's simple words were all that was required. They served as a kick up the pants to everyone. As individuals we knew we had to improve and produce the goods, and we set about doing exactly that.

John Toshack, a former Anfield favourite, had done a remarkable job as manager of Swansea, guiding the club from the Fourth Division to the top of the First. The team was a blend of experienced players who had done the business at the highest level, with a younger element in Robbie James, Nigel Stevenson and Chris Marustick. Following Bob's pointed talk, however, we were fired up for match.

Alan Hansen put us ahead and, just before halftime, Kenny played me in and I made it 2–0. After the break I added a third and by the time Mark Lawrenson chimed in with a well-placed header Swansea were already a well-beaten side and we were in round four.

My two goals was real fillip to me. I'd not been scoring as regularly as I would have liked and, seeing as Bob wanted goals from me, my erratic goal-scoring had made me anxious about my place.

We had not been playing well as a team, and the fact the lads had not been carving openings in previous games was something of a relief to me; a striker can't score if he doesn't get the ball. I felt I had made the best of what chances had come my way and sensed Bob thought this, too.

The resounding FA Cup win at Swansea buoyed everyone. I was aware of a different atmosphere amongst the players on the coach journey home from Wales. Nobody suggested we had turned a corner, but there was a marked confidence amongst the players I had not detected for some time.

The feelgood factor carried over into our next games. Wolves were beaten at Anfield (2–1) then it was up to Sunderland for the FA Cup fourth round. Under new manager Alan Durban, Sunderland had begun the season losing just one of their opening five League matches. Just enough of a good start to give their sizeable following optimism but, like many a Sunderland side before them, having offered their supporters hope of better things to come Sunderland's season had gone pear-shaped. Before Christmas, Sunderland had a twelve-match run during which they failed to win a game and scored just two goals. They had picked up a little form over December, however, so we expected a hard battle.

Roker Park was only half a mile from the sea. It was a cold January day and the wind off the North Sea that was blowing over the Roker End would have penetrated the thickest over-coats like a knife through butter. Before the game we had gone out to inspect the pitch, which, surprisingly, given the freezing weather, had a little give in it. When I returned down the tunnel a guy I took to be the Roker groundsman said, 'Not bad, is it?' I agreed and told him I had expected the pitch to be hard given the weather.

'Aye,' he said, 'it's freezing all right. I've just come out of the social club. It's so cold in there the one-armed bandit has a glove on.'

As with their near neighbours Newcastle, when we went up to Sunderland we did so with the intention of shutting up their supporters as soon as we possibly could. Both clubs enjoy tremendous and vociferous support, and once those fans get behind their team it can make life difficult for opponents. Our intention was for Kenny, Graeme and Terry Mac to control the game from the off, which they succeeded in doing.

After fifteen minutes Kenny took a return pass from Sammy Lee and slid the ball past Barry Siddall in the Sunderland goal. Just before halftime, Terry Mac crossed from our left. I had managed to lose my marker, Jeff Clarke, and arrived at the far post unmarked to slot home number two. When the ball nestled in the back of the net it suddenly became so quiet you could have heard dust settle around Roker Park. Job done. To make sure, Kenny added a third in the second half, from which point we were coasting by the coast.

Back in the dressing-room my hands were so numb with cold I had trouble undoing the laces on my boots. Somebody remarked about how cold it was and Alan Kennedy, who hailed from the north-east, replied, 'Aye, they only have two seasons up here – June and winter!'

Against Swansea, Wolves and Sunderland there had been a cohesion and fluidity about our play that had not been in evidence in the first half of the season. Next up was Notts County in the League. We knew if we were to make up ground on the teams above us, particularly Swansea City and Ipswich Town, who had been playing leapfrog with the top two places, it was imperative we produced the sort of performances in the League we had displayed of late.

These days it may appear incongruous to think of Notts County in the Premier League but in the early days of the Premier League, its membership included the likes of Oldham Athletic, Wimbledon, Swindon Town and, more recently, Reading. It was no different in the days of the First Division. Notts County had battled their way to the top-flight from the Fourth Division under that wily old manager Jimmy Sirrell. In players such as Brian Kilcline, Pedro Richards and Ray O'Brien, County boasted a defence more physical than most, and more than a touch of quality in Don Masson, John Chiedozie and Trevor Christie.

The issue, however, was never in doubt. We were positive from the start against County, and not inhibited by the blustery cold wind. Kenny provided more than the occasional moment of devastating inspiration, Phil Neal and Sammy Lee combined to null the threat of Chiedozie, while Graeme Souness clamped down on Masson. Such was our dominance that the final scoreline of 4–0 could have been more but for some fine goalkeeping from Raddy Avramovic. As it was, we were more than happy with the result and I was absolutely delighted to score my first hat-trick for Liverpool.

None of the goals was spectacular but, as Jimmy Greaves famously said, 'Come May they all look the same in the record books.' I was now feeling a lot more relaxed, and, if not certain, then confident of my place in the team.

Temperament is important to all players but particularly where strikers are concerned. Having had chances created for me, I never felt panic. I did what I had to do, instinctively and, happily, incisively. My acceleration took me away from defenders and into space. When the ball came it was a simple matter of quickly sizing up the gap and angle. I was never blessed with the physical build to power my way through defences, but used my pace to get into space or else to thread my way past opponents and tuck the ball away neatly. My hat-trick against County was a tremendous boost to my confidence. Not only was I proving I could score goals regularly in the First Division, but every goal helped to erase fears that I might not be included for the following game.

A few days after the victory at Notts County, Bob called me into his office to discuss a new contract. On the wall to my right was a fixture planner and three plaster cast ducks of diminishing size. Above the modest pine desk was a photograph of piglets scrambling over one another to reach the teats of their mother's belly. A printed line under the photograph read 'It's easy to stay on top'.

'OK, we think you've earned the hundred pound a week rise,' he said in his quiet voice.

I felt I had established myself in the team and that, by selecting me, Bob had displayed confidence in my ability to score goals. I had settled into life at Anfield and my teammates had become good friends. The last thing I wanted to do was to move but I didn't want Bob to think I was what players called a 'patsy' when it came to discussing wages and a contract.

'Thanks, it's much appreciated, but I'm not sure I want to sign a new contract right now. I would like time to think it over,' I told him.

It took a lot to surprise Bob but his jaw dropped. 'Aye, well, you'd better go away and think about it, then,' he said with more than a hint of suspicion.

So I did.

A couple of days later I was back in Bob's office.

'I've had a good think, boss. The offer of the extra one hundred is appreciated, but I also want the extra ten per cent I'm entitled to,' I informed him.

'My, my, you have been giving it some thought, haven't you? That it?'

'Yes.'

'I don't think so,' he said.

'Well, thanks for your time, boss.'

I got to my feet and began to make my way out of his office. At the door I glanced back at him. He was leaning back in his chair, arms folded behind his head, a thoughtful look on his face.

'Aye, you've settled into this club right enough,' he said.

The following day, I paid yet another visit to his office.

'I've been doing some thinking as well,' said Bob. 'The hundred plus ten per cent it is. Think you're just about worth it.'

'Thank you very much.'

He pushed the new contract across the desk for me to sign, which I did without reading it.

'And just how do you intend to justify this rise?' he asked.

'By scoring goals.'

'That'll do for me.'

'Starting against Villa on Saturday,' I said.

'Oh, I thought you'd already started. That's why I'm giving you the rise,' he said with a wry smile.

Looking back, I don't think Bob ever intended to sell me. He had assessed my character, was aware that I was unhappy during my first year at the club, and had lectured me about not scoring enough goals, in so doing offering a golden nugget of advice about being selfish. He knew I was an essentially shy lad not given to extreme displays of emotion. To get me worked up and angry, he had told me some home truths, with the veiled threat of getting rid of me. I'm sure all this was intentional on his part, geared towards provoking the required reaction in me and getting me to do exactly what he wanted me to do. The more I watched him over the next two years before he retired, the more I saw him get the required reaction from a player by this means or that. On one occasion I heard Joe Fagan compliment Bob for the tactful and diplomatic way he'd handled David Fairclough, who was unhappy at not being able to hold down a regular place in the team.

'When dealing with players with grumbles, you use tact until you can lay your hands on a big stick,' replied Bob.

I never found Bob the easiest person to talk to. He was quiet and introverted, but he certainly knew football and how to deal with players. A player knew when Bob was happy with how he was performing, simply because he picked him for the team. On the other hand, he would always talk to players he was leaving out (unlike Shanks). I think the reason Bob did this had much to do with the fact he himself had been dropped by manager George Kay for the 1950 FA Cup final. Bob had been a mainstay of the Liverpool team but, for reasons known only to himself, Kay left Bob out for the final against Arsenal. Apparently Bob was devastated and never forgot it.

Bob was not an emotional man and I think this had much to do with his roots and his particular generation. He hailed from the appropriately named Durham mining village of Hetton-le-Hole, but served an apprenticeship as a builder and bricklayer. He played for Bishop Auckland, appearing in an FA Amateur Cup Final and in 1939, at the age of twenty, signed for Liverpool. Due to the war he didn't make his Liverpool debut until 1946, establishing himself in the team as an uncompromising but skilful wing-half.

His roots were deeply embedded in the north-east working class where it wasn't the done thing for men to display emotion other than anger, as it was deemed unmanly. He grew up during the Depression of the 1930s and, just when it appeared he had made something of himself by signing for Liverpool, war was declared. He served in the Royal Artillery and, as he once told me, lost a lot of good friends. It was little wonder he talked straight and had no compunction in telling home truths to well-paid players who told him they were not happy with their lot.

The undoubted wisdom he possessed was not imparted with a sharp wisecrack as with Bill Shankly, but often through softly spoken, sometimes muttered asides in the County Durham accent he never lost. He exuded sagacity, often with gentle humour such as advice he once gave to Ronnie Whelan: 'Assuming you have the talent, you only need three sentences to survive in football: "Not my fault, I was tight on my man"; "I was in space, you should have passed to me"; and, "That's a great idea, boss".'

He remains Liverpool's most successful manager but none of his monumental successes ever impinged upon the solidity of his personality. I sensed his feeling for football was so deep it made him immune to its occasional romance. Certainly glory and success meant less to him than satisfaction of a job well done. He achieved much success, but his character was never tainted by a sense of superiority, glamour or materialism that often descends on those who find sudden affluence through football. The phrase 'down to earth' could have been coined for him.

His management was all about basics. He once told the team, 'Champagne only comes along if you get the bread and butter values right.' Keeping possession of the ball was all-important to him. We were all told to keep a hold the ball until an opening was created or presented itself. One of the main problems the opposition had when facing Liverpool was getting the ball off us.

His knowledge of the game, players and particularly opposing teams was phenomenal, yet he was never one for complicated tactics. In all my time at Liverpool we never man-marked nor did we adopt zonal marking. When defending corners, Ronnie Whelan had the job of covering the near post. Apart from that we each took the responsibility of picking up opponents as we thought fit.

In all my time under Bob I can only recall us once working on a set-piece, a corner routine, on the training ground. We tried it against Aston Villa and it worked. After the game all Bob said was, 'That corner routine. That was good. We should do it again some time.'

For all he was quietly spoken there was a steeliness about him which could flash dangerously at times. No one was exempt from a terse word, which, though quietly spoken, was always sharp enough to perish complacency. In one match against Notts County we were winning 4–0 and had taken our foot off the gas in the remaining minutes. In the dressing-room after the game, Bob was quick to denounce our laxness. 'OK, the game was won, but after the fourth went in, you started to play as if you were in a testimonial. That's not on, not at this club it isn't. We teach and we display good habits here. We only play the testimonial stuff in testimonials. Don't want to see that again.'

No one responded.

'Do you hear what I say?' asked Bob, the tone of his voice still soft.

A chorus of 'Yes, boss.'

'Good.' Satisfied his point had been made, he offered the briefest nod. 'Is there any more tea in that pot?' he then asked Ronnie Moran, the moment of tension in the room disappearing as suddenly as it had evolved.

Bob Paisley signed good players, sometimes great players, but he never hesitated to give youth its chance, as shown by the opportunity afforded to Ronnie Whelan and myself. He had faith in his players and we had faith him because he had acquired such a bountiful knowledge there was hardly a situation he didn't know how to tackle. His knowledge of players was phenomenal and often displayed exacting detail. Before one match against Ipswich Town he made casual mention of Frank Thijssen.

'Duggie Doings in midfield, Dutch lad?' he said, characteristically unable to remember names of the opposition.

'Thijssen,' Ronnie Moran reminded him.

'Aye, him. When he receives the ball, always takes it on the inside of his right foot. So, if he's yours, don't allow him to turn so he can receive the ball his favourite way. Be ready to step up and come across him. Oh, aye, and midway through the second half, he'll take a rest for ten minutes or so. Seems to run out of puff. Doesn't put it in till he's got his second breath. So when you see him coasting, down the middle we go. Have I mentioned their keeper?'

'No.'

'Cooper,' advised Ronnie.

'That's the lad. Not the biggest, not bad in the air, but weak when balls are played in from his left, especially when he has to come to that point between his six-yard line and the penalty spot, which he does because his centre-backs tend to leave him to it. So, you know what to do to get the worst out of him.'

All these little titbits on opposing players were gold dust. Liverpool had the players to expose such weaknesses, but we would never have been alerted to them but for Bob's knowledge. He never spent time talking of the strengths of opposing players, only their perceived weaknesses. He appeared to have such faith in us as individuals and a team, he expected us to go out and beat any side irrespective of who they were.

As a team we had faltered at the end of 1981, but only by Liverpool's previous high standards. Come January we began to gel and were still sufficiently in touch with Swansea and

Ipswich to engender a belief in us all that we would continue our good form and overhaul both clubs.

Having been beaten at home by Manchester City on Boxing Day, our season took off. At that point we had not quite reached the halfway stage in League fixtures but for the remainder of the season victory followed victory as the Liverpool juggernaut gathered momentum.

Following the City defeat we won seven of our next nine League matches, a surprising defeat at home to Brighton on 6 March serving to remind us nothing but the best in the way of performance and application was acceptable. In our following game we beat Stoke City 5–1 at the Victoria Ground, from which point we remained unbeaten in our final sixteen games of the season, a run which saw us win eleven consecutive League matches. On 2 April we beat Notts County 1–0 at Anfield, a win which saw us top the First Division for the first time in the season.

I was scoring regularly both in the League and League Cup. As a consequence of this, I felt my place in the team was as secure as it could be. I was benefiting from the improved form of all the players around me, particularly Kenny Dalglish and Graeme Souness who were in imperious form, and also Ronnie Whelan who, like me, had established himself in the team that season.

Though Kenny and Graeme received the plaudits from the press, Ronnie had emerged as a player of considerable note. Not an out-going lad, Ronnie had, nevertheless, given full scope to his vast array of skills. Unlike Thijssen, for example, Ronnie was happy to receive the ball any which way. As with Kenny, with one swift touch of either foot, chest or thigh, he had the ball under control and rolling forward for him to move on to. One of Ronnie's other strengths, often overlooked, was that he was good in the air. He was a very good header of the ball, not only in attacking goal but also when having to drop back and defend. His timing in the air was immaculate, enabling him to win aerial battles against opponents much taller than him.

Some players are busy on the field, covering a lot of ground without ever making the most of it. Ronnie was different. He did a lot of running but had such nous and vision he always moved into space that enabled him to receive the ball then use to it good purpose, which, I have to say, benefited me greatly. Ronnie's presence in the team also allowed Kenny to move up and play just behind me. Having such a world-class player alongside me brought my game on in leaps and bounds, as he was forever offering advice.

As with Graeme, Sammy Lee and Kenny, Ronnie Whelan would play the ball into space for me to run on to. What was more, he played it early. I had to be alert and on my toes all the time, constantly looking for spaces in the opponents' half of the field, particularly in the penalty area, because I knew Ronnie, Kenny and co would spot them, too, and that was where the ball would be going.

Our form in the New Year was such we lost only two of twenty-two League matches and eventually clinched the First Division Championship, four points ahead of runners-up Ipswich Town and nine ahead of third-placed Manchester United. Early pacesetters Swansea City had to settle for sixth. It was Liverpool's thirteenth league title and the club's fifth in seven seasons.

After such a faltering start why had our fortunes changed in such dramatic fashion? Though I wish to emphasise the following, it did not, to my mind, affect individual performances or that of the team: in September the club had been rocked by the death of Bill Shankly.

Bill died on 29 September, aged sixty-seven, following a heart attack. He was the man who had laid down the foundations and instigated the culture of Liverpool football club. While it is true Shankly had been ably assisted in this by Bob and his backroom staff, particularly Joe Fagan and Reuben Bennett, the fact remains that he turned a Second Division club in decline into one of the most successful football clubs in the world. In addition, he was responsible for transforming players, often recruited from lower division teams, into fine footballers, Kevin Keegan being a case in point.

Bob had not only continued Bill Shankly's work but built upon it. Looking back, for all he never let it show in his work as manager, perhaps the death of Shanks affected Bob for a time. Certainly it coincided with a drop in the team's form for a few months. That said, I think the main reason for Liverpool's stuttering form before Christmas 1981 was down to Bob re-building the team and the time it took for the newly introduced players to bed in and make an impact, and here I include myself.

I didn't make my first appearance of the season until October but, once given a chance, did my utmost to justify my inclusion at the expense of David Johnson. When I got into the side, Ray Kennedy was on the left of midfield where he played superbly, a position he also fulfilled admirably for England on seventeen occasions.

As I have previously said, Bob's knowledge of players was incredible. He knew how to get the best out of us, which he had done with Ray. Bob, however, also knew when a player had reached the tipping moment in his career, and I think he felt Ray had reached that moment. Ray, although a fantastic player, was never the quickest, and in 1981 that was beginning to show. Having got into the side I wasn't setting the world on fire and scoring goals, one reason for which was that the ball, when played from the left, wasn't arriving early enough. I believe Bob was aware of this and that it was the prime reason he brought in Ronnie for Ray. When Ronnie, with his constant running and, more importantly, great vision came into the side, the service I received improved. Not only that, but Kenny, Graeme and Terry Mac also benefited from Ronnie's presence. For one thing, when an attack broke down they didn't have to come across to supply cover as Ronnie was always there.

People often ask me to reveal the secret to Liverpool's success. There was no secret as such, but one factor was attention to detail. The cumulative effect of attention to detail was considered by Bob and his backroom team to be the difference between success and failure. Ray Kennedy still had a lot of top-flight football in him, but the fact he wasn't playing the ball quite as quickly as Bob would have liked prompted change. At the time Ray would have won a place with any team in the First Division, as he did with Swansea, but Bob's standards were so exacting that Ray lost his place at Liverpool.

It is an old saying in football that you should never change a winning team. During our tremendous run of unbeaten games in the New Year, Bob went against that old adage by replacing Terry Mac with Craig Johnston. Craig, like Ronnie, brought an extra dimension as far as pace was concerned. Again, Terry still had much to offer in top-flight football, but had found himself the victim of Craig's younger legs. With Craig and Ronnie in the side, the tempo of our play increased. Some teams increase the tempo of their game but do not possess the quality of a player whose brain and skills are such they can produce optimum performances at the increased speed. Liverpool did have those players. Kenny, Graeme and Sammy Lee had no difficulty in adapting to our new tempo. What was more, their personal game improved as result. Our build-up from defence was quicker, and opposing teams had great difficulty in coping. Often we swept forward with opponents struggling to get back behind the ball. The fact we were able to counter-attack so swiftly benefited me, too. The ball arrived earlier and, having exploited space, I did my best to inflict maximum damage on the opposition.

I finished the season with seventeen goals from thirty-two league games. It says much of the contribution and quality of Terry McDermott that, although he lost his place to Craig Johnston, he finished with fourteen league goals to his name, four from the penalty spot. Such a strike rate would have guaranteed him a place with any other First Division club, but not at Liverpool.

The First Division title was sealed in our penultimate League game of the season with a 3–1 victory over Tottenham Hotspur at Anfield. As I joined my teammates in celebration I couldn't help but think how much things had changed for me at the club. I was absolutely overjoyed to have won a Championship medal and felt quiet satisfaction from the fact I had proved I could score goals for Liverpool.

The Championship won, a relaxed and celebratory atmosphere pervaded Melwood when we reported for training the following Monday morning. We did some light training as we had one match remaining, the following evening, away to Middlesbrough, who were already doomed to relegation.

Usually when playing a mid-week away game we would travel on the afternoon of the day preceding the game. With the title won, we didn't travel to Teesside until the Tuesday morning. We checked into a hotel in North Yorkshire where rooms had been booked so that we could get some sleep before the game in the evening. Normally everyone would get their heads down for a couple of hours at least while Bob, Joe and Ronnie Moran would sit downstairs in the hotel lounge sharing a pot of tea, talking football.

I was about to get ready for bed when Graeme Souness and Alan Hansen appeared in the room I was sharing with Ronnie. Graeme told Ronnie and I that Bob and his backroom staff were in the hotel restaurant having a 'good lunch' and had ordered some bottles of wine. Graeme wanted us to report to the hotel lobby but didn't say why. With the team assembled in the lobby, Graeme suggested that as Bob and co were taking things a little easy, we might go for walk to a nearby park. I didn't feel much like sleeping so I fell in step with the rest of the lads.

We were heading in the general direction of the park Graeme said he knew when we came across a pub. It was a Cameron's house, Cameron's being the Hartlepool-based brewery. Graeme asked if any of us had tried Cameron's beer and when the majority said no, he suggested we should sample it.

We strolled into the pub, broke off into groups of four in order to buy rounds and I suddenly found a pint of lager in front of me. We talked football for some fifteen minutes before another lager appeared. I had never done anything like this so close to a game before but, as the senior players went at it, so did I. Having drunk two pints of lager, Alan then said, 'Your shout, Ian?' I took to my feet, made my way to the bar and ordered another round of lagers.

We stayed chatting and drinking in the pub until just after two when Graeme suggested we ought to be getting back to the hotel as Ronnie Moran would be making his rounds at four to wake everyone up. Back in our room I jumped into bed and managed to get just over an hour's sleep before Ronnie walked in at four to tell us it was time to get up. Ronnie, of course, wasn't taken in, of that I am sure. He must have smelled beer in every room he entered, but to the best of my knowledge never said anything to Bob or Joe.

Needless to say, I was far from my best against Middlesbrough. The lunchtime drink didn't seem to affect Graeme too much, though. He dominated midfield and was running about as if he had never been to the pub at all. My performance was so lax during the first half that he came up to me and said, 'You are allowed to kick the ball, you know!' Usually at halftime players leave the field at a leisurely stroll. Not on this day. As soon as we heard the referee's whistle all eleven of us sprinted off the pitch and down the tunnel like rattled rats down a drainpipe. I can still picture the startled look on the face of a Middlesbrough official who pressed himself against the wall as the Liverpool team sprinted past him in the corridor and burst into our dressing-room. Once inside we all made for the loos. There wasn't enough, so, rather than standing on ceremony, we stood three around a toilet bowl as we brought much-needed relief to our bladders.

The game ended goalless and I am not sure there was a tackle of note, either. If the game had counted for anything, even if Middlesbrough could have stayed up by beating us, we wouldn't have gone to the pub. But it was a fag-end game to the season with nothing at stake and, at the end of a long, gruelling season, with the Championship trophy and League Cup in the Anfield trophy room, for once we relaxed our normally impeccable standards.

It had been a terrific season for me, but my mettle as a striker was under constant scrutiny and I knew I had to score even more goals the next season. I wasn't content with what I had achieved thus far, and wanted to work hard and develop my game so that more goals would be forthcoming. I was as interested as anyone in seeing what I was capable of in front of goal because, in truth, I still didn't know what I could really do.

At Liverpool we wanted to win every competition we entered. Bob instilled in us a winning mentality. Just as I wanted to explore what I was capable of as a striker, collectively we wanted to find out what we were capable of as a team. No competition took precedence over another, though it is true to say the one competition we wanted to win above all others was the First Division Championship. Yes, we wanted to win the European Cup because to do that would mean Liverpool was the best team in Europe and we all desired that, not just for ourselves but for the club and our supporters. We saw the First Division Championship, however, as the mark of our quality as a team.

As opposed to the Premiership these days, the First Division in 1981 was more democratic in terms of which team might win it. This had been Liverpool's fifth title in seven seasons but in that time five different clubs finished as runners-up, namely QPR, Manchester City, Nottingham Forest (champions themselves in 1977–8), Manchester United and Ipswich Town. Liverpool's success in winning League Championships had been anything but a foregone conclusion.

Liverpool's title success of 1980 came courtesy of two more points than Manchester United, and there had been a single point between the club and Manchester City in 1977 and QPR in 1976. Likewise, our title success of 1982 was a close-run thing, in that we had not clinched the Championship until our final home game of the season.

At the time clubs were still very much dependent on gate receipts for revenue. Clubs did receive money from television but such money did not constitute anywhere near the lion's share of annual income as it does now. Likewise, revenue from commercial activities, though growing, did not come anywhere near that of match receipts, and the Liverpool strip bore not a single sponsor's or manufacturer's logo. Liverpool was financially better off than most other First Division clubs because attendances at Anfield were joint second-best (with Spurs) behind those of Manchester United.

The financial disparity between clubs within the First Division was not as great as it is in the Premiership, and the financial gulf between top-flight clubs and all other Football League clubs not the vast chasm that exists today. Liverpool might have enjoyed a bit of support throughout the world but it did not financially benefit the club. These days Liverpool, along with Arsenal, Manchester United and Chelsea, who owe their resurgence to Abramovich's billions, boast thousands of supporters throughout the world, particularly in the Far East. In 1982 it was very different. Though Ipswich had fallen short of Liverpool by four points it was still possible for a club with the suffix of 'Town' to be in with a real chance of winning the Championship, and for clubs such as Swansea and Southampton to contest the title throughout the season. This appears to me to be a more healthy and competitive situation than exists nowadays.

It was a great disappointment to everyone at the club that we failed to make any great impact upon the European Cup that season. Following successes over Oulu and AZ Alkamaar we came unstuck in the quarter-finals against the Bulgarian side CSKA Sofia. A Ronnie Whelan goal gave us a slim advantage to take to Sofia but a second-half strike from Miadenov took the tie into extra time, during which the same player sounded the death knell to our hopes of winning the European Cup. We didn't play well in either of those two legs, principally because we lacked that little bit of experience in Europe. Bruce Grobbelaar, Mark Lawrenson,

Craig Johnston, Ronnie and myself had few European games between us and it showed against a team who, though far from the best, had a lot of European experience.

Having despatched Swansea and Sunderland it was a blow to be beaten in round five of the FA Cup at Chelsea. It was in the League Cup, or Milk Cup as it was then termed, that we excelled. As I previously said, our quest for it began with a resounding win over Exeter City. There followed victories over Middlesbrough, Arsenal, Barnsley and Ipswich Town before we were rewarded with a Wembley appearance against Tottenham Hotspur.

I had scored seven goals in the League Cup to equal the existing record and, needless to say, was looking forward to adding to that tally in the final. Though I already had a League Cup winners' medal, this, of course, was my first appearance in a Wembley final. In the week leading up to the match the atmosphere on the training ground began to bubble as the prospect of playing at Wembley drew nearer. I had only twenty minutes experience of playing at Wembley, as a substitute for Wales against England. The prospect of playing a full ninety minutes there served to instil in me a sense of achievement. As a boy I had read of Wembley finals in books, and had seen them on television. I had even attended Liverpool's last appearance in a Wembley final against West Ham United, but to actually take part in one made me feel I was making a very small, but none the less indelible mark on the history of the League Cup.

True to form there were no special arrangements for the final. We simply donned our usual clothes and travelled down to London on the Friday afternoon, just as we would do for a League game in the capital. Each player was on a bonus of £850 to win the League Cup. I am quite aware that every former player who writes a book says money was not all-important during his career, that the joy of playing football and winning was the reason they were in the game. Money was important to me because I wanted to make something of my life and provide for the family I hoped to have with Tracy. That said, I can honestly say that none of the Liverpool team was driven by the thought of the bonus in our desire to win the League Cup. We wanted to win it as a team, for the club and our supporters.

Such a lack of ceremony was in sharp contrast to how I was feeling. I was so keyed up at the prospect of playing at Wembley that I found trouble concentrating on my newspaper during the journey down to London. I found myself having to read the same paragraph twice, sometimes three times, before it eventually sunk in.

My altered state stayed with me at the hotel. I roomed with Ronnie but, for once, had great trouble getting to sleep. I remember looking at the clock, seeing it was almost midnight and softly cursing to myself. Some time later I looked at the clock again and saw it was now half-past. I must have dropped off some time after 1am.

Despite my unsettled night I woke early, as did Ronnie. Our itinerary stated we had to report for breakfast by 8.30am but I never took breakfast, preferring to eat a light meal at around noon. So keen were we to get going that Ronnie and I found ourselves in the hotel lounge reading the morning newspapers just after 7am.

At Anfield the crowd is so near you can have contact with supporters. Not so at Wembley. Supporters seemed a long way away but due to their sheer number and the fact they were all under cover, the sound of the fans resounded down on to the pitch. This cacophony of noise from people so far away, who were not even caught in one's peripheral vision, induced in me a feeling of the surreal.

For me the marked difference I found of playing at Wembley as opposed to say, Anfield, was the sense I had of this being an event, a real occasion of pomp and circumstance as opposed to a game. I was conscious that whatever I did at Wembley would live in the memories of all present – and certainly in my own memory.

The Spurs team included Ray Clemence in goal, Steve Perryman, Ossie Ardiles, Glenn Hoddle, Steve Archibald and Garth Crooks. The mark of Spurs' strength as a team was clear in the fact that Ricardo Villa had only made the bench. We knew Spurs to be a very good team that liked playing purist football. Wembley's large pitch and pristine surface of Cumberland turf (it was like playing on close-clipped moss) would suit their style. We were expecting the game to be a close battle. In the event, that proved to be an underestimation.

After eleven minutes we were given a true indication of how difficult Spurs were going to be when Steve Archibald gave them the lead, which they fought manfully to hold to halftime. In the second half we poured forward in search of an equaliser, but although some pundits considered the Spurs defence to be a soft underbelly, it continued to hold firm. I had a few efforts that Clem took comfortably but though we dominated we couldn't find the all important breakthrough.

With only five minutes remaining I thought our number was up. Steve Archibald received the ball in front of goal and, with Grob scampering to make up ground, fired wide. Had Archibald scored, as he invariably did from such a position, it would have knocked the stuffing out of us. As if often the case in football, such a crucial miss served to energise us. We began to think it may be our day after all.

I am sure I was not the only Liverpool play suddenly to find an extra spring in my step and edge to my game. We began to buzz and laid siege to the Spurs goal. Our opponents failed to clear their lines and the ball bounced around their six-yard area before falling to Ronnie Whelan, who scooped it past Clem. We went wild with delight and, when looking about at the Spurs players around me, their abject faces told me they didn't think they could do it all over again.

In extra time Spurs still give it all they had, but I sensed something was missing from their game – their belief that they could win. Ronnie capped what was an outstanding performance by drilling past Clem to give us the lead. Spurs' heads drooped yet again. Two minutes from the end of extra time, David Johnson, who had come on for Terry Mac, made progress down our left, cut inside, served as a magnet for Clemence, then unselfishly squared the ball across the box. I had made the ground, lost my marker Paul Miller and, the hard work done, had the simple task of side-footing the ball into the net.

What tiredness had beset my legs suddenly vanished. I carried on running across the stamina-sapping turf with one arm aloft, as if reaching out for the trophy I now saw at the front of the Royal Box. It was game over. I knew it and Spurs knew it.

I was tired but feverishly excited as I followed Graeme, who had assumed the captaincy, up the thirty-nine steps to the Royal Box to receive my winners' medal, my second in as many seasons. Again we had the curious distinction of running around Wembley on the traditional lap of honour brandishing two trophies, the League Cup and the rather 'handle-challenged' sponsored Milk Cup.

Back in the dressing-room as the champagne flowed, Joe Fagan reminded me I had set a new record of eight goals for the League Cup. Up to that point, the fact I had created a new goal-scoring record hadn't entered my mind as I had been too preoccupied with helping to win the trophy. I thought I might only hold the record for a year, but as fleeting as it might prove to be, felt I had made a little mark in the illustrious history of Liverpool football club.

I had quite a lot to contemplate at the end of my most successful season to date. I felt I had improved in leaps and bounds and gone some way to repaying Bob's faith in me to score goals with a total of thirty in all competitions. When I agreed to sign for Liverpool from Chester, a mate of mine in Flint told me that after you are offered a new job and before you actually start is the best feeling you will have in relation to that job. At the time I said he was totally right. Given the season I'd had at Liverpool, I now had cause to disagree.

CHAPTER FIVE

Business As Usual

The Home International Championship that took place at the end of 1981–2 had an added edge for England, Scotland and Northern Ireland. All three nations used the Championship as preparation for their respective appearances in the World Cup finals taking place in Spain that summer. Wales was the only Home nation not to have qualified for the World Cup but any disappointment I felt at that was tempered by once again being called upon to represent my country.

Wales began with a home match against England at Ninian Park. I partnered Swansea's Robbie James in attack but the only goal of the game came from Trevor Francis. Not the start we had hoped for but we took some consolation in the fact we had run England close. A similar scoreline befell Wales at Hampden Park, only on that occasion it was Asa Hartford who inflicted the damage.

In terms of winning the Home International Championship, Wales were out of it, but we rescued some pride by beating Northern Ireland 3–0 at the Racecourse Ground. Swansea's Alan Curtis gave us a first-half lead and some fifteen minutes into the second half I met a cross from Brian Flynn and directed a header past Jim Platt, who had come as a substitute for Pat Jennings. I was always very proud to score for Wales, but arguably the most important goal I scored for my country came a week later.

Following Wales's victory over the Irish we travelled to Toulouse to face France. The game represented France's final match preparation for the World Cup, which the bookies had made them favourites to win. No one outside the Wales camp gave us a chance in hell of getting a result. At the time, France and Brazil were considered the best teams in the world.

Today Toulouse's Municipal Stadium is as good as any in Europe, but in 1982 it seemed rather run-down and seedy. When I joined my teammates to inspect the pitch, I can recall feeling a little down. The stadium looked dreary and dilapidated. The roof of the main stand had obviously been patched up over the years and all stands were dotted with immense concrete pillars, which must have obstructed the view of many supporters. I was told, however, that the atmosphere generated for an international match was fevered, which was why the French FA liked to stage games in Toulouse when not playing in Paris.

I was a little in awe of the French team, which contained such outstanding players as Battiston, Trésor, Bossis, Tigana, Giresse, Six, and the player many considered at the time to be the best in the world, Michel Platini. I couldn't wait to pit myself against players whose stature and achievements were already well known in the UK. I reasoned that if I could perform well against these players in such a volatile and partisan atmosphere, I could play against anybody.

Roared on by a capacity crowd of 35,000, France took the game to us from the start. International matches usually begin with both teams sounding one another out, but France did not seem to care one iota about how we were going to play. From the referee's first whistle they went on the attack and proceeded to dominate.

For a good twenty minutes we were on the back foot and there was little doubt goalkeeper Dai Davies was in for a very busy evening. We were so much on the defensive I found myself dropping deeper and deeper in search of the ball. At one point Chris Marustick said, 'If you come any deeper, Rushy, you'll be playing behind Dai.'

Having failed to breach us, France appeared to lose their initial momentum and we came more and more into the game. Ten minutes before halftime Brian Flynn drew the French midfield towards him and played the ball behind them. I outstripped Trésor, latched on to the ball and fired across Castenada only for the ball to smack against the foot of his left-hand post. Hope sprang eternal.

During the halftime interval, Mike England urged us to keep it going, telling us that if we produced a similar effort in the second half we could 'nick it'.

We expected France to come out and give it a go in the second half and we weren't disappointed. Prompted by Michel Platini, France continued to prod and probe, and when not doing that, used the speed of Didier Six for the hell-for-leather approach. Still we held out. With some fifteen minutes remaining our midfield simultaneously found their touch and seized the initiative. Taking a throw-in from Chris Marustick just inside the French half of the field, Brian Flynn surged forward down the right-hand side. There was an exchange between Arsenal's Peter Nicholas and Leighton James before the ball returned Brian.

A killer ball for defenders is the one played in from wide behind their back four but in front of the goalkeeper. It requires accuracy and has to be weighted properly, and the striker running on to the ball has to time his run to perfection if he is going to have any chance of scoring. Get it right and few defences can cope with this type of ball. Brian's raking pass curved behind Trésor and co. Having started running as soon as I realised what he had in mind, I sprinted between Trésor and Lopez to sweep the ball past Castaneda. I don't think the French lads or their supporters could believe what had happened, and I'm not sure Mike England could, either. We had the lead.

Try as France did, and Platini gave it all he had, we not only held out but could have increased our lead when Leighton James's late effort was cleared off the line by Alain Bossis.

The Wales dressing-room was euphoric after the game. We had played what was one of the top international teams in the world and beaten them on their home turf. As Peter Nicholas remarked, 'Why the hell are we not going to Spain when we can play like that?' Indeed.

During the post-match reception I fell into conversation with Michel Platini, little knowing that our meeting was the beginning of what would be a long and lasting friendship. Despite my scoring the winner, in his presence I felt like a schoolboy meeting his hero. During the game I had marvelled at the way he dictated from midfield. Every French attack stemmed from him. Given I had spent a lot of time on my own upfront while my teammates valiantly defended, I was able to observe him at close quarters. He had a unique ability to read the game, was able to size up a situation in a flash and demonstrated complete mastery of the ball. He also possessed great powers of acceleration combined with cunning to veil his real intentions. He kept the ball constantly flowing and brought so many other players into the picture. A truly brilliant and inspirational player. Platini was so good I was left wondering how the hell we had managed to beat France with him in the side. That said, I was to play seventy-three times for my country and, as I write this, I'm pushed to recall a better Wales performance. To a man we were superb that night.

Michel told me he was quietly confident of France's chances in the World Cup, that he thought they would surprise a lot of teams. Their opening game was against England and he plied me for information on the England team, which put me in something of a dilemma. Although he was a hero of mine, I didn't want to say anything that might give France an edge over England.

Michel went on to tell me he felt he had played his last game for St Etienne, that if he had a good World Cup he believed one of the big Continental clubs would make a move for him. He said he would be sad to leave France, but should an opportunity come along with, say, AC Milan, Juventus or Real Madrid, he would accept. He felt he would never find out what he was truly capable of as footballer unless he was playing against the best week in and week out. Years later, I would have cause to remember those words.

In the event Michel had a tremendous World Cup in Spain. I think most would agree he was the best player in the tournament by some distance. I felt France were the best football team in the finals but, as is often the case, with the notable exception of Brazil in 1970, the best and most entertaining football team in a World Cup invariably doesn't win it.

France were beaten in the semi-finals by West Germany in a penalty shoot-out, after extra time finished with the score 3–3. They were exceedingly unlucky. You may recall Battiston being felled by the German goalkeeper Schumacher in what was a scandalous yet unpunished challenge.

The day after that game I contacted Michel and offered him and his teammates my commiserations. We talked of how close France had come to appearing in the final, if not winning the World Cup.

'You have heard of Icarus?' he suddenly asked.

'Yeah, Greek legend, the man who flew too close to the sun and his wings melted,' I replied

'Yes, and what is the moral of that story, Ian?' he asked.

'I'm not sure.'

'Most believe it is, don't fly too close to the sun,' he said. 'But I think the moral is you have to build better wings. In France, regarding our football, that is what we are going to do.'

When I reported back to Melwood for pre-season training I couldn't wait for 1982–3 to get underway. But we were greeted with sad news. Bob gathered the players together in the Anfield dressing-room and told us this season would be his last.

'I'm getting too old for this game,' he said. 'Management, that is, not football. I've been too old for football for donkey's years. I've had a fantastic time, but I'm calling it a day come May. Just thought I'd let you all know that.'

We were all stunned, though for some time there had been rumours of Bob going 'upstairs', perhaps to a position on the board (which later transpired). It didn't seem the time or place for us to thank Bob for all he had done because we were going to have another season together. So we all said we understood his reasons for retirement and that we hoped we could make his last season at the club one to remember.

We were keen to build on the achievements of the previous season. For my part, with the experience I'd gained through an extended run in the team, I was confident of getting somewhere near, if not exceeding, my previous season's tally of thirty goals.

The optimism and general feeling of well-being I shared with my Liverpool teammates was in sharp contrast to the general state of the English game. There were positives. Aston Villa had won the European Cup to further emphasise English dominance of Europe's major club trophy. The FA and League Cup finals had attracted record TV audiences as it was the first time both finals had been beamed 'live' to a worldwide audience. By and large, the football being played was dramatic, fast and skilful, and the introduction of three points for a win in this season did induce more attacking football and produce more goals.

Set against this was the threat of financial ruin for many clubs and the continuation of a decrease in attendance. In the summer of 1982, Wolves, once as dominant a force in English football as Liverpool now were, came to close to extinction. Bristol City, Oxford United and Hull City announced they too were close to bankruptcy, while a number of lower division clubs were struggling to survive, principally Rochdale whose average attendance had dipped below 2,000.

Just over 20 million spectators had attended Football League matches in 1981–2, almost 2 million down on the previous season, and 10 million less than 1972. It was a far cry from the immediate post-war years when more than 40 million spectators attended League games.

There is little doubt hooliganism had had a detrimental effect on the image of the game. Yes, there were some serious incidents, but even minor disturbances were given lurid headlines and columns of newspaper space that were out of all proportion with the actual incident. One would have thought there was trouble on the terraces at every ground every Saturday, but this was far from the case. I talk to numerous supporters who were fans back in the early 1980s, and the vast majority never witnessed trouble at games.

The term 'football hooligan' never rested easy with me. It's an emotive term. I objected to the use of the word 'football' because the minority who did cause trouble were criminals using football as a theatre for their moronic activities. In the early 1980s there was footage on TV of so-called 'football hooligans' purporting to support Nottingham Forest and Manchester United clashing in Nottingham city centre. The incident took place while the Forest–United game was in process.

I don't want to sweep the hooliganism problem under the carpet, it happened and there were some sickening incidents, but football at the time was not so infested with the problem as the media would have one believe. But the result was that a lot of people turned away from football, particularly family groups and the elderly. In the wake of the Taylor Report and in these days of fine stadiums some people also cite the poor state of many grounds as a reason for the decline in attendances in the 1980s. While trumpeting the facilities now on offer and saying some of the facilities on offer in the 1980s were woeful if not downright degrading, I have never come across anyone who said he or she stopped going to games because the ground wasn't up to scratch. It's almost as if those who now charge supporters the earth to attend games are using that argument to justify their high prices.

The Taylor Report was right in saying football had to take a long hard look at the way it treated its 'customers'. It took the terrible tragedies of Hillsborough, Bradford and Heysel for the game to get its act together, and only then under pressure from government and other authorities. But the financial peril which beset the game and many clubs in the 1980s was not simply down to incidents of hooliganism and shabby facilities. Due to its poor image, football was not as attractive to television and the corporate sector as it is now, so there was nowhere near the amount of money coming into the game, even in relative terms, as there is today.

But although English football was in a poor state of health, the game was not diseased as all that, and there was plenty of top-class, skilful football being played. Nowhere more so than at Anfield, which, incidentally, never suffered from problems of hooliganism.

Before pre-season training began, all the Liverpool players were subjected to a medical. Those considered to have put on a little weight were given two weeks to lose it. The pre-season training was geared to building strength and stamina as well as fitness. I always found it something of a chore as there was no game to look forward to at the end of the week, albeit, in keeping with Liverpool tradition, plenty of five-a-side games.

In keeping with most top clubs, Liverpool played a number of pre-season games on the Continent. Many clubs chose to travel to Scandinavia where the opposition might not be of the highest quality, particularly in the case of part-time professional clubs. As a consequence, matches were easily won and often by a sizeable scoreline. Many managers believed it best to ease players gently towards match fitness. Teams would then move up to the next stage of their preparation by playing sterner opposition.

Bob, however, never saw the point of playing inferior opposition in pre-season games. He wanted us to be tested from the start. Secondly, he and his backroom staff were always interested in learning new methods and techniques which they might be able to adapt for use at Liverpool. As far as Bob was concerned, there was more likelihood of this happening should we play quality opposition than part-timers from Sweden or Finland. Also, the majority of the teams Liverpool faced were already some weeks into their domestic season, hence were fully match fit and provided us with a game at a tempo and pace more in keeping with what we would encounter once our season started.

Due to the World Cup in Spain, the English league season would not begin until the end of August, so we set off for on our pre-season tour at the beginning of the month. Our first game was in Switzerland against Servette who, in recent years, had done comparatively well in European competition. The game ended goalless. Then we were off to Spain.

Our first match there ended in a 2–0 victory over Real Betis, our second goal coming from David Hodgson, signed from Middlesbrough while we were on tour. David could play as a striker or in midfield and I think it was primarily because of his versatility that Bob signed him. He could provide cover not only for Kenny and I but also any of the midfield positions. Such a player is a godsend to a manager because he doesn't have to sign two or even three players to cover positions. Rather than doing him a disservice, I feel it was a compliment to describe David as a 'job lot' squad player, he was so versatile.

The downside for such a player is that he never seems to hold a regular place in the team, which would prove to be the case with David. The upside is that he will, in all probability, always be involved with the first team. If not actually playing, then on the bench, as his versatility enables him to cover a variety of positions. David and I became really good pals. His knowledge of the history and tradition of English football was phenomenal, and he was an avid collector of football memorabilia, having the foresight to collect many match programmes, team sheets, press sheets, pennants, shirts and autographed footballs from Liverpool games.

We rounded off our pre-season programme with a 1–1 draw against Malaga, then it was back home to prepare for the Charity Shield against Spurs at Wembley. It's funny how often seemingly inconsequential things seem to stick in your mind for years to come. Flying back from Spain I can recall reading in the newspapers that Kevin Keegan, then of Southampton, had held talks with Manchester United manager, Ron Atkinson. Three days later, Kevin, still worshipped by Liverpool fans, signed for Newcastle United, then of Division Two. It was reported in the press that Kevin's proposed move to Old Trafford fell through because the club wouldn't meet his personal terms. I found it strange, however, that a club of the stature and, even then, wealth of United were unable to match Kevin's salary demands, yet a Second Division club did. It suggests to me there may have been other reasons for Kevin not joining United, or, should the press have been correct, that the financial state of football in the 1980s was not quite as bleak as some would now have you believe.

A crowd of 82,500 was present at Wembley to see us get our season off to a satisfying start by winning the Charity Shield against Spurs. The game had only one goal in it. It occurred in the thirty-second minute and I managed to score it. In so doing I made a mental note: 'One down, twenty-nine to go.' I had set myself a target of equalling my thirty-goal haul of the previous season. It was a tough ask but, barring injury, I was quietly confident of achieving my aim. Goals had been my lifeblood since early childhood. If I wasn't scoring goals, I was never in a truly happy frame of mind and I wanted the season ahead to be a very happy one.

Liverpool took to the field for our first game of the season at Anfield against West Bromwich Albion sporting a variation of the traditional all-red strip. It was still all-red, of course, but the shirts incorporated a pin stripe and the logo of the club's first sponsor, Crown Paints. The sponsorship had been in place the previous season and we had intermittently worn shirts bearing the logo as television refused to broadcast games featuring teams wearing sponsored shirts. Now television seemed more flexible. In the event, TV executives and the Football League would still insist we wore non-sponsored shirts when playing major games that attracted large TV audiences. The game may have been in a poor financial state, but the powers that be were still reluctant to embrace ideas that would inject much-needed money into the game.

The West Brom team included Martin Jol. He was not your archetypal Dutch player, as he was a powerful, tough-tackling midfield player who, even then, came across as rather humourless. Jol was one of a small, but growing number of foreign players who had entered the English game. Spurs, of course, had for some years boasted Ardiles and Villa, whose names were familiar to most through their exploits with Argentina. Now overseas players whose names were not familiar to many supporters were beginning to ply their trade in English football.

At the time Nottingham Forest had another Dutchman, goal-keeper Hans van Breukelen, and the Norwegian Jan Einar. Notts County had goalkeeper Raddy Avramovic from Yugoslavia. Dutchman Arnold Muhren was at Manchester United, having formerly been at Ipswich, for whom Franz Thijssen still played. There were other overseas players but in reality none were massive stars of European football. Foreign players were coming in increasing numbers to English football but our game did not have the riches to attract the really big names, who still gravitated to

(Right) Me, aged five. I was quite a chubby lad before I contracted meningitis. Afterwards I lost a lot of weight and was to remain lithe.

(Below) Deeside District Primary Schools XI. I'm second from left in the front row wearing white 'Alan Ball' boots previously worn by some of my brothers. My record for the most goals scored in a season for Deeside was eventually broken – by Michael Owen.

(Right) With my brothers all set for a kick-about on the back field. Left to right: Peter, Francie, Gerald, Graham, (front) Stephen and me (holding the ball).

(Left) In my first season with Chester. Today, Premiership clubs wear a new strip for every game. In all my time at Chester the first team wore the same set of strips.

(Below) Chester line-up for 1978–9. I'm an apprentice, seated front, far right. On the back row, far left, is manager Alan Oakes who, along with coach Cliff Sear, helped me enormously.

(Below) My dad was a lifelong Liverpool supporter and a member of Deeside Liverpool Supporters Club. This was a very special moment for us both. Dad gets to present me with the Liverpool S.C. 'Young Player of the Year Award'.

(Above) With my mum (and something else for her to polish). My whole family were incredibly supportive of me. Given the size of my family, that was some support.

(Right) Looking for space to exploit (with hair like Simon Le Bon's).

(Above) Terry McDermott demonstrates the close marking I will be subjected to when I move to Italy.

(Below) In action against Manchester United, a club I never seemed to do well against.

(Right) Being presented with the Matchman of the Month Award in 1982. Now whatever happened to that award?

(Below) Signing autographs in Tokyo prior to the World Club Championship against Flamengo of Brazil. Little did I know then how much time I would spend coaching in the Far East when my playing days were over.

(Right) Some fans are on the pitch, they think it's all over … In fact, it was just the start. Hoisting the League Cup aloft in only my third first-team game for Liverpool. I don't look very happy but, believe me, I was.

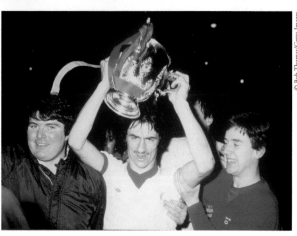

© Bob Thomas/Getty Images

(Above) I never considered myself a great header of the ball but I managed to score quite a number with my head simply by finding space, such as here against Benfica.

(Left) My face says it all. With the European Cup following victory over Roma in the Stadio Olimpico. I scored in the penalty shoot-out, my fiftieth goal of the season.

(Below) After victory over Roma we pose for the press singing the club's anthem, 'You'll Never Walk Alone'. Seemingly Alan Hansen (back row, far left) has trouble remembering the words.

© Bob Thomas/Getty Images

© Bob Thomas/Getty Images

(Left) Liverpool and Everton players at Wembley with the Charity Shield. Despite the fierce rivalry on the pitch, the players of both clubs have always socialised and got on well.

(Right) I celebrate my goal against Everton in the Charity Shield with a characteristic raise of a finger. The goalkeeper on this occasion is Bobby Mimms.

(Above) Craig Johnston displays his fear of riding on the upper deck of an open-top bus as Steve McMahon and I show off the FA Cup to our fans.

(Left) With Tracy, my 'Match of the Day' and life.

(Below) For a short time I owned a Porsche (but apparently no socks). Then we had a family and that lovely Porsche had to go.

(Left) Taking my turn to look after the boys! At my testimonial with Jonathan (right) and Daniel. I was thrilled to be able to take them on to the Anfield pitch for the pre-match kick-in.

(Left) With the Golden Boot Award in 1984 – awarded to the top goalscorer in Europe.

© Bob Thomas/Getty Images

(Below) I leave the field following my last game at Anfield for Liverpool before joining Juventus. I had thrown my shirt into the Kop and some fans joined me as I made my way to the tunnel.

© Steve Hale

Italy and Spain. Though no one realised it at the time, sponsors' logos on shirts and the trickle of foreign players into the game were the seeds of change that would, in time, see English football alter irrevocably.

We began the season with a 2–0 victory over West Brom and our good start evolved into good form. We remained unbeaten in our first seven league matches, but it wasn't until our fourth game, a 4–3 home win over Nottingham Forest, that I managed my first League goal of the season. We were, however, scoring regularly as a team and in September hit a purple patch, scoring fifteen goals in four League matches, the pick a 5–0 win at home to Southampton.

Amazingly, fifty goals were scored in the eleven First Division matches played that day. In addition to ourselves, seven other teams scored four or more: Watford (8–0 winners against Sunderland); Ipswich (6–0 winners against Notts County); Stoke City and Luton Town (drew 4–4); Coventry (4–2 winners against Everton); West Ham (4–1 winners against Manchester City); Spurs (4–1 winners against Nottingham Forest). Of course, there was always Arsenal, who featured in a drab goalless draw with Manchester United, but the open, attacking football being played by the majority of teams was producing goals and this was being reflected in an upturn in attendances.

I had picked up an injury in the Southampton game, nothing serious but enough to keep me out of our next game at Ipswich where we suffered our first defeat of the season (0–1). In footballers' parlance, it was a good one to miss. After such a promising start to the campaign, it all went a little pear-shaped for us in our next three games: a 3–1 defeat at West Ham followed by draws against both Manchester United (0–0) and Stoke City (1–1).

Bob, however, kept with the same team for our next game at home to Brighton and we repaid his faith with a 3–1 win. Up to this point I thought I had been playing reasonably well but was still unhappy as I hadn't been scoring anywhere near as regularly as I had hoped. My tally was just four in eleven League games.

You hear people talk about confidence being important to strikers and it's true. I hadn't lost faith in my ability to score goals. Every time I crossed the white line I expected, rather than hoped, to come off with a goal to my name. That this had not been the case didn't wreck my confidence but it did take an edge off it. In such circumstances you have to maintain a steely mindset. It's all too easy for a striker enduring a barren run to tell himself, 'I've got to score in this game.' When he doesn't, self-doubt grows within him and he starts to think back to previous games and goals he scored. Dwelling on such things is never good, because you are in danger of thinking, 'That last goal I scored sneaked in at the post. I was lucky. A couple of inches the other side and it would have gone wide.' One thought leads to another, and he begins to re-assess all the goals he scored: 'I hit that one on the turn without looking. Don't know how it went in'; 'So-and-so set me up for that one. My grandmother would have scored it'. The self-doubt increases and confidence begins to evaporate. He begins to try too hard and when he misses another chance, gloom descends.

I remember once talking to Tom Ritchie, who had joined Sunderland for a sizeable fee from Bristol City in 1981. Tom was bought in to score goals but, following his move, couldn't hit the back of the net. He became something of a target for Sunderland fans, frustrated that the club's new striker couldn't score. When presented with an opportunity the thought flashed through his brain that he must put it away and he became afraid of missing.

The longer it went on the worse it got. Then, against Birmingham City, he managed a tap-in. 'It was as if a millstone around my neck had suddenly been lifted,' Tom said. Having finally opened his account after five goalless months, Tom went on to score a hat-trick against Birmingham.

So come November, although I hadn't been scoring as regularly as I hoped, I didn't beat myself up about it. The goals were being shared about in the Liverpool team, which is a mark of a good side. I never felt my place was under threat because, generally speaking, my performances had been good. On several occasions I had been making goals for teammates. Not for one moment had I ever been afraid of not putting the ball in the net when presented with a chance; it just didn't happen for me regularly. I knew the goals would come and so did Bob who, before our next game, which was against Everton, told me, 'Don't worry. You have goals in you. Just keep playing the way you are doing and they'll come. No Liverpool player has scored a hat-trick against Everton for over fifty years. I think you can help yourself to one.' It was unusual for Bob to make such an outlandish statement, but his words filled me with confidence.

Many supporters have a love–hate relationship with a derby match. It is the biggest game in the fixture calendar but there is so much local pride at stake and fans are so desperate for their team not to lose, that tension renders enjoyment of the game almost impossible. Until, that is, the final whistle signals that your team has won.

A Merseyside derby is full of fervour, partisanship and tension. What makes the Merseyside derby different from others, however, is the almost total absence of hate for the opposition and their fans. This has much to do with the city itself. Whereas in Glasgow or Tyne and Wear, for example, there is a clear divide between the groups of supporters, in Liverpool you are likely to find supporters of both clubs within one family, my own family being a prime example, or amongst close friends. It is because of this that the vitriol so often presented on the terraces at other derby matches is noticeably absent when Liverpool take on Everton. That is not to say the games lack atmosphere; on the contrary, the games raise the roof, and to play in one is an unforgettable experience.

On the morning of the derby, 6 November 1982, Liverpool sat at the top of Division One. Everton were mid-table. Not that League positions meant anything. Merseyside derbies were traditionally tight, irrespective of how either team was faring.

In previous seasons Everton had not enjoyed the best of times but, under Howard Kendall, were now beginning to show signs of revival. Their team contained some top-quality players: Neville Southall (whom I knew from the Wales squad), Adrian Heath, Steve McMahon, John Bailey, Graeme Sharp, Andy King and my old Liverpool team-mate Kevin Sheedy.

The noise within Goodison Park as we kicked off was immense. Instantly, we went on the attack and within seconds came within a whisker of taking the lead. I made ground down the middle, Sammy Lee crossed low, I met the ball on the run and it flew past Southall only to thud against the Everton crossbar. The red contingent within Goodison let out a collective 'Go-ahhhhh!' only for this to be followed by a sonorous roar that almost popped my eardrums as our supporters smelled blood.

In the opening stages Everton were struggling to contain us. There was another roar of exasperation from our fans when Sammy Lee rapped a shot against the Everton woodwork, then came the game's first controversy.

Alan Kennedy went down the Everton right on one of his maze-like runs, lifted the ball into the jaws of the Everton penalty area where Kenny, having made up the ground, bulleted a header past Southall. Goodison, or at least the red contingent within it, erupted.

I ran up to congratulate Kenny. In so doing I glanced across at the referee, Mr Civil, who was signalling 'goal' by pointing back towards the centre spot. He then set off towards the halfway line for the re-start and, having congratulated Kenny, the Liverpool players followed suit.

I was on the centre circle in our half of the field ready for the re-start when I suddenly noticed the Everton defenders Billy Wright and John Bailey were also up on the halfway line. Both were manically gesticulating towards the linesman on the far side and, when other Everton players saw this, they all went at it.

Bowing to this pressure, Mr Civil began walking across to the linesman, who was waving his flag in the air. Behind me I heard the gruff voice of Graeme say, 'What the fucking hell's he on about?'

When Kenny's header went in, I'd also glanced across to the linesman, something I invariably did when a teammate scored, just to assure myself I hadn't missed anything and the goal was good. The linesman's flag had been down by his side. Seemingly, there had been a change of mind.

For a few moments Mr Civil took on the role of the Pied Piper as blue and red-shirted players fell in behind him as he made his way over to the touchline and his linesman. Suddenly aware he had an entourage, Mr Civil turned and indicated we should all keep our distance; the conversation between him and his linesman was going to be private.

When a referee consults his linesman, two things will happen.

Either the referee will have made up his mind that the goal was legitimate and, irrespective of what the linesman has to say, will overrule him, believing he had a clearer view of the incident.

I'd even known situations when a referee, bent on absolute certainty, didn't even ask the linesman's opinion but would simply make conversation to look as though he had taken another view into consideration before confirming his award of the goal. Either way consultation serves to quell the protests of dissenting players.

The other thing that will happen is, having consulted with his linesman, the referee will take on board what is said and change his decision, which is what Mr Civil did.

That got Kenny going. He was absolutely livid at having his goal disallowed, firmly believing himself to have been onside when Alan Kennedy played the ball. Having been surrounded by Everton players, Mr Civil now found himself besieged by Liverpool players or at least a number of us, Kenny, Graeme, Alan and Sammy having crossed over to the linesman to vent their displeasure with him.

The crowd was in uproar, the red contingent angry at the decision, the blue sections directing us to get on with the game. Perhaps prompted by their baying supporters, the Everton players came across and began giving us verbals for contesting the referee's re-appraisal of the incident.

'Shut the fuck up!' snarled John Bailey at me.

I began laughing. Up to this point I hadn't said word. I was leaving it all to Kenny and co. When Kenny got angry he reverted to a very strong Glaswegian accent, so strong even fellow Scots such as Graeme and Alan couldn't understand a word he said. So Mr Civil had no chance.

'Yedinnafackingiitthenathenafackinchingeyemeenditsafackin-teerabledeeshionyadiasgracethatwhoolonyerlefttit,' raged Kenny, or words to that effect. Who knows what he was actually saying?

John Bailey and 'Inchy' (Heath) then started on Kenny, who was so outraged that his face, rosy at the best of times, turned an even deeper red than a Liverpool shirt.

Mr Civil had had enough. He ordered everyone to retreat and signalled a free-kick deep in the Everton half, while the linesman did his best to get into row G for cover.

'Offside. Free-kick. Now get on with it, the lot of you, or I'll get the book out, gentlemen,' he ordered. Despite the barrage of criticism aimed his way, he was living up to his name.

I have known players who, in such a highly charged atmosphere, would allow their anger and frustration to get the better of them. They begin to get involved in personal battles with the opposition, the shape of the team suffers, they get more frustrated and angry, their concentration goes, as does their chance of getting something from the game. We were made of sterner stuff. We put disappointment behind us and got on with it only for pandemonium to descend on Goodison yet again.

An exchange of passes between Graeme, Sammy and me ended with Kenny bursting through the Everton back line with a clear run on goal.

Glen Keeley was on loan and making his Everton debut, which, it would transpire, would also constitute his last game for the club. Unable to cope with Kenny's pace, Glen hauled Kenny to the ground a yard or so from the Everton penalty box. Kenny sat on his backside, arms outstretched and looking in the direction of Mr Civil as if to say, 'What the hell was that?'

Mr Civil was in no doubt. His hand was reaching into his pocket as he ran towards Glen. The Everton debutant centre-back was off.

We were not to be denied. We continued to pour forward and, minutes after the Keeley incident, I received the ball on the right. As Neville Southall came rushing out to close me down, I slipped the ball wide of him and into the net. It was now an incendiary atmosphere.

During the halftime interval, Bob told us to 'keep going', as he felt Everton would crumble and there were more goals in the game for us. 'Keep making those runs into space. The ball will come, and you'll get another, at least,' he told me.

We were really on song in the second half. We pulled the Everton defence this way and that. Six minutes after the re-start I received a pass on the edge of the area and went for goal. The ball took a slight deflection off an Everton defender but, to my mind, it was goal-bound anyway. Our fans, massed behind Southall's goal, were elevated to mass hysteria. We were two goals to the good, but we upped the tempo still further.

Some five minutes later Phil Neal took a throw-in on the right. Kenny received the ball, looked up and, on seeing Mark Lawrenson gliding towards Southall's far post, sent the ball unerringly towards him. Lawro swept the ball into the net to the further delight of our fans. The Everton players, seemingly catching the mood of their supporters, appeared sullen and silent. There was no berating of his defence by Southall. It was if they had resigned themselves to the inevitable.

Kenny and Graeme's skilful repertoire of passes, timed and executed to perfection, probed ceaselessly into the home defence. Chances came and went, then, having stifled a rare Everton attack, Alan Hansen strode majestically out of defence with the ball at his feet before playing a pass up to the halfway line. I let the ball run, turned and headed for the lonely Southall. I could hear the '*thick-thick-thick*' of Everton studs in the turf behind me but I kept going, and that noise didn't get any louder. Entering the Everton penalty box I hit a low shot wide of Southall's dive and kept running, which proved the right thing to do. The ball cannoned off the foot of the post and, with Southall spreadeagled behind me, I stroked the ball into an empty net.

A hat-trick in a Merseyside derby. I was consumed by a feeling of happiness I had never known. The feeling was terrific, not least because the hat-trick re-affirmed what I always believed to be true – that I could score goals. It was as if my mind were suddenly rid of the possibility of self-doubt.

Five minutes from time the ball was played quickly out of defence to me yet again, and again I turned and headed for Southall, behind me the now familiar *'thick-thick-thick'* noise. Southall came out of his goal to narrow the angle. I dropped my left shoulder. He made to spread himself across the ground. I swayed the other way and, looking up, aimed for the far stanchion. It didn't quite hit the spot, but it was good enough. I couldn't believe it. To say I was 'made-up' with my four goals would be an understatement. I was on an absolute high.

Dad could not have been happier had he won the jackpot on the pools. He was beaming although he didn't say much, almost as if he was unable to find the right words to express his delight. But I knew he was happy all right from the way he kept looking at me – proud but at the same time seemingly disbelieving of what I had managed to achieve.

After the game we enjoyed a drink with the Everton lads, though I'm not so sure they enjoyed it as much as we did. One of the first of the Everton lads to congratulate me was John Bailey. 'Well done,' he said. 'You killed us.'

A score of 5–0 against Everton away from home is the stuff of Merseyside folklore. The fact I had managed to score four of those goals was something to savour and I began to feel really bullish about the prospect of more.

In the following league game, at home to Coventry City, I

bagged another hat-trick in a 4–0 win. A four-goal haul and a hat-trick in successive league games had the newspapers writing all manner of good things about me. I was compared to 'Dixie' Dean, Jimmy Greaves and Roger Hunt but, as young as I was, I never deluded myself. I was mindful that, before my hat-tricks, I had scored only four goals in eleven League games. Curiously, no newspaper thought fit to mention this.

We continued to post good results. Those convincing victories over Everton and Coventry were part of a run of twenty-seven League games of which we lost but one, at Norwich City. There were other handsome wins posted during that run, too, including 5–1 against Notts County (in which I scored another hat-trick). Stoke City were beaten 5–1 while Manchester City succumbed 5–2 at Anfield. There were also four-goal victories against Aston Villa and Manchester City. In all we scored 63 goals in those twenty-seven matches. No other team could keep up.

We were presented with the First Division Championship trophy following our 3–0 win over Swansea City on 9 April when we still had seven matches to play.

Having wrapped up the title so early, the steam went out of our engine and we failed to win one of those remaining seven games, yet so commanding had been our lead at the top of the table that we still finished eleven points ahead of runners-up Watford.

Looking back I feel sorry we didn't finish on a high note for Bob, though I don't think he felt let down. He was, after all, the most successful manager in the history of English football and, to this day, no other manager of a British club has won more European Cups. Yet, for all his unparalleled success, Bob remained modest to the end. At the end of the season Sammy Lee remarked that now Bob had retired he might write his autobiography.

'Some autobiography that would be,' remarked Alan Hansen.

'Bob's so self-effacing he'd probably only mention himself twice.'

Bob never did get around to writing his story, but if he had done, I bet Alan's throwaway line wouldn't have been far off the mark – Bob was that sort of guy.

Having clinched the title against Swansea, the *Daily Mirror* ran the headline: 'BUSINESS AS USUAL'. But a hell of a lot of hard work had gone into running the 'business'. It had been a team effort and by that I don't mean just from the players. Management and backroom staff had all contributed in no small way to our success. When football writer Frank Butler suggested to Bob that Liverpool's success was primarily down to him, now English football's most successful ever manager, Bob was quick to refute such a notion with characteristic modesty. 'I don't think so, Frank,' he said. 'Good football management is all about taking credit for other people's hard work.'

I finished the season with twenty-four league goals to my name. I also scored two in each of the FA, European and League Cups. Added to the goal I scored in the Charity Shield (and why not?), my total for the season was thirty-one. I had exceeded my target for the season.

The downside to what had been another fantastic season for the team, the club, our supporters and me was our failure to make any real headway in the FA and European Cups.

In the FA Cup, we dispensed with Blackburn Rovers (2–1 at Ewood Park) and Stoke City (2–0 at Anfield) only to be beaten 2–1 at home by Brighton in round five, Brighton's winner coming from former Anfield favourite Jimmy Case, who, not for the first time, had come back to haunt us. Brighton were managed by another former Red in Jimmy Melia, not that the old Anfield connection proved any consolation to us. Brighton went on to reach the FA Cup final that year and were minutes away from beating Manchester United when Gordon Smith missed the chance of a lifetime to score the winner. It proved very costly as United won the replay at something of a canter.

Football can be cruel and fickle. Gordon's goals had been instrumental in Brighton reaching Wembley but on the big day he missed an opportunity to write himself into the record books. This, to me, sums up a striker's lot. A forward can score regularly throughout his career. He can make a telling contribution to the clubs he plays for, but all that is forgotten by supporters should he fluff his lines at a crucial moment in a crucial game. I guess Gordon was left wondering why fate had suddenly dealt him such a cruel hand. I say this because earlier in the season he had been on the losing side in the Scottish League Cup final when on loan at Rangers. Gordon did create football history but of the unwanted kind. I can't think of another player who, in the same season, ended up on the losing side in English and Scottish Cup finals. It is an unusual story but I should imagine it's not one Gordon has dined out on too many times.

Our exit from the FA Cup was a disappointment to us, but our failure to make an impact upon the European Cup was an even bigger blow. We began in comfortable fashion with victory over Dundalk of Ireland. In the second round we were paired with HJK Helsinki and, after a 1–0 defeat in Finland which irked us but didn't unduly concern us, we won the return leg 5–0 at Anfield.

In the quarter-final we travelled to Poland to meet Widzew Łódź, who were minus their star player Zbigniew Boniek. (Following the World Cup he had joined Juventus.) Poland also appeared to be minus any hotels with soft loo paper. Polish football was enjoying something of a golden period. The national team had reached the semi-finals of the World Cup – coincidentally, Boniek had been unavailable for that game, too – and, in sharp contrast to the state of the nation, Polish football was buoyant.

Łódź had won successive Polish League titles. They were a decent side with some very good players but were not one of the European Cup's heavyweights. We were expected to progress to the semi-finals without too much bother. If only. On the night Grob made a terrible error that resulted in Tlokinski giving Łódź the lead. When the home side scored a second we knew we would have a job on our hands at Anfield.

However, we had so much confidence in our ability to beat any team and turn around any tie, I firmly believed we would progress, particularly when a penalty from Phil Neal gave us an early lead in the second leg. Then an uncharacteristic mistake by Graeme led to Łódź being awarded a penalty, which they converted. With an away goal to their name, we now had real task on our hands. We laid siege to the Łódź goal. With every Liverpool player but Grob in the opposition's half of the field, Łódź won possession of the ball and mounted a swift counter-attack. To our dismay, Smolarek despatched the ball past Grob with just about every one of us in his wake. The tie wasn't totally beyond redemption, so we kept going at them. I pulled a goal back and David Hodgson scored another to give us a 3–2 lead on the night, but with the tie 4–3 to Łódź on aggregate, we ran out of time.

It had been a case of too little too late and that of Liverpool paying a very high price for uncharacteristic, silly errors. With holders Aston Villa also going out to a Platini-inspired Juventus, the European Cup left England for the first time in six years.

Business as usual was an apposite way to describe 1982–3 for, as in the previous season, Liverpool also retained the League Cup.

Our defence began with a victory over Ipswich Town, now without the management skills of Bobby Robson, who left the club to manage England. There followed victories over Rotherham United, Norwich City and West Ham United before a place at Wembley was secured with the defeat of Second Division Burnley over two legs (3–0 and 0–1) in the semi-finals. Burnley also reached the sixth round of the FA Cup but, curiously, fell well short of repeating their fine cup performances, and were relegated to Division Three.

The League Cup final against Manchester United proved Bob's twelfth and final visit to Wembley in charge of a Liverpool team. It also proved to be a match full of drama and good football, too, even if, at times, the play had a frenetic air.

United took the lead after twelve minutes through Norman Whiteside. Despite the early setback we never lost our composure and attacked methodically for the rest of the game. United were almost constantly on the back foot and, seemingly deciding this was not an occasion for the finer rudiments of football, hacked the ball to all corners of Wembley in order to relieve the pressure on Gary Bailey's goal. Yet they held out until what was to prove a dramatic final quarter.

With twenty minutes remaining, United's central defender, Kevin Moran, twisted his ankle and had to leave the field. United reshuffled, with Lou Macari replacing the injured Moran. Five minutes later Alan Kennedy tried his luck from twenty-five yards. The ball took enough of a bounce in front of Gary Bailey to throw the United keeper and we were level. I felt not a little relief and thought now that we could go on and win.

Five minutes later, United's Gordon McQueen pulled up

suffering from cramp and a hamstring problem. With United having used their substitute (only one allowed at the time), McQueen bravely decided to carry on, or, rather hobble on.

Then in the final minute of the game, McQueen found himself free on the right and bearing down on our goal. Grob came sprinting out of his area and, as McQueen tried to go round him, Grob body-checked him.

During the season there had been a lot of debate about what was termed the 'professional foul'. Having retracted their decision that 'deliberate handball' constituted 'serious foul play' meriting immediate dismissal, an advisory committee chaired by Sir Matt Busby, and including Jimmy Hill and Bobby Charlton, suggested a 'professional foul' committed on a player outside the penalty area that prevented a likely goal should result in a penalty being awarded. This was rejected by the FA and Football League, though both bodies took on the suggestion that the perpetrator of such a foul 'could be dismissed by the match official'. As far as United was concerned, there lay the rub when referee George Courtney from Spennymoor opted only to book Grob.

The United players and their manager, 'Big Ron', were furious. To a man they were calling for Grob to be sent off, but the referee was not, strictly speaking, out of order.

The wording of the directive handed down to referees concerning the professional foul was woolly, the key wording being the perpetrator of a 'professional foul' '*could* be dismissed', as arbitrary a ruling as the current offside law. The ruling didn't state the player *must* be sent off, and Mr Courtney had decided Grob's foul didn't warrant his dismissal, hence all the hullabaloo and United's anger and frustration.

With the score 1–1 the final went into extra time, which, I imagined, was the last thing United wanted. Credit to Ron Atkinson's side they continued to battle and make life difficult for us. Ten minutes into the first extra period, Ronnie Whelan set off on what must have been his umpteenth sortie down our left side.

I was trying to get into space to receive the ball but Ronnie had other ideas. Cutting in from the left, rather than trying to find me, he hit a dipping shot past Bailey and into the net. Ronnie's fine solo effort signalled the end of United's brave rearguard action. The League Cup was Anfield-bound once more. Liverpool had joined Nottingham Forest in becoming the only teams to play in three successive League Cup Finals but, unlike Forest, we had won all three.

As we gathered beneath the Royal Box in preparation for ascending the stairs to receive the trophy, skipper Graeme Souness made a marvellous decision. Turning to Bob, he insisted the boss, in this his final appearance at Wembley with Liverpool, lead us up the stairs and collect the League Cup. Bob, dressed in a fawn flat cap and light grey mackintosh, at first declined, but we all gathered around and insisted he must do it and so, not without reluctance, Bob eventually bowed to our pressure.

It was a wonderful and wholly appropriate gesture on the part of Graeme and I think even dyed-in-the-wool traditionalists didn't begrudge Bob a rare moment of glory.

I shared everyone's appreciation and pleasure when Bob walked forward to climb the steps to the Royal Box, only for him to set foot on two steps and then be hauled back by Graeme.

'Whoa! Might be a good idea if you took off your cap and mac, boss,' he suggested.

Although I knew he was right, a part of me wanted to see Bob accept the cup wearing his flat cap and mackintosh. For him, it would have been wholly appropriate.

Bob handed his cap and mackintosh to Joe and then went up to accept the League Cup on behalf of Liverpool. He had achieved many a 'first' during his long career in the game, and now added to that long list by becoming the first, and to date only, manager to receive a major trophy at Wembley. When Bob took the cup he did so to thunderous applause from both sets of fans. And they say there is no place for sentiment in football.

That evening we partied. Wives and girlfriends were present, and we had a whale of a time. There may even have been one or two lagers consumed. We were staying over in London as we were all due to attend the PFA's annual dinner and awards ceremony the following day.

When I came down to breakfast on the Sunday morning I could barely walk. During extra time against United I had stretched to meet the ball and felt a pang in my groin. I didn't think anything of it at the time and, to be honest, after the initial twinge, felt no discomfort to speak of. But on the Sunday morning I felt it all right. I went for a swim in the hotel pool in the hope that it would relieve the stiffness. It seemed to help, so I was quite relaxed when, in the evening, wearing best bib and tucker, I joined everyone at the PFA dinner.

We were midway through the meal when Graeme sidled over to the table where Ronnie and I were sitting and told us Kenny had been awarded Player of the Year.

'Well, you'd think they would make a bit of a ceremony of it,' I joked. 'We didn't even see him get the award.'

Graeme made as if to clip me round the ear. 'When you arrived at this club, we couldn't get a word out of you. You start scoring a few goals, and now you're taking the piss,' he complained.

Then he delivered the bombshell.

'Let's see if you're so lippy in ten minutes. You're Young Player of the Year.'

I was totally stunned.

To be chosen as Young Player of the Year by all the other players in the country after only two full seasons in the First Division was a tremendous, but unexpected accolade. Ask any player who has won a PFA award and he will tell you how much he treasures it. Of course it is a great honour to be voted the Football Writers' Footballer of the Year, but to receive a top award from your fellow professionals is recognition of your efforts from your peers and this made me feel humble.

Ronnie Whelan leaned across to me. 'You'd better jot some notes down about what you are going to say,' he advised.

I suddenly froze. I was still shy about speaking in public and the prospect of making a speech in front of hundreds of people turned my legs to jelly. I downed what wine was remaining in my glass, immediately poured another and downed that. My stomach was churning so much I couldn't finish my meal. I scribbled some bullet points down on paper, crossed them out, then hastily made another list, only to also cross that one out as well.

When they announced the winner of the Young Player of the Year, I took to my feet and forced my legs to walk towards the podium. With the spotlight trailing me I nervously made my way on to the podium to generous applause.

Fortunately, the presentation was being made by Mike England, the Wales manager, which made me feel a little more relaxed, but only a little. I stood feeling very abashed as Mike waxed lyrical about me, saying what an excellent young pro I was, a striker with tremendous potential, and being generally over the top with his praise.

When Mike finally concluded, he turned to me.

'Thanks, Dad!' I said, and the room erupted into laughter.

I kept my acceptance speech short. I simply thanked my fellow professionals, my teammates, Bob and his staff, Tracy and my family for all their support. It wasn't the best speech I have ever made but it was sincere.

I really did feel honoured – I even came third behind Kenny in the Player of the Year award, which I didn't think I merited. The mark of how high Liverpool's standing was among our fellow professionals was that Graeme and Lawro also featured in the top six players. We all felt honoured and not a little chuffed.

CHAPTER SIX

Welcome to the Pleasure Dome

We held a leaving party for Bob, during which I thanked him for all he had done for me.

'You did it yourself,' he told me with characteristic modesty. 'I gave you a helping hand to get started, that's all, and you've made a very good start, but now you have to build on that, work hard, keep progressing.'

I told him I knew I still had a lot to learn about football.

'So have I,' he said.

As with his predecessor, Joe Fagan was something of a reluctant Liverpool manager. It was widely implied that when it came to appointing a new manager, it was club policy to appoint from within, and to a degree this was true. The feeling was there should be continuity, but only if the right man for the job was already on the staff. Liverpool was not adverse to appointing a new manager from another club, but it was deemed preferential to appoint someone who knew the players, the workings and culture of the club. The players all wanted Joe to succeed Bob. We all thought he was the best man for the job.

When Bob Paisley replaced Bill Shankly, he gathered the players together and told them Shanks had recommended him to the board as his successor. Then he asked the players for their opinion. To a man, Tommy Smith, Ian Callaghan, Kevin Keegan and co had urged Bob to accept, saying there was no other candidate.

'Well, that's that, then,' Bob had told them. 'Somebody has to do the job and I suppose it might as well be me.'

The passing of the Paisley to the Fagan era of management at Liverpool was very similar. If there had been a better candidate available at the time, Joe would have been happy to serve under him. The board had counselled Bob for his opinion as to who should succeed him. Apparently Bob told them, 'I think Joe would like a crack at it, though he's never said as much. But he'd be right. He knows the players and he knows the game.'

Joe had actually been on the books of Liverpool as a player during the post-war years, but manager George Kay had told him he wasn't good enough to make it at Anfield. He played for a number of clubs, including Manchester City, and had gained some management experience as player-manager at non-league Nelson (according to Joe, Nelson matches were always reported in the newspapers because 'they were always good for a column'), also as trainer and assistant manager at Rochdale, before returning to Anfield in 1958 to take charge of the reserves a year or so before the arrival of Bill Shankly.

Joe was promoted to first-team trainer in 1966 and, when Shanks retired, stepped up to become Bob's assistant. But Joe was always more than simply an assistant to Bob. He was Bob's sounding board and, along with Ronnie Moran, acted as a conduit between Bob and the players. If a player had a problem he could refer it to Joe, who would process the matter in his sharp brain, then advise Bob accordingly. That is, tell Bob the player in question had a point, or else tell Bob the player was trying it on and should be given short shrift. Rarely, if ever, was Joe wrong.

One of the many qualities Joe possessed was that he was scrupulously fair. He was also an objective thinker, so whenever you went to see Joe with a beef, if he said you were wrong, you reappraised your situation. If he said you had a point, you knew he would do his best to present your case to Bob and, in all likelihood, your request would be granted or the problem solved.

Like Bob, Joe was very knowledgeable about football. He didn't quite possess Bob's in-depth knowledge of players and tactics, but was perhaps a little more streetwise about the game, in that he was perhaps a little more clued-up about the tricks and ploys employed by players in an attempt to make life easier for themselves, such as requesting treatment for a knock that didn't merit physio. In short, Joe could suss out the genuine from those who were trying it on. He didn't suffer fools gladly, either. He would sound off more often than Bob and, on the rare occasion of a Liverpool defeat, would have no compunction about verbally laying into a player he felt hadn't performed well. He was also very witty. Once he had a go at Stevie Nicol, who blamed an under-par performance on the fact he was carrying a knock.

'I should be getting treatment not being bawled out,' said Stevie defensively.

'Maybe,' replied Joe, 'but we're on an economy drive and shouting obscenities is cheaper than sending you to physio.'

The curious thing about Joe and Bob was they always appeared to me to be stuck in late middle-age. I know that sounds silly, but when you saw photographs of them in the early 1960s alongside Shanks, they looked no different from how they did twenty years later. As such, they always gave the impression of being venerable old sages of football .

Having served under Shanks and Bob, Joe was therefore far from a rookie when he stepped up to the manager's job. He devoured the game's lore and its emerging tactics and techniques with an insatiable appetite, yet could call also upon considerable experience. His opinions were valued, and his views on tactics and players held up as gospel. He would not tower over English football, or indeed Liverpool football club, as Shanks and Bob had done. Nevertheless, Joe's tenure as manager, though brief, was to be highly effective and successful.

I liked Joe a lot, as did all the lads. Taking nothing away from Bob, who had proved himself one of the greatest managers ever to have graced English football, while he offered the impression of being a kindly grandfather the reality was often somewhat different. Joe, however, came across as a favourite uncle in his dealings with players. As managers must, both he and Bob kept their distance from players, but the distance was less marked where Joe was concerned.

In preparation for 1983–4 we embarked upon a busy pre-season. In previous years Liverpool had usually played four pre-season friendlies against quality opposition. That year our programme in August comprised six matches plus the Charity Shield at Wembley.

Joe was not slow in asserting himself as manager. During the summer he signed striker Michael Robinson from Brighton for the relatively modest fee of £250,000. It seemed an excellent piece of business on the part of Joe as Michael was a very good player who had cost Brighton £400,000 when they had signed him from Manchester City. Another new recruit was defender Gary Gillespie, signed from Coventry City for £325,000. The only major outgoing was David Fairclough who, though a number of English clubs had expressed interest in signing him, surprised a lot of people, including myself, by opting to join the Swiss club Lucerne.

The strangest move that summer was Watford's Luther Blissett to AC Milan for £980,000. During the previous season Luther had made quite an impact as a striker at Watford, scoring nineteen league goals, albeit this had included nine penalties. He was physically powerful, a handful for opposing defences, and his strike rate was more than decent, but his move to Milan surprised many, even though Milan had previously signed another striker of the battering ram variety in Joe Jordan. While everyone wished Luther well, the joke at the time was that Milan had signed the wrong man because their scout had confused Luther with John Barnes and filed the wrong name back to the club. However, I should imagine it came as some relief to Liverpool as word of mouth also had it that our scouts were keeping a close eye on Barnes's progress.

Our pre-season began with a testimonial match against Manchester United, which was played in Belfast. Both teams were still very much in the process of shedding ring rust. United's 4–3 victory was of little, if any, consequence, though I was pleased to have netted twice. Subsequent pre-season games included matches against SV Hamburg Feyenoord and WAC Morocco (another testimonial) and Dinamo Bucharest, which all served to help us achieve match-fitness for the Charity Shield showdown against Manchester United at Wembley.

The Charity Shield had been the first major trophy Bob Paisley had won as manager of Liverpool and we dearly wanted Joe to begin his stint as manager in similar fashion. On a blistering hot day, sadly United won 2–0. Unbelievably, this led to some football writers' prophesising the demise of Liverpool as major force in domestic football.

The groin injury I had suffered towards the end of the previous season flared up again during our pre-season. I had got through the training and friendly matches without too much discomfort but before the Charity Shield felt a nagging pain in my groin, particularly when twisting and turning, of which I did a lot during the course of a game.

I wasn't happy about facing United and told Joe and Ronnie Moran as much.

'The only way we'll find out how serious it is is for you to give it a real go,' said Joe. 'Those friendly games are just looseners. Now we're coming to the real business of the season it's no use messing about. If the groin's gone, you'll just have to rest it for three to four months.'

This knocked me back. I had been working very hard because I knew the season ahead would pose a severe test of my mettle as a striker. I had enjoyed two very successful seasons in front of goal, but was very mindful that opposition managers and players would be working on ways to counteract me in and around the penalty area. This in mind, I knew I had to up the ante should I wish to continue my previous level of goal-scoring. I didn't fancy playing with a nagging groin injury, but four months on the sidelines was a terrible prospect.

Before facing United at Wembley, Joe and Ronnie told me they had observed me at close quarters and were of the mind my groin injury was not going to be a source of trouble to me. 'It's bugger-all,' said Joe. 'Go out there and play your normal game. There'll be no problem, you'll see.'

Against United I can't say I had one of my better games in a Liverpool shirt but, true enough, following the game I felt no discomfort from the groin whatsoever. I was puzzled because I had been feeling it twinge throughout the pre-season build-up.

Joe Fagan was already calling on his vast experience with players. I believed what he had told me about my nagging groin, that it would clear, and it did. Ronnie later told me, 'We watched you closely in training and games and figured the injury was not serious, that it was mainly in your own mind. Because you had never been injured before, it got to you, made you feel it was something far more serious than it actually was. It was a tweak rather than a strain or a tear, only we had to convince your mind of that.'

We began the season with a 1–1 draw at Wolverhampton Wanderers. I partnered Michael Robinson in attack, apart from which, it was the usual suspects – Grob in goal, Phil Neal, Alan Hansen, Lawro and Alan Kennedy at the back, with Graeme, Kenny, Sammy and Craig Johnston across the middle. A draw away from home on the opening day was a satisfying start, as was the fact I managed to get our goal.

By the time we travelled to Old Trafford in late September we had managed four wins and two draws from six matches. I had four goals to my name, and Liverpool were third in the table behind Southampton and table-topping West Ham (not often you see those words in the same sentence).

All appeared to be going well for Joe in his first season as manager. Those football writers who had been so quick to criticise following our defeat in the Charity Shield had been silenced, but they were about to sharpen their pencils again.

For some reason Old Trafford was never a happy hunting ground for me. I never seemed to score regularly against United and the meeting between the two clubs in late September proved no exception. Liverpool lost 1–0.

Teams, and their supporters, never relished meeting Liverpool after we'd been defeated. Invariably it served as a kick up the backside, a pertinent reminder that nothing but 100 per cent would ever do. Having tasted defeat at Old Trafford, we were expected to put lowly Sunderland to the sword in our next game at Anfield.

But this was not to be. Sunderland took the lead in the first half through a penalty from Gary Rowell, from which point it was one-way traffic. Try as we might, we couldn't breach the Sunderland rearguard, which featured a young full-back who caught the eye – Barry Venison.

The following Monday there was no great inquest as to why we had suddenly lost successive League matches. That is not to say Joe wasn't concerned; he did remind us that quality is all well and good but that it has to be combined with the right attitude. I wouldn't say his delivery was fuelled with anger, but there was audible annoyance in his voice.

The fact there was no prolonged debate and diagnosis of our defeats against United and Sunderland was typical. In the wake of defeat, many managers discuss at length with their players the reasons for their loss; conversely, little, if anything, may be discussed following a win. At Liverpool it was different. We often learned more from a victory, as we would talk about what had worked well, how we could improve on a certain move and so on. It was the victories, not the occasional defeats, that spawned debate – we concentrated on the positives and how to improve upon them.

Some players wait until the team talk in the dressing-room for motivation, or else, before kick-off, for a teammate to encourage and urge them to deliver. I knew I had to motivate myself. Joe, like Bob, used to say, 'You can't leave it to your teammates to produce the necessary to win games – YOU must do it.'

The more games you get under your belt, the more responsibility you feel. Playing for Liverpool was all about winning. Every player wanted to be a winner and the team to be winners. As an individual I knew I had to work hard to make a difference. My teammates knew what I was capable of, and vice versa, but I was always conscious of the fact I had to push myself that little bit harder than the previous game in order to keep developing and progressing, to become a better player. In football, at any level, you must be hell-bent on trying to better your last performance rather than just maintaining the same standard. It doesn't always happen, but by making the effort you motivate yourself.

In our following game at table-topping West Ham, I, along with every member of the team, was determined to put in a performance that was better than the one against Sunderland.

Our performance at Upton Park was indeed a great improvement. Michael Robinson scored his first league goal for Liverpool and didn't stop there, going on to score a hat-trick in a 3–1 victory. Generally speaking, our victory at West Ham was seen as clear evidence of our ambition to retain the title. It was a time when the tabloids were beginning to revel in excruciating puns and the *Daily Mirror* gave full vent in their headline: 'ROBINSON SQUASHES HAMMERS'.

With only nine league games played it was too early to write off any team but, with our win at Upton Park elevating us to second in the table, we were gathering momentum. QPR were next up and had title aspirations of their own, but Steve Nicol, a second-half substitute for Craig Johnston, scored late in the game to give us a narrow win at Loftus Road.

There followed Luton Town, at the time sixth in the table. Under David Pleat, Luton played a lot of entertaining and attacking football. In goal was Les Sealey, in the heart of defence, Paul Elliott and Mal Donaghy, and in front of them the experienced Brian Horton. But it was going forward that Luton really excelled. In players such as Brian Stein, Paul Walsh, Ricky Hill and

Trevor Aylott, Luton possessed the quality to open up even the very best defence.

We signalled our intentions from the start. Phil Neal made progress down our right and, to everyone's surprise, cut inside and fired a shot from some twenty yards. I couldn't get out of the way and the ball cannoned off the back of my legs to Sammy Lee. Sammy reacted quickly but his effort hit a thicket of Luton defenders only for the ball to then fall kindly for me. A yard from the goal-line, I had the simple task of tapping the ball into the net.

As a striker I expected to get about nine such goals a season, tap-ins when the ball breaks after a goal-mouth mêlée. Joe used to call them 'bread and butter goals'. It was all about anticipation, being there on the spot when and where the ball breaks. You can't really teach that. It is something you are born with. Of course, as you grow in experience, your anticipation improves; it's almost as if you acquire an extra sense, and even though the ball may be ricocheting around like a pinball, you somehow know where it will end up.

Before Luton could recover from their early setback, we had them rocking again. Sammy Lee played a short free-kick to Kenny on our right side. Kenny floated the ball into the Luton penalty area and Graeme met the ball with the meat of his forehead only to see his effort twang the crossbar. When the ball came down, I was there to side-foot it past Sealey for number two. Yet again, it was anticipation. As soon as I saw the trajectory of Graeme's header I was on the move. I wasn't certain, but it looked as of the ball wasn't going to get under the crossbar and, in flash, I was able to assess where I thought the ball would end up if it rebounded off the bar. Sometimes you're right, sometimes you're wrong, but the trick is always to get in position. Minutes later I was inches short of completing an early hat-trick. Kenny played a great ball through the Luton backline and, in what would be the old inside-left position, I was on to it. Sealey came out to narrow my angle of vision. I went for the far corner but the ball clipped the outside of the post. The groans of disappointment around Anfield sounded like 40,000 bicycle tyres simultaneously being let down.

But we were relentless in our pursuit of further goals. Sammy Lee had Sealey at full stretch to save an effort from twenty yards, only to repeat the scenario minutes later. This time his effort beat Sealey but skimmed down the side netting. It was one of those incidents when the crowd on the far side actually thought the ball had entered the net and roared, 'Goahhhhh!'

Luton just couldn't get a hold of the ball, and rather than play pretty football amongst ourselves, we continued to go for the jugular. On thirty-six minutes Stevie Nicol reached the by-line on the left and whipped the ball across the face of Sealey's goalmouth. As crosses go it was perfect. All I had to do was re-direct the flight of the ball with my head.

Three-nil to the good, me with a hat-trick to my name, and little over half an hour of the game gone. It was exhilarating stuff.

Still we poured forward. I had a shot tipped over the bar by Sealey, Mal Donaghy hacked an effort from Stevie Nicol in the general direction of the Liver building, then Graeme had an effort which streaked past Sealey's left-hand post. Minutes before half-time, Kenny cut in from the right and fired low. Sealey appeared to have Kenny's effort covered but, to compound what was already proving to be a miserable afternoon for Les, the ball bounced in front of him, over his prostrate body and into the net for goal number four.

During the interval Joe told us not to ease off. 'The job isn't done,' he said. 'Keep going at them. The crowd are loving it.' Historically, no team had ever come back at Anfield from having been four down at halftime. Even with another forty-five minutes to go, Luton were a beaten side. I imagined they would come out in the second half and do the pro thing – a damage limitation job. But we did the pro thing, too, by keeping the pressure up.

Kenny and Stevie Nicol both went close, Sealey mustered saves from Graeme and myself as our attacking play relentlessly continued. Ten minutes after the re-start, Alan Kennedy floated a long ball into the Luton penalty area. I was making ground fast, and had managed to time my run so that when the ball began its descent I was there to meet it. When you're taking the ball out of the air and attempting a volley it's important to get your body in the correct position, to meet the ball with the meat of your boot – that is, the top your foot where the talus and navicular bones meet – and get your head over the ball so as not to blast it over the goal. On this occasion I met the ball just right and it arced past Sealey, rocketing into the net.

We felt we should have had a penalty when Paul Elliott brought down Stevie Nicol, but at five goals to the good our protests were rather muted. As a result of Elliott's challenge we won a corner. Kenny played it short to Stevie, who turned on a fivepence piece and curled a shot that looked to be goal-bound all the way, only for Sealey to take off and claw the ball to safety.

Still we went at Luton and with just under five minutes remaining we scored goal number six. In trying to relieve yet another bout of pressure, Brian Horton played the ball out of defence but only as far as Michael Robinson, who roasted and basted this pig's ear of a clearance by jinking along the Luton line seeking an avenue for a shot. When the shot it came it rebounded to Graeme, who promptly despatched the ball back towards goal. Again the ball came off Luton legs and, happily, I was there for more 'bread and butter'.

I had managed to score five of our six goals. Of course, the newspapers went overboard in their praise of both Liverpool and me. Naturally I was delighted with my effort, but was conscious too that my feat would result in opposing teams keeping an even closer eye on me. I was going to be a 'marked' man.

There is, quite literally, a footnote to the Luton game. I was wearing a new pair of boots as I had signed a boot deal with Nike. (I was the first player ever to sign up with Nike and am still with them today. Over the years I've had numerous offers from other boot companies, many more lucrative than the Nike deal, but because the company has stayed loyal to me, I have wanted to return their loyalty.) Before the game, when I'd tried my new boots on in the dressing-room, the new leather felt stiff and uncomfortable. I didn't want blisters, so I went into the bath and shower area, filled a sink with water, soaked the boots and continued to bend and twist them in the water. This softened the leather. When I tried the boots on again they felt much more comfortable.

I have never been given to superstition, but after scoring five against Luton in the new (wet) boots, I took to soaking my boots in water before every game I played. I convinced myself that I liked playing in wet boots, as they seemed to fit better and hug my feet, and I continued with this pre-match routine for the remainder of my career as a player.

Following the rout of Luton our next league game was at home to Everton, who, though mid-table, were beginning to evolve into the excellent team they would become under the management of Howard Kendall and his coaches Colin Harvey and Mick Heaton.

It was yet another thunderous Merseyside derby and to my delight I gave us the lead in the first half. You won't be surprised to hear my goal was not a stunning shot from thirty yards, but a left-footer from three yards after Neville Southall had blocked a shot from Sammy. I can't honestly tell you how many goals of mine were scored like that but, during my entire career, I should imagine it was getting on for a third.

With us a goal to the good, I couldn't see Everton getting back in the game and so it proved. Further goals from Michael Robinson and Stevie Nicol gave us a 3–0 victory, which saw Liverpool assume top spot for the first time in the season.

It proved to be yet another exhilarating season. Following our surprise defeat at home to Sunderland at the beginning of October we gained a head of steam and roared on like an express train.

In fourteen League games leading up to the New Year we lost just one, a 0–4 defeat at Coventry in mid-December. We began the New Year with an unconvincing display against Manchester United at Anfield which resulted in a 1–1 draw. We had not been at our best that day and, in our following League game, contrived to produce a performance that was even worse. We lost 1–0 at home to Wolves, who had been glued to the foot of the table all season.

Joe was fuming and when Joe was angry he didn't give a monkeys about reputations. If he felt you had let the side down, you were in for it. In the dressing-room after the Wolves game both Kenny and Graeme were subjected to Joe's wrath, but it was Craig Johnston who really got it in the ear.

'As for YOU,' roared Joe, 'you're always telling me when you've played well. Let's hear from you now after that shambles.'

'I didn't think I was that bad, boss,' replied Craig.

Joe's face was crimson, the veins on his temples stuck out like biros. 'Not that bad? Which game were you at? Let me tell you, son, you were bloody useless. You reminded me of Road Runner, darting about all over the place, except you were like a headless chicken.'

'You're starting to piss me off now, boss,' said Craig.

'Better to be pissed off than pissed on, which is what happened to you out there this afternoon,' retorted Joe.

'You're having a right go at me,' intoned Craig, 'You once told me I was one of the best midfield players in the country.'

'It must have been once. I wouldn't make the same mistake twice!'

By now I was struggling to contain my laughter. Alan Hansen was holding a towel up to his face, as if pretending to wipe away sweat, but his eyes were full of tears of laughter. Seeing Alan like this served only to make me worse. I was in agony trying to my suppress laughter.

Eventually Joe simmered down and, having said his piece, much to the relief of everyone, took off for the boot room.

Wolves were eventually relegated, having won only five matches all season. I'm at a loss to explain how they managed to take six points off us, but that's football. Wolves endured a terrible time of it. As their manager, Tommy Docherty, later quipped, 'It was so bad, with no hope of things getting better, that the club held its end-of-season dinner in November.'

When we travelled to Aston Villa in late January, we did so hell-bent on getting our title challenge back on track. The thing about Joe was, having bollocked a player, he would then give that player a chance to prove him wrong by staying with him for the following game. Having had a go at Craig after the Wolves débâcle, Craig kept his place for the match at Villa.

Joe never liked the press talk of Liverpool's title challenge being, more or less, a 'foregone conclusion'. As players we didn't believe such nonsense, either, but before the game at Villa Park, Joe was at pains to remind us to ignore the stuff in the press about us being favourites for the title, even though we had lost to lowly

Wolves. He was of the mind that premature claims about the desti-nation of the Championship could give players a false impression of their task ahead.

'We can't stop people from talking,' he told us, 'but really it's an exercise in futility for anyone to suggest a particular club – and I mean ANY club – will win the title when there are some twenty games to go. So keep things in perspective. I know you will, because I also know you are a great bunch of pros, and that you'll be professional to the end.'

Joe had total faith in us, not only in terms of our ability and quality as players, but also with regard to our attitude, application and desire to see the job through. Bob would occasionally say to us, 'Don't go out with your big heads on.' We were so professional in our approach to games I don't think we ever did.

I managed yet another hat-trick against Aston Villa – I was scoring goals with some regularity – and our 3–1 win consolidated our position at the top of the table.

We lost just two of our remaining nineteen matches to win the Championship for a third successive season and give Joe the title in his first season as manager. During the run-in, West Ham were beaten 6–0 and Coventry 5–0 at Anfield, the latter a game in which I managed to help myself to a four-goal haul. The *Daily Mail* wrote that I was 'scoring goals for fun'. Well, it was fun, but it was hard graft all the same.

Liverpool finished the season on 80 points, three ahead of runners-up Southampton, and six in front of Nottingham Forest, who finished third on goal difference ahead of Manchester United, who, in turn, were but one point better off than fifth-placed QPR. Liverpool had become only the third club in the history of the Football League, after Huddersfield Town and Arsenal, to achieve a hat-trick of Championships, but our final winning margin of three points represented a single victory. That clubs such as Southampton, Norwich and QPR could mount a serious challenge for the title says much about the open, competitive nature of top-flight football at the time. Even in relative terms, a club didn't need to spend an enormous sum of money on transfers or pay astronomical wages in order to be real contenders for the Championship. Manchester United and, to a lesser degree, Liverpool, were financially better off than other First Division clubs, but that is what we were, clubs, not brands, and the relative wealth enjoyed at Old Trafford or Anfield was such it did not preclude other First Division clubs inhabiting the same football universe.

I finished the season with thirty-two league goals, fourteen of which I scored with my head, which pleased me no end, as I had never thought of myself as being particularly good in the air. Kenny finished the season with seven league goals to his name but such a modest goal tally does not paint a true picture of the contribution he made to our season.

I would say that Kenny, more than any other Liverpool player, had been responsible for my success. We had developed an almost telepathic understanding. I would make a run, instinctively knowing that he would find me with an inch-perfect pass. A lot of people are under the impression that Kenny joined Liverpool at a young age, but he was coming up to twenty-seven when he arrived at Anfield from Celtic in the summer of 1977. He had now been with the club for seven years and, although he had lost a bit of pace, his astute football brain and superb technique more than compensated for his advancing years. To my mind he was the most complete and all-round player I ever had the privilege of playing with – and that's saying something given the many fine players I knew over the years. The phrase 'genius' is often over-used in football. Very few players are truly worthy of that epithet but, without doubt, Kenny was one. Doing easily what others find difficult is talent; doing what the talented find impossible is genius. Many times I saw Kenny perform something on a football pitch that I had thought impossible. He was everybody's ideal of the thinking footballer and a lot more besides. His inspired reading of play and sublime passing created many goals for me, but above all he encouraged me, and every player, to go out and enjoy ourselves and entertain supporters. I shall always be grateful to him for that.

When I first joined Liverpool I bought an Austin Allegro from former Chester player Alan Tarbuck, who owned a garage in Chester. What attracted me to the Allegro was it had an open-top roof. As soon as I saw the car I envisaged Tracy and me going out for drives in the country on a hot summer day and sliding back the sun roof. Which I did once, I think. I was still living at home with my parents, and continued to do so until Tracy and I were married. Initially I gave my parents board and lodging, and paid for one or two things for the house, but around this time I decided Mum and Dad deserved a better quality of life. I bought them a new detached house, but continued to live with them there. I still had a reasonable amount of disposable income, so I sold the Allegro and splashed out on the type of car all top-flight foot-ballers wanted to be seen driving around in – or so the salesman told me: a Morris Ital, the first new car I ever owned.

It was while I had the Ital that I won a competition organised by a national company for having scored thirty goals the previous season. My prize was the very latest model of Rover. One winter's night I was driving Tracy and a friend of hers back from Liverpool. It was a cold, frosty night and, not far from Flint, we approached a part of the road on which there was a sharp bend. The road had not been gritted and, rather than taking the bend, the Rover lived up to its name and went 'a-roving', sliding across the road. I instinctively wrestled with the steering wheel and, for a moment, thought the car was going to straighten up, only for it to turn sideways, straighten again, then smash headlong into a post.

I was OK and so too was Tracy's pal. Tracy was injured but, thankfully, not seriously. The police eventually arrived and, having seen for themselves the surface of the road, the incident was dealt with as an accident, which it obviously was.

My first thoughts, of course, were for Tracy. I was just relieved she was OK. I then began to think of how lucky we had been. A serious injury could have ended my career. That night I offered a heart-felt prayer of thanks.

The following morning the Liverpool media carried the story that I had been involved in a car crash. One of the people asked for reaction was the former Everton centre-half Mick Lyons, who was then with Sheffield Wednesday but still lived locally.

'What's your reaction to Ian Rush having hit a post?' asked the radio reporter.

'It must be a first,' said Mick. 'He usually scores, especially against Everton.'

It was a fantastic season, and the League Championship was not the only major trophy we won. The one disappointment was again our failure to make any sort of impact in the FA Cup. Having convincingly beaten Newcastle in round three, a game in which I managed another two goals, in round four we fell foul of our bogey team, Brighton. A Second Division team they may have been, but they saw us off 2–1 at Anfield.

Regarding domestic cups, it was the League Cup in which we excelled. We had a difficult run to the final, having to dispose of Brentford, Fulham, Birmingham City and Sheffield Wednesday and eventually Walsall in the semi-final. Many believed our semi-final against Walsall would prove easy; it was anything but. Alan Buckley's Third Division side put up a tremendous performance in the first leg at Anfield to earn a 2–2 draw and make the semi-final finely balanced. A full house of just under 20,000 was at Fellows Park for the replay, which proved tougher for us than the 2–0 final scoreline suggests. We may have laboured against Walsall but we had made it to Wembley to produce a dream final: Liverpool versus Everton.

Wembley took on all the atmosphere of a huge family party. I was aware of numerous Liverpool and Everton fans who had travelled down to London together, yet once inside the stadium the rivalry was as keen and fierce as ever.

Despite the competition between the two clubs, Liverpool and Everton players have always mixed together socially. In the 1960s Liverpool and Everton players, even after a Merseyside derby, would meet for a night out with their respective wives and girlfriends in the Royal Tiger, a club situated near the mouth of the Mersey tunnel and owned by the father-in-law of Liverpool full-back Chris Lawler. I often met up with Everton players for drink, particularly Neville Southall and Kevin Ratcliffe, who were my Wales teammates. Kevin, in fact, was my room-mate for many years with Wales, and one of my best friends in the game. But there is, of course, precious little friendship to be seen when players find themselves opposing one another on the pitch, and this was never more so than on the occasion of that League Cup final.

Throughout my career, for all I scored regularly against Everton, I never relished playing against Kevin. We seemed to know too much about one another. I found him difficult to shake him off as he was one of the quickest defenders in the First Division.

I had got used to defenders wanting to clatter me in the opening minutes of a game. It's part and parcel of football. The defender wants you to know he is there, so he whacks you the first chance he gets. He's not out intentionally to injure you. He just hopes that, having given you a good whack, every time you go looking for the ball you'll do so looking over your shoulder, half expecting him to come in with another crunching tackle.

In the opening exchanges Kevin hit me hard, not once, but twice. On each occasion when I crashed to the ground, I looked up to see his grinning face. I wasn't having this. By no stretch of the imagination was I ever what you could term a physical player, but I knew how to look after myself in games. The next time Kevin and I challenged for a high ball I flung out my arm to keep him at bay. My arm caught him full on the nose. I'd hit him a bit harder than I meant to, and turned to see his nose streaming with blood.

The referee didn't halt play or say anything because it appeared my arm had just been raised to effect balance as I raised myself off the ground and Kevin had jumped into it – which is the way to elbow away defenders, not the obvious way in which you often see it done now.

When Kevin managed to get his breath back, the ball had moved up to the Liverpool end of the field and he came racing towards me. I didn't think for one moment he was going to belt me. I just burst out laughing. Kevin suddenly ground to a halt and laughed, too.

'Better we just get on with it, eh?' I suggested.

'Aye, I reckon,' he said.

We did.

Everton enjoyed the lions' share of the play and, to be fair, were unlucky not to beat us on the day, the game finishing goalless. Peter Reid was outstanding in midfield for Everton, and Kevin Richardson not too far behind him. Yet for all their endeavour and enterprising play, I can't recall Grob ever being stretched. If anyone had the opportunity to wrap up the game it was me. I was presented with three good chances in the second half only to be denied by super saves from Neville Southall. People often make mention of how many goals I scored against Everton – I hold the record in Merseyside derbies with twenty-five goals – but, believe me, it could have been ten or fifteen more but for Neville.

Though the game at Wembley had been goalless it produced a lot of entertaining football, but the replay at Maine Road was a thriller. Again Everton played extremely well without creating any clear-cut opportunities, whereas when we went forward I always felt we could score.

There had been just over twenty-minutes of cut-and-thrust Cup football when we broke down an Everton attack and swept forward on the break. A four-man move that began with Graeme ended with him when he received the ball from Phil Neal and fired low past Neville Southall.

Everton gave it their all, but we remained unbowed, and in the end, Graeme's strike was all that separated the two teams. Liverpool had won the League Cup for a record fourth successive season.

It was Joe's first trophy success as a manager, though it was far from being the only cup he would guide us to that season. I hear managers and some players today complain about the heavy fixture schedule they have to endure, and this in an era of squad rotation. Though Liverpool were contesting the League

Championship and European Cup, we fielded what Joe considered our best eleven in every round of the League Cup. In winning it we played a total of thirteen ties, one of which included extra time. Due to penalty shoot-outs, that wouldn't happen now, but I never heard any player complain about having to play too many matches. Quite simply we loved playing football and, provided we got sufficient rest between games – say, three days – we were all far happier to be playing games than having a full week on the training field. I wanted to be successful in football, to win trophies, and to do that you have to play a lot of games. As far as I was concerned, the more games Liverpool were involved in, the more it was a mark of our success as a team.

In 1983–4 we played a total of seventy-five competitive matches and Joe called upon the services of just fifteen players. In all probability it wouldn't have been that many but for injuries.

In addition, the state of the pitches, for much of the season, proved a real test of stamina. In the 1980s a season consisted of basically four types of pitch. Early in the season the pitches were like bowling greens; the grass was lush, cut short and pleasure to play on.

In winter, pitches were either heavy – some grounds such as Leicester's Filbert Street or Vicarage Road at Watford resembled molasses – or, in extreme weather, frozen. I can recall going to Sunderland in January 1985 on a bitterly cold day with a freezing wind blowing in off the North Sea (nothing new there then). The Roker Park pitch was frozen solid and so icy we were all teetering around. It was so cold my hands were numb and blue, and the strong wind so relentless it gave me earache. As we players walked down the tunnel at halftime, we passed what I took to be the Sunderland groundsman, carrying a garden fork, seemingly off to do some work on the pitch. He was wearing just jeans and a T-shirt, and tucked into one sleeve was a packet of fags.

Conditions were so bad the referee abandoned the game at half-time. Later, as we left our dressing-room, we passed the match referee in the corridor being harangued by T-shirt man.

'Frozen? Dangerous ?' he gasped incredulously. 'Ye soft shite!'

Come spring, the pitches began to dry out, leaving them bone-hard and bumpy. Reserve teams also played their matches on the home pitch and, at this stage of the season, every pitch was barren, the only grass of note being on the wings.

During wet winter weather some clubs resorted to covering their pitch with sand. White Hart Lane and the Dell at Southampton used to be covered in so much sand come the end of a season it was like playing on a beach.

Given the number of competitive matches Liverpool played, the physical nature of the game back then and the heavy pitches, I find it remarkable that Liverpool called upon just fifteen players in 1983–4. What's more, this was not unusual. So consistent was the Liverpool team over the years that it was the norm for less than twenty players to be used in the course of a season.

I have heard it said that today's players are much fitter and stronger than players of yesteryear. I didn't hang my boots up until 2000 and I don't believe that statement to be true. Players in the 1980s, 1970s – and 1960s, come to that – were every bit as fit and strong as players now. What has contributed to the speed of the contemporary game are the pristine pitches and lightness of the balls. The pitches in particular lend themselves to a more fluid, speedy type of game. It is, of course, much easier to run at speed on a bowling green surface than on a pitch resembling a Christmas pudding.

Generally speaking, the technique now displayed in the Premiership is of a higher standard than the old First Division. But this has much to do with the fact that the Premiership now attracts the top players in the world. Whether the technique displayed by today's home-grown players is markedly different to that of players in the 1980s is debatable. I think today's home-grown players do benefit from playing alongside top-quality overseas players – something has to rub off – but the likes of Kenny Dalglish, Graeme Souness, Glenn Hoddle, Bryan Robson, Alan Hansen and John Barnes would make a similar impact upon the Premiership today as they did back in the 1980s. Their skill and technique apart, they would adapt.

During that season one of the injured first-team players was Ronnie Whelan, who had suffered a knock to the pelvis. An appointment was made for Ronnie to attend Fazackerly Hospital (players then were left to attend to such matters on their own). Coincidentally, I had also taken a knock in the same region, so I went along, too.

At the hospital we were both subjected to X- rays, told to wait until these were processed, after which the doctor would offer his diagnosis.

When we were called back in to see the doctor, he held an X-ray up to the light.

'Good news, Mr Whelan,' announced the doctor brightly. 'Your X-ray is showing nothing serious. You've had a knock. It must be bruising. There's no pelvic trouble at all. Carry on playing!'

I was really pleased for Ronnie, and could see he was delighted by the news.

'Now, Mr Rush,' said the doctor, holding another X-ray up to the light. The serious tone in his voice made me suddenly concerned. 'I'm afraid the news I have for you is not so good.'

The doctor went on to tell me the X- rays revealed my pelvis had tilted, probably the result of a direct blow when playing. Not only that, he was concerned there might also be some damage to internal organs, such as the bladder. To my utter shock and dismay, the doctor informed me I would be out of football for three to four months.

I was stunned. I had a little soreness in the pelvis but had only really attended the hospital to keep Ronnie company, and I'd asked for an X-ray just to put my mind at rest. My mind was suddenly buzzing with what I had to do – phone Joe, Tracy, my parents – when, suddenly, a nurse in some state of fluster entered the room.

There followed a muttered conversation between her and the doctor, at the end of which a very embarrassed-looking doctor turned to Ronnie and me.

He was full of profuse apologies. There had been a mix-up regarding the labelling on the X-rays. It was Ronnie who had the problem, not me.

Ronnie was distraught. I was relieved but, given Ronnie's diagnosis and sudden and understandable change of mood, couldn't display it.

I did my best to console Ronnie, as did the doctor, who was still full of apologies for the mix-up. The doctor went on to say Ronnie would make a full recovery and would be fit again to play within four months.

'Funny thing,' said Ronnie as we left the hospital, 'I'd been feeling a lot of discomfort, but when the doctor told me I was OK, I suddenly felt OK.'

However, the doctor was right. Ronnie made a full recovery and was playing again in just under four months.

In addition to contending the League Championship and League Cup, we were also keen to do well in the European Cup.

Our European Cup sojourn began with a comfortable 6–0 (1–0

and 5-0) aggregate victory over Danish champions Odense BK which set-up a tie against Atletico Madrid.

I was still finding my feet in terms of European football. We adapted our style when in Europe, slowing the tempo, trying to keep possession, because Continental teams were very good at hitting you on the break. I found myself subjected to man-marking of a much tighter variety than I ever experienced in the First Division. There was also a very different interpretation of the rules.

Most Continental referees allowed defenders to get away with the sort of obstruction that was never tolerated in our domestic game – whereas hard but fair tackles, so much a part of our football, were invariably given as fouls against us. Fortunately we had cerebral defenders such as Alan Hansen and Lawro, who, rather than winning the ball through crunching tackles, possessed such vision and reading of a game they won much of the ball through interception. Then, rather than humping the ball forward, they had the ability to bring the ball out of defence, allowing us to maintain possession and effect better movement upfront.

Experienced players, such as Kenny, Graeme and, when he came forward, Phil Neal, would be forever talking to me and offering advice, but it's only with experience that you learn what is required when playing on different stages in distant countries.

Today Spanish football is held up as having the best league in the world regarding skill and technique. In the 1980s Spanish teams were capable of displaying breathtaking technique and skill, but there was also a cynical, often brutish side to their play that happily appears absent from La Liga today.

Atletico Bilbao were the epitome of Spanish style at the time, capable of wonderful skills but also of the most cynical football you could imagine. They proved stern opposition in the first leg at Anfield. They were very well organised, particularly at the back, and we found opportunities very limited. The game ended goalless and I could see by the faces of the Bilbao players as they left the pitch that they were delighted with that result.

When we arrived in Bilbao, we got an idea of what sort of reception would be awaiting us at the San Mames stadium. Having checked into our hotel, I joined the rest of the lads for a leg-stretcher to a nearby park where Michael Robinson, Sammy and I fell into conversation with a local who spoke good English.

'We Basques, we do not like the Spanish,' he told us. 'We despise the Italians, we hate the Germans and can't stand the French. So you can imagine what we think of you British.'

The Bilbao coach, Javier Clemente, had created a very physical and intimidating side. Without putting too fine a point on it, they had kicked their way to the Spanish title in successive seasons. Just about every player in the Bilbao side was fearsomely aggressive but by far the most volatile player was Andoni Goikoetxea whose nickname was 'the Butcher of Bilbao'.

Before the game Joe reminded us to stay calm and not retaliate, whatever the provocation, while at the same time emphasising that we should not be intimidated or bow to rough-house tactics. Liverpool had a lot of quality in the side but we also had players who, when the occasion demanded, could dish it out as well as take it. Graeme could be frightening when he wanted to be, and Kenny could more than handle himself in physical situations, but perhaps the hardest player we had in the team at that time was Alan Kennedy, affectionately known in the dressing-room as 'Barney Rubble'.

The game against Bilbao was, as we expected, a tough battle. I was kicked up hill and down dale but kept my cool, hoping my response to such treatment would be to score. That way the Bilbao defenders would know their rough-house tactics hadn't made an impression on me. We weren't scared of Bilbao, far from it, but I gained the impression they were a little shaken by the fact we could handle the rough stuff and out-play them.

The first ten minutes were hairy as the Bilbao players attempted to knock us off our stride. They hacked and kicked irrespective of where the ball might be. After ten minutes of this, Sammy Lee sidled up to me and asked, 'Is there a ball on the pitch?'

Having dealt with Bilbao's initial onslaught we gradually began to assert ourselves. Just before halftime, I had a shot that skimmed the home crossbar and Kenny also went close. In the second half we picked up the same script, dealt with what Bilbao could muster in the way of attacks and hit them on the break. Coming up to the sixty-sixth minute of the game, Sammy crossed from the right and I managed to steer a header wide of the Bilabo keeper. There was a capacity crowd of 50,000 inside the stadium but when that ball hit the net it went so quiet I heard Alan Hansen, on the halfway line, shout, 'Yes!'

One-up away from home in Europe with less than half an hour to go, we did what we normally did: we played the possession game, getting forward when we could. Panic set in to Bilbao's play. We could have added to our tally and nearly did. Seeing Zubizzaretta off his line, Kenny chipped the home keeper from twenty-five yards. It looked a goal all the way only for Zubizzaretta to back-peddle like crazy, arch his body into the air backwards, and fingertip the ball to safety. It really was a magnificent save, but in the final analysis, in vain.

We had endured two bruising encounters against Bilbao but our opponents in the next round promised to be a team who would play more fluid, enterprising and sporting football – Benfica.

Benfica's pedigree in European competition was not in doubt. Past winners of the European Cup, they had high hopes of once again establishing themselves as one of Europe's premier sides under their coach, a young Swede by the name of Sven-Göran Eriksson.

The Benfica squad included six players – goalkeeper Bento, Bastos-Lopes, Humberto, Sheu, Chalana and Nene – who had played against Liverpool when the two teams had last met in Europe back in 1978. Rather than being an ageing side, however, Benfica had achieved a fine balance between experience and youth. Young players such as José Luis, Carlos Emanuel and the Swedish under-21 international Glenn Strömberg were often the subject of rumours of big moves to Italy.

I still have the match programme from our first leg against Benfica at Anfield in which Sven-Göran Eriksson is described as a 'former ski-jump' star. Eriksson had enjoyed considerable success as a coach with IFK Gothenburg, leading them to UEFA Cup success, and had been at Benfica for two seasons during which time they had won the Portuguese league and cup 'double' and had been beaten finalists in the UEFA Cup. Sven was beginning to make a name for himself.

The game at Anfield proved tough, but of a different type to what we had experienced in Bilbao. Benfica were not cynical or physical, but they did play very good football and were a handful. There was only one goal in the game and I managed to score it. Curiously it was timed at sixty-six minutes, exactly the time I had scored against Bilbao.

Having left Anfield with only a 1–0 defeat, Benfica obviously fancied their chances at home. For our part, we travelled to Portugal believing we could beat them again. Benfica had played a good defensive game at Anfield but now that they were chasing the tie at home in front of 70,000 of their fans, Joe felt they would come at us more and that we could exploit the gaps they left behind.

On the night it was Liverpool, rather than Benfica, who started well. Ronnie Whelan put us ahead after only nine minutes. Losing 0–2 on aggregate, Benfica knew it was all or bust. They launched attack after attack but, just after the half-hour mark, we broke from defence and Craig Johnston's clinical finish made it 2–0 on the night. To all intents and purposes it was over. I added a third in the second half and though Benfica did pull a goal back we continued to dominate and so it came as no surprise when Ronnie added a fourth. When the final whistle sounded we received a standing ovation from the home fans as we left the pitch. A far cry from what had happened when we had beaten Bilbao. On leaving the pitch that night we had been pelted with fruit, stones and seat cushions.

Victory over Benfica took us into the semi-finals, where we were drawn against Dinamo Bucharest of Romania. Having gone out to teams from Eastern Europe in the two previous seasons, we were determined it would not happen again. Although we had beaten Dinamo back in August in a pre-season friendly in Bucharest, we knew that would count for nothing in the semi-final.

We had expected a rough-house tie against Atletico Bilbao but our games against Dinamo were the most brutal of my entire career. We'd been told Dinamo were a physical side, and had had a little taste of this during our friendly in August, but nothing prepared us for the way they applied themselves in the first leg at Anfield.

The Dinamo players hacked and kicked at us from start to finish, so much so we seemed to spend most of the game leaping in the air to avoid late or over-the-top tackles. I was punched, kicked, elbowed and spat at so many times that at the end of the game my shirt was covered in spit.

Everyone seemed to be engaged in, quite literally, a running battle with their opposite number, no one more so than Graeme with Movila. Their heated exchanges boiled over on several occasions and, eventually, exploded. Graeme challenged Movila for the ball, there was a tussle, which ended with Graeme winning the ball and playing it forward. As Graeme began to move forward Movila had a go. Through the corner of his eye Graeme saw it coming and instinctively ducked, but the blow caught him on the temple. Movila had picked on the wrong guy. Graeme swung round and let him have a haymaker. Movila immediately hit the ground like a bag of spanners. We were mounting an attack so neither the referee or the linesman saw the incident, which was just as well. When play was eventually stopped, Movila still hadn't moved. He was taken from the field and treated by medics, who discovered his jaw was broken.

The only goal of this brutal game came in the first half, a header from Sammy Lee. Not being the biggest of lads, it was rare for Sammy to score with his head. He put it down to all the practice he had on the night, leaping to avoid late tackles.

The game at Anfield was bruising, but the return in Bucharest was enough to make your blood curdle. With a volatile crowd of 70,000 we knew we would be in for tempestuous night. Once again, Joe reminded us to keep our cool, not to become involved in trouble, to keep our minds on the game and do the job we had come to do.

I needed eyes in the back of my head that night. Once again I was kicked even when the ball was nowhere near me, punched and spat at. It was so bad that it was a relief when the defenders simply reverted to pulling my shirt, which they did at any given opportunity. I don't like saying this of another team, but in my opinion the behaviour of the Dinamo players that night was disgraceful.

However, I had the last laugh, scoring in the first half and again in the second. A 2–1 victory gave us the tie 3–1 on aggregate and Liverpool were bound for another European Cup final.

Happily, we were too much the professionals, too intent on maintaining discipline and the standards that had been set at the club, ever to resort to the mindless aggression displayed by the opposition that night. Every team will have an off-day, but nobody could ever beat Liverpool by resorting to intimidation. We could take care of ourselves.

We had been hoping for an all-British European Cup final as Dundee United also reached the semi-finals. Unfortunately, the Scots fell to Roma and, as luck would have it, the final was to take place at Roma's home ground, the Olympic Stadium.

No one at Liverpool was bothered about the prospect of playing Roma in their own back yard. We had won every one of our away games in the competition and saw no reason not to continue with this feat. I had watched European Cup finals on television and the prospect of playing in one thrilled me beyond belief and made me think about how far I had come in such a relatively short period of time.

For some weeks there had been stories in newspapers that Italian clubs such as AC Milan, Juventus, Napoli and Sampdoria were interested in signing me. (Significantly, not Roma.) None of this unsettled me in the least. As I have said, I never believed my own publicity, let alone the rumour mill. I had just signed a new contract at Anfield and was very happy at the club. My new contract had built-in clauses regarding bonuses. In simple terms, if Liverpool stayed at the top and continued to win trophies, I could earn £500,000 over four years.

Five years previously I had been as happy as Larry earning £20 a week for doing what I loved. I was now twenty-two and the prospect of earning half a million pounds over the next four years was beyond my wildest dreams. Though this was not a conscious thought at the time, I think Liverpool offered me a new contract when my existing one still had eighteen months to run, because they felt the press stories of interest in me from Italy had substance. All I wanted to do was to carry on playing for Liverpool and scoring goals.

The fact I wasn't officially available for transfer and had also made it clear I was very happy at Anfield cut no mustard with the Italian press. When we touched down at Rome airport before the European Cup final, I was mobbed by reporters as soon as I set foot in the arrivals hall. I was bombarded with questions but didn't say a thing, simply because there was nothing to say.

As we prepared to board the coach which would to take us to our hotel just outside Rome, Graeme suggested I say something to the posse of journalists, as to say nothing could well further fuel speculation.

'When will you be coming to Italy?' I was asked.

I looked round, as if to check the name of the airport. 'I was under the impression I'm here?'

Ripples of laughter. 'Yes, yes, but when will you be coming to play here and who will you sign for?'

'I'm very happy at Liverpool and have no intention of leaving the club. Now, if you'll excuse me, we have a European Cup final to win.'

I thought that was clear enough. Seemingly not. The following day carried news I was about to sign for AC Milan, Inter, Juventus, Napoli and Lazio, depending on which Italian newspaper you looked at.

The mood amongst the Liverpool players was buoyant. As our coach made its way towards our hotel we began singing, song after song. When our coach drew up at the hotel there was quite a crowd of reporters, photographers and local fans there to meet us. We were singing Chris Rea's 'I Don't Know What It Is, But I Love It' and, much to the bewilderment of the crowd, continued with our song as we disembarked. Our singing, though not great, was loud and proud, partly because we enjoyed it, partly to convey to the Italian press we held no fears of facing Roma in Rome.

Liverpool was looking to win the European Cup for a fourth time. The night was warm and sultry, and we emerged from the bowels of the stadium into the night air to an ear-splitting cacophony of noise. The Olympic Stadium seemed decorated for the occasion, fireworks and flares engulfing the alp-like terraces with a maroon and grey hue, and was brought alive by the guttural sound of 80,000 fans, the vast majority of whom, as we were soon to be made aware, not on our side. As we walked towards the pitch we were showered by coins, stones and plastic cups whose contents were, let's say, dubious. I can remember thinking, 'If this was happening at Wembley or Anfield, there'd be hell on at UEFA. But, because this is Italy, I bet nothing will happen.' Nothing did.

The teams lined up as follows:

LIVERPOOL: Grobbelaar, Neal, Kennedy, Lawrenson, Whelan, Hansen, Dalglish, Lee, Rush, Johnston, Souness

ROMA: Tancredi, Nappi, Bonetti, Righetti, Nela, Di Bartolomei, Falcao, Cerezo, Conti, Pruzzo, Graziani

There was an electric start as both sides went in search of an early goal. Within two minutes of the start Graziani gave warning as he stung Grob's fingertips with a rising drive. At the other end,

Sammy played me in and I managed to hold off Nela to fire a shot across Tancredi's goal to signal our intent.

Kenny, Graeme, Sammy and Craig began to exert themselves in midfield and we gradually took control of the game. After a quarter of an hour of play, during which we had been in the ascendancy, we drew first blood.

Roma got into a muddle trying to clear their lines. Sammy won the ball, played it to Phil Neal who advanced before firing past Tancredi – a typical threading of the needle under pressure when defenders are closing down and the goalkeeper narrowing the angle. Phil was the only survivor of the Liverpool team that had won the European Cup in 1977, and the thought occurred to me that it would be entirely fitting if Phil's goal was the only one of the game.

We were playing a 4-4-1-1 formation with myself upfront and Kenny in 'the hole'. Kenny was superb at this because he possessed the brains, the skill and the know-how to be the conduit of the team. He was the hub around which everything revolved and, of course, when we were on the attack, his experience was of great benefit to me.

My job involved a lot of running. I was constantly criss-crossing along the Roma back-line, always looking for the ball to be played into space. I would run some eight miles during the course of a game, much of that in short bursts, and spend the majority of the time with my back to the way I wanted to go, so I was forever glancing over my shoulder to see where defenders were and where the space was going to be created.

I'd come off my man, receive the ball, play it back or wide, then move up again as we gained territory and defenders fell back. I always made myself available and there was always a big defender right behind me. The tight marking never bothered me, however.

My mind was focused on the play and looking for the space where I felt the ball would played.

I was grafting hard and all seemed to be going well. We were in control but an uncharacteristically sloppy piece of defending let Roma in just before the break.

Roma had broken down one of our attacks. They worked the ball down their right-hand side. I dropped back to just beyond the halfway line, but there was no need to track back as we were very quick in getting men behind the ball. There appeared to be cover on when the ball was swung across into our penalty area, but when Pruzzo made a run nobody went with him. Pruzzo, relishing his newfound freedom, buried a header into the back of the net.

The Olympic Stadium erupted. Instinctively I looked down at the grass. It was shimmering with dew under the floodlights. When a goal was scored against us, particularly during an important game away from home, I couldn't bear to look at the opposition or home fans celebrating.

When that goal went in I heard Righetti say something behind me. As I didn't speak Italian I didn't understand what he said, but gained the impression it was for my benefit, perhaps something on the lines of, 'Now we're going to put you to it.' Most defenders did that. Following a goal for their team they'd say something in the hope of putting doubts into your head. It never did for me. I was always confident of scoring, always confident of us as a team. No amount of verbal haranguing ever swayed me from what I had to do.

We carved out a number of openings in the second half, and were the better side, but we couldn't find a breakthrough. When Roma did forage into our half of the field, they too found clear-cut chances at a premium. On one rare occasion when they did breach our rearguard, Falcao found Grob at the top of his game. A swerving low drive from the Brazilian took a deflection off Lawro, but Grob adjusted his position in an instant and, having originally began to move to his right, got down low to his left to tuck the ball into his chest.

With no further goals the final went into extra time. I felt we were the stronger team and we dominated that extra period but, credit to Roma, they held out. Kenny was tiring so Joe replaced him with Michael Robinson, and Stevie Nicol came on for Craig. Fresh legs gave fresh impetus to our cause, but still no breakthrough. With the game 1–1 after 120 minutes of play a little football history was created. We were in the first European Cup final to go to a penalty shoot-out.

I'm down on one knee, composing myself. There is the soft buzz of conversation from 80,000 people in the stadium. I know this momentary quiet won't last for long. Soon there will be wild celebrations – and tears. I can smell sweat, fag smoke and some sort of food, I think it might be pizza, but from my position close to the ground the prominent smell is that of grass. Not the sweet, heady aroma of newly mown grass but a more earthy smell. I look up. Though it's late it is still an oppressively warm night but the floodlights catch the evening dew in the blades of grass. In different circumstances it could appear magical, but for some reason I'm seeing every blade as a potential hazard. A bead of sweat has run down my forehead on to my nose. I wipe it away with the back of my hand and take to my feet. I'm now on the same level as the rest of the lads. I should never have knelt down – it made me feel out of things. We all need to be together.

I take a few steps forward to where the lads are bunched. Joe approaches with a clipboard. Alan Hansen suddenly moves towards the back of our group; he obviously doesn't fancy his chances. Kenny would, but having been substituted he can't now take a penalty. Who's going to take the fifth?

'Steve Nic?' enquires Joe.

'Yeah, boss.'

Joe makes a note on his clipboard. 'Phil?'

Phil Neal nods.

Joe writes down his name. 'Graeme?'

For once Graeme doesn't say anything, he just nods.

A note. 'Rushy?'

'Yeah, OK.'

Joe is looking about for a volunteer.

Come on, somebody, for God's sake.

'Barney? You gonna be OK?' asks Joe.

'If you want,' says Alan Kennedy.

Bloody hell. Barney? I just hope he's up for it.

My mind goes back the last training session we had before leaving for Rome. Joe had us practising penalties. The reserves took five penalties against Grob and he didn't save one. Five of us then took penalties against reserve goalkeeper, Bob Boulder. Unbelievably, not one of us scored. I can only recall Barney ever having taken two penalties for Liverpool, both in pre-season friendlies, and he missed on both occasions.

I put those thoughts out of my mind. I have to be positive.

'Hey, come on, lads, let's be big!' says Graeme, clapping his hands.

'Yeah, let's be confident. This is ours. We're gonna do it,' says Lawro.

The referee is in position. He seems edgy but that's normal for referees in this situation, especially a European Cup final. It's tense all right.

Steve Nicol is first up.

'Good luck, Stevie, son.'

'Put it away Nicko.'

Stevie places the ball on the penalty spot and glances up. At what? Goalkeeper Tancredi? The spot where he intends to put the ball? The spot where he hopes Tancredi thinks he's going to put the ball?

I am watching the ball sailing beyond the bar. Having passed the bar, it continues to rise before smoothly beginning its descent when I momentarily lose sight of it against the massed backdrop of faces. Happy faces, ecstatic faces, whose owners are jumping up and down and cheering.

Steve's shoulders are hunched. He stares down at the ground and holds his head. He turns and looks at us . . . Bloody hell, he's gonna cry.

'Hey, never mind, Stevie, son.'

'Get your head up, we'll win this.'

Stevie begins his long walk back to us. Kenny steps forward and puts a comforting arm around his shoulder.

Bartolomei is first up for them. He's a swarmy so-and-so. *Go on, show some nerves. Bottle it . . .*

'Come on, Grob!'

'Oh, no. Shit.'

The stadium has erupted again. I look down at the grass, still shining, like shards of glass.

Phil Neal.

Never says much. Mr Dependable when it comes to penalties. Has he ever missed? Can't think that he has. *Come on, Phil.*

'Yes!'

We're back in it. Bring it on.

Bruno Conti.. Fantastic player . . . amazing touch . . . *fuck it up, go on . . .* he has!

'Yes!'

'No use putting it away now, mate, doesn't count!'

That's got us all going. Lawro, Kenny, Barney, even Stevie Nick . . . and our lot, look at them, they know it as well.

It's 1–1 with two gone.

You wouldn't think Graeme's going up to take a penalty in a European final. Looks like he's off for a stroll in the park. Talk about cool. Wonder what he's feeling. I never can tell, not with him . . .

Bloody hell, it's gone quiet . . . Don't listen to the silence, Gray, just do it.

'Yes!'

I glance across to the Roma lads. Plenty of strained faces. That's a good sign.

Who's next for them? Righetti. Never seen him take one. If he misses . . . that'll make it . . . shit!

The stadium erupts again.

Bloody hell, it's me.

'Come on, Rushy, do the business.'

'Good luck, Ian.'

'Stick it away, Ian.'

Lord God, please, let me score this. Ball feels slippery, like a bar of soap. Wipe it on my shirt, place it on the spot, maker's logo facing me. Usual job. Glance towards the corner to keeper's left, he might go for it, then hit it to his right . . . What if he's seen me take one?

Should I switch? Put it to his left? No, no, forget that . . . as normal . . . Must concentrate . . . clear my mind of all thoughts . . . two seconds .and I'll be done . . . Bloody hell, can't seem to get my breath . . . deep breaths . . . Yes, OK, ref . . . ready. Got to clear my head . . . get rid of this spit in my mouth . . . don't even look now at where it's going . . . don't even think . . . here I go . . . running OK . . . must hit it clean . . . no thoughts now. Tancredi's moved . . . to his right . . . put it in the other corner . . .

'Yes!'

Thank God. Bloody hell, the sense of relief is so great. Thank you, Lord, thank you!

God, if I'd missed I couldn't have lived with it. All those nights lying awake thinking, 'If only I'd done this or that.' Got loads of career left but to have missed . . . How long would that have taken to get out of my system? Months? Years? For ever?

'Well done, Rushy, son.'

'Topper take, Ian.'

'Nice one, Ian.'

'Who's next? Graziani . . . bloody hell.'

Grob's playing him up. He's taking the piss. Wobbling his legs and knees like they're jelly and he's bricking it, which he isn't. Or maybe he is, but wants Graziani to think he is so confident he can make a joke of it . . .

Graziani is steaming in . . . He's hit the bar! He's hit the bloody bar!

'Yes!'

Graziani is on his knees. He knows. He bloody well knows.

'Wazzat make it? Wozissit?'

'3-2 to us.'

'3-2? Four gone. Hey, if we score now, that's it.'

'That right, Kenny?'

'Aye, if Barney does the business . . .'

'Come on, Barney Rubble, son.'

Bloody hell, Alan, don't look at him like that . . . give the lad some confidence.

'Nivver scored one in me life.'

'Well, now's the fucking time to start. Go on! Put it away!'

'You can do it, Barney.'

'Why aye, nee problem.'

Never scored one in his life. Let tonight be the night. Go on, Barney . . . go on . . . He's backing away, wiping his hands on his shorts. What's he gonna do? Throw it in? Stay calm, Barney.

Barney's running to the ball, stops. Little dummy, running again . . . keeper's gone to his left . . . side-foot . . . ball to his right . . .

'YEEEEEESSS!'

We're jumping all over each other. There are clammy shirts all over me. I've got other people's sweat rubbing into my face. Steve Nick has just head-butted me. Don't care. We've done it. Won it! And look at those blades of grass, shining like polished silver. Brilliant. Olympic Stadium? Welcome to the Pleasure Dome!

CHAPTER SEVEN

Bring on the Dancing Horses

I t had been another incredible season for Liverpool. In guiding us to the League Championship, European Cup and League Cup in his first season as manager, Joe had written himself into the record books as the first British manager to win three major trophies in a single season. We were delighted for him. True, Joe had inherited a very good side from Bob, but that has never been a guaranteed recipe for success. After Bob, we needed not only a superb manager but a strong character to keep us going and maintain progress. As Bob had done before him when replacing Bill Shankly, Joe had opted for evolution rather than revolution. The spirit of Liverpool football club was still very much in place. If anything, it had become stronger, and much of the credit of that goes to Joe.

It was also an incredible season for me. I couldn't quite believe how good it had been. I scored forty-nine goals in competitive matches as well the penalty in the European Cup final, which made it a round fifty. My exploits earned me the Golden Boot, the award afforded to the top goal-scorer in Europe. In addition to which I had the honour of being voted the Football Writers'

Association Footballer of the Year. 'We'll be keeping Duraglit in business for years,' quipped my dad.

To be voted Footballer of the Year thrilled me to bits. When I thought about the great players on whom this honour had been bestowed – Stanley Matthews, Tom Finney, Bobby Moore, George Best, Bobby Charlton and Pat Jennings, to name but a few – I felt very humbled. I was the sixth Liverpool player to receive this honour, the others being Kenny Dalglish (twice), Ian Callaghan, Kevin Keegan, Emlyn Hughes and Terry McDermott.

When accepting my award I was at pains to pay tribute to my teammates, Joe and his backroom staff. I told the assembled guests that the secret of my success was teamwork. This was true, though I didn't think it prudent to confess that I was also continuing to adhere to the advice given to me by Bob – that of being selfish in front of goal.

My success resulted in a number of offers for commercial deals. For various reasons I declined most of them, though I did sign a boot deal. The money from this, I hasten to add, was nothing compared to what footballers receive from such deals today.

I did sign up to other commercial deals but by far the most exciting offer came from *Shoot* magazine. As a boy I had loved *Shoot*, and even collected the League Ladders which, in the weeks leading up to a new season, came free with the magazine. I particularly enjoyed the 'Super Focus' feature in which footballers answered a series of questions that, supposedly, gave an insight into their character and their lives. (The answers were often bland. For example, in response to 'favourite food' the answer would invariably be 'steak'. With regard to 'favourite drink', the answer nearly always would be, 'lager'.) So it was not without some excitement that I agreed to take part in this feature.

While rummaging around my home for items for this book that

would help me recall my days as a player, unbelievably, I came across the questionnaire *Shoot* sent me in 1983–4. At the time I was delighted to complete it. Looking back at my answers now, the over-riding feeling is one of embarrassment. In mitigation let me say I was twenty-one, and what do you know of life at that age? Seemingly, in my case, very little.

MARRIED: No
CAR: Renault Fuego
PREVIOUS CLUB: Chester
JOB OR TRADE BEFORE TURNING PRO: None
NICKNAME: Rushy
FAVOURITE NEWSPAPER: *Daily Mirror*
FAVOURITE PLAYER (S): Frank Stapleton (Manchester United),
    Michel Platini
PLAYER FOR THE FUTURE: Ronnie Whelan
FAVOURITE OTHER TEAM: Chester
FOOTBALL HERO OF CHILDHOOD: Jimmy Greaves
FAVOURITE OTHER SPORTS: Snooker and tennis
OTHER SPORTSPERSON YOU MOST ADMIRE: Snooker player Alex
    Higgins
MOST MEMORABLE MATCH: 1981 League Cup final replay v
    West Ham
BIGGEST DISAPPOINTMENT: Not going to the World Cup Finals
    with Wales
FRIENDLIEST AWAY FANS: In England all of them are friendly
BEST STADIUM PLAYED IN: Wembley
FAVOURITE FOOD/DRINK: Steak and chips, lager shandy [What
    did I tell you?]
LIKES AND DISLIKES: Music and winning . . . losing and traffic
    jams

FAVOURITE SINGERS: David Bowie, Human League

FAVOURITE ACTOR/ACTRESS: Clint Eastwood, Susan George

FAVOURITE HOLIDAY DESTINATION: Spain

BEST FILM SEEN RECENTLY: *Escape to Victory*

FAVOURITE TV SHOW: *Not the Nine O'Clock News*

FAVOURITE ACTIVITY ON DAY OFF: Snooker

HOBBIES: Music and reading

BIGGEST INFLUENCE ON CAREER: Cliff Sear, Chester's youth
    team manager, and my dad

SUPERSTITIONS: None [Seemingly written before the Luton
    game]

INTERNATIONAL HONOURS: Welsh schoolboy, U-15, U-18,
    Youth, U-21 and full international caps.

PERSONAL AMBITION: To become a regular for Liverpool and
    win the European Cup [written before European Cup final
    against Rome].

IF NOT A PLAYER, WHAT JOB WOULD YOU DO: Don't know,
    perhaps painter/decorator.

CAREER AFTER PLAYING: Haven't though too much about that.

WHICH PERSON IN THE WORLD WOULD YOU MOST LIKE TO
    MEET: Bjorn Borg

Regarding proposed deals, I have always trusted my own judgement and, in the main, have dealt with everything myself, referring actual contracts to a solicitor to read the small print. In 1984 just about every Liverpool player had an agent and, being only twenty-two, for a short time I too went down the road of having an agent, a guy named Charles Roberts.

Following our victory in the European Cup I was over in Ireland doing some promotion work for the club's sponsor Crown Paints. While in Ireland I received a call from Charles Roberts. His news rocked me. A representative of Napoli had been in contact with him. Napoli wanted to sign me.

I was very happy at Liverpool and had no desire to leave the club. Liverpool were, after all, European Champions. In football terms how could I possibly move to a more successful club? Charles told me I should not dismiss the opportunity outright until he had outlined the bones of the deal on offer, so I agreed to meet with him on my return to Liverpool.

When Charles Roberts told me what Napoli were offering it made my eyes water. I was to receive £1 million as a signing-on fee. I was aware of my knees trembling and nearly fainted when Charles told me the 'bones of the deal'. In addition to the signing-on fee, Napoli was willing to pay me another £1 million over a three-year contract, just over £333,000 a year.

It was one Dickens of an offer. Should I accept I would be able to look after my whole family for the rest of their lives, and Tracy and I would also be sitting pretty.

It was a Thursday and the Italian transfer deadline for their new season was forty-eight hours away. Charles told me that if I did not sign by Saturday all bets were off.

Given I was very happy at Liverpool, I knew I had to give some serious thought to this offer as I believed it to be the chance of a lifetime. I agonised. The money was fantastic. While I agonised, Charles made frantic efforts to get in touch with Liverpool chairman, John Smith, who was in London watching the tennis at Wimbledon. This was a time before mobile phones and Charles didn't manage to get in touch with Mr Smith until the Friday morning. Mr Smith listened to what Charles had to say, then told him he needed time to think and refused to discuss the matter of my possible transfer until the Monday morning, which, of course, was two days after the Italian transfer deadline.

I managed to contact Mr Smith, asked if I could come down to London to discuss the matter with him only for him to refuse point-blank. Though still not 100 per cent sure about whether I wanted to move or not, I was angered by Mr Smith's reaction, given the urgency of the impending deadline.

The deadline came and went. As a consequence, the deal collapsed. I then received a call from Charles to say Napoli had been in touch. Having been unable to speak with Mr Smith, they'd had no alternative but to look elsewhere and had signed Diego Maradona.

John Smith and I did, in time, bury the hatchet and become good friends. But I wasn't the only one to have had a run-in with him. Tommy Smith told me how, towards the end of his career, he received an offer to play in America for Tampa Bay Rowdies during the close season. Tommy had rung John Smith to ask permission as he felt a summer of football would, given his age, maintain his fitness. John Smith refused Tommy's request and, as Tommy was in the process of explaining why such a move would be good for him and the club, the chairman put the phone down. Needless to say, Tommy was furious at this treatment. He had, after all, given some sixteen years of unstinting service to the club. Coincidentally, John Smith was about to go to London. Tommy, determined to say his piece, caught up with the chairman at Lime Street station only for John Smith to refuse to discuss the matter further. The chairman then boarded his train with Tommy tracking him from the platform and saying what he thought of him as John Smith made his way along the carriage to his seat. Knowing Tommy, this would not have consisted of plaudits. (For the record, Tommy did play for Tampa that summer. Bob intervened and, apparently, told John Smith that, as manager, he made the decisions on such matters.)

As for myself, I was so upset with the chairman's belligerence and rudeness in not even returning Napoli's calls that for a long time afterwards I refused to acknowledge him. If he walked into a room, I would walk out. If we passed each other in the corridor, I'd stonewall him.

This had all happened while Joe had been on holiday. When he returned he called me into his office and asked me what had been going on. I was straight with Joe, as he always was with me. I told him for all I never wanted to leave Liverpool the deal on offer had been just too fantastic to ignore.

'I understand, Ian,' he told me. 'Football's a short career and you have to make the most of what's on offer while you can. Nothing wrong in that.'

I told Joe that the money would have enabled me to look after my family for the rest of their days.

'You're a good lad and I like you. Your heart's in the right place,' said Joe. 'Bottom line, they didn't want you to go and put the mockers on it. It's the way it was done that was wrong. Have no idea how to treat people.'

As I was in the process of leaving, Joe offered a parting shot.

'A lot of money, but just think how much would go in tax. There'd be more deductions than in an omnibus of Sherlock Holmes stories.'

Good line, but it didn't make me feel any better.

In purely financial terms, Liverpool were wrong to keep me. Napoli were prepared to pay £4.5 million for my services. Even if Liverpool had won every trophy going for the next three seasons, the club would never have realised that sort of money. Ironically, when I eventually did go to Italy three years later, I did so for a fee of £3.2 million. Without even taking inflation into account, the club had let £1 million slip away – as, to all intents and purposes, had I.

When a team has achieved significant success, as Liverpool had done, supporters expect all the players to remain with the club. The notion being that a team at the top of the tree consists of contented players who are enjoying the pinnacle of their careers and would consider a move to another club as a step back. By and large this is true, but by his very nature a footballer relishes challenges, and footbridges to new pastures can provide not only a new and exciting challenge but also an opportunity to achieve financial security for his family for life. My proposed move to Napoli had incited this desire in me and, in the summer of 1984, Graeme Souness was presented with a similar opportunity. Graeme moved to Sampdoria for a fee of £650,000, in so doing teaming up with Trevor Francis and two emerging stars of Italian football, Roberto Mancini and Gianluca Vialli.

Without doubt, Graeme's decision to join Sampdoria was a blow to Liverpool. It was also something of a watershed. Since the early days of Bill Shankly's reign, the manager had decided who left Liverpool football club. Graeme's move was an indication that such power was swinging away from managers and towards players and their agents.

Graeme was a key member of the Liverpool team and, understandably, Joe didn't want him to leave. When Kevin Keegan had left Liverpool, Bob had negotiated a ready replacement in Kenny Dalglish. Initially it was difficult to see who could possibly replace Graeme in the side. Joe was upset and this came out during a press conference when asked how he was going to replace the player who had made an invaluable contribution to the team in his 358 appearances for the club.

'Souness is Souness,' replied Joe, irritated. 'Forget him. We have. He's gone. The three trophies we won last year, they've gone. It's the past. Now we're starting afresh.'

I think part of Joe's frustration stemmed from the fact that he had not expected Graeme to go. To the best of my knowledge he had no replacement in mind, let alone one ready in the wings, because Graeme's move came out of the blue.

Graeme was an outstanding player with terrific all-round ability but perhaps his most important contribution was that he provided the 'fight' in the team. If I scored a hat-trick, he would be on at me to score a fourth. He was never satisfied. His desire and will to win was absolute and he radiated this to every other player in the side, urging us all on to bigger and better things. When the going got tough, Graeme was tougher than tough. He led by example and such was his commitment and fight, we players were incited to battle harder, too, not least because we didn't want to be the subject of his wrath after the game.

Graeme never stood on ceremony and pushed himself to the limit in everything he did. When he first joined the club from Middlesbrough he lived in the Holiday Inn hotel for nine months. After morning training and lunch at Melwood, he'd return to the hotel, have a few beers, sleep from 4pm until 7pm, have dinner then go out into the city for more drinks. Yet this routine never affected his training or performances in games. He trained, played and lived harder than anyone else at the club.

By his own admission he wasn't the most popular player in English football and he wasn't the most popular in the Liverpool dressing-room either, but everyone respected him, not simply because of his physical prowess but because he was both a tremendous individual and team-player. I owe much to Graeme. When I got into the side he was one of the players who constantly offered help and advice. I listened to him during games because what he said made sense and I became a better player as a result. The fact he would never win an award in a popularity contest never bothered him. To Graeme, being successful was always much more important than being popular. We were going to miss him, but I was confident we would continue to flourish without him.

As part of our preparation for 1984–5, Liverpool embarked upon a short tour of the Continent. I scored the only goal of our first game against Borussia Dortmund and netted again in a 6–0 victory over Belgian side RSC Charleroi, which we followed with victories in Switzerland against BSC Young Boys and Grasshoppers. Our final pre-season friendly was in Ireland against Home Farm.

Our pre-season appeared to be going well. Joe had spent the summer in the onerous task of finding a replacement for Graeme and appeared to have found a likely candidate in Ajax midfield player Jan Molby. Jan had begun his career with FC Kolding in his native Denmark, before moving to Ajax where his performances had been brought to the attention of Joe. To be truthful, Joe didn't know much, if anything about, about Jan, other than the recommendations he had received from an agent. With the new season only a fortnight or so away Joe was desperate to plug the hole in midfield, but knowing little of Jan, insisted he came to the club on trial. Impressed with what he saw of Jan in training Joe included him in the side for the game against Home Farm.

The match took place as part of an agreement reached between the two clubs when Liverpool had signed youngsters Ken de Mange and Brian Mooney from Home Farm some months previously. The club had also been Ronnie Whelan's first, so there was a friendly air to the game.

It had been a particularly dry summer and the Tolka Park pitch was hard. During the game I turned quickly and jarred my foot. My momentum caused my knee to twist. I felt a twang of pain and immediately knew something was wrong. I signalled to the bench and was immediately substituted.

We won the game 3–0 at something of a canter, our final goal being scored by trialist Jan Molby. The other two, fittingly, came from Ronnie Whelan. The result, however, was of little consequence to me. Back in the changing room, Ronnie Moran had a look at my knee and shook his head. 'It's not looking good, Ian,' he told me. 'I think we should have a specialist view.'

Back in Liverpool I underwent an examination. The diagnosis was that I had sustained a hairline fracture and other damage to the cartilage which would necessitate an operation.

I have never liked hospitals. I know the people who work in our hospitals do a fantastic job and our National Health Service is admired throughout the world (though, curiously, never imitated) but I find even the smell of a hospital off-putting. The thought of going under the surgeon's knife in an operating theatre filled with me with dread, as did the general anaesthetic. I'd rather have faced the most ruthless defenders in the world than endure it, particularly when I heard the surgeon who was to perform the operation was called Mr Carver and that one of his assistants was a Nurse Butcher.

In the event Richard Carver did an excellent job. I was delighted when he told me the operation had been a complete success and I would be able to play football again within two months. There was nothing left but for me to begin the slow process of rehabilitation and work my way towards achieving match fitness.

Liverpool's first game of note that season was the Charity Shield against Everton at Wembley. On the day, our near neighbours exacted revenge for the defeat we had inflicted upon them in the previous season. It was a game during which Bruce Grobbelaar offered further evidence of his eccentricity. Everton were deserved winners and but for Grob, who made a string of superb saves, would have won by more than a single goal. But this goal came in bizarre circumstances.

On fifty-five minutes Grob made an excellent save from a close-range shot from Graeme Sharp. Then something unusual happened. The ball pinballed about the box as our defenders failed to clear their lines and, when the ball ricocheted back to Grob, he instinctively reacted by sticking out a foot, only to succeed in diverting the ball into the net.

The press put it down to Grob's tendency to drop the occasional clanger (tell me the goalkeeper who hasn't) and they said as much to Joe during the post-match press conference. Joe was having none of this. He recognised that but for Grob Everton would have had the game won long before the only goal was scored.

'The defeat wasn't simply down to a goalkeeping error,' snapped Joe. 'If it wasn't for Bruce it could have been a lot worse. What I saw out there today was a collective failure. Players I expect to do the business didn't, simple as that. I'm glad it happened today. It gives us a week to put it right.'

In the event it was to take somewhat longer than a week to rectify the problems that had beset us as a team.

I was out of action and Graeme had gone, but I still believed we had quality in depth to make an excellent start to the season. However, other circumstances contrived to see Liverpool make their worst start to a season since the 1950s.

My place in the team was taken by Paul Walsh who, in the close season, Joe had signed from Luton Town. Paul must have wondered if he'd actually come to the right club as Liverpool won just two of the opening ten league matches, and were beaten by Spurs in round three of the League Cup.

'Fortress' Anfield proved anything but. Only one of the first five home matches were won, prompting the press to write articles comparing the so-called 'Liverpool dynasty' to empires of old, in that all empires eventually crumble and fall.

I thought the reports of our demise were grossly exaggerated. That said, it was a very worrying time for everyone connected with the club, particularly for Joe.

Jan Molby was doing OK in midfield but he wasn't Graeme. Jan had superb skills, wonderful vision and was a great passer of the ball, but he couldn't match Graeme's presence and work rate. We needed two players to replace Graeme not one. Jan would go on to become a superb player for Liverpool but in those early days at the club I think it fair to say he struggled to adapt. Never the quickest (he would always be fighting to keep his weight down) there were times when the tempo of the game appeared too much for him.

It would have helped Jan enormously had Kenny been on song, but he wasn't. Kenny was enduring, by his own high standards, a poor run of form. I think he missed Graeme. Then again, we all did.

Craig Johnston was also out of the side and out of contract. During the summer he had returned to his native Australia where his wife was due to give birth to their first child and hadn't returned for pre-season training or by the start of the season. The story going around the club was that Craig might not be coming back to Anfield. A story given some credence when we heard Chelsea chairman, Ken Bates, was prepared to fly out to Australia in an attempt to lure Craig to Stamford Bridge. Craig eventually did return in late September when he signed a new three-year contract. However, I never sensed he was truly happy that season. He later requested a transfer which, though granted, happily came to nothing.

Craig's protracted absence gave rise to all manner of dressing-room jokes, the pick of which came from Alan 'Barney Rubble' Kennedy, who said he'd been to see Joe to ask if he could have a couple of days off as his wife was also going to have a baby. The story went that Joe agreed to this and, three days later, on Barney's return to the club, asked him, 'Well, was it a boy or a girl?' Only for Barney to reply, 'Oh, it takes months, boss.'

Sammy Lee, like Kenny, was also suffering a poor run of form but, to be honest, just about every player was struggling to find the imperious form they had shown the previous season. David Hodgson left to join Sunderland for a fee of £125,000. Michael Robinson also left the club to try his luck in Spain where he would subsequently go on to become something of a celebrity football presenter on Spanish television. The combination of no longer having Graeme to boss midfield, Kenny and Sammy struggling to hit form, and other mainstays not playing as well as they could contrived to produce some below-par performances and the poor set of results.

It was an anxious time for everyone at the club but I also had anxieties of my own. My rehabilitation was going well and I never doubted I would play again and soon. What did concern me was whether my cartilage would be the same as it had been before the injury. I'd heard lots of stories of players with a similar injury who, when they resumed playing, discovered they had lost a yard of pace or the ability to turn sharply, in some cases, both. I prayed that when I returned to the fold I would not be a shadow of my former self. I spent a lot of time indulging in such anxious thoughts, and because I was not playing I had the time to dwell on them.

In mid-October I was given the news I had been yearning to hear: I was fit enough to have a run out with the reserves. I played for the 'ressies' in a 2–0 win over West Brom and managed to score our first goal. The following day, a Sunday, Liverpool faced Spurs at White Hart Lane and did so without Kenny, dropped for the first time in his Liverpool career. Sammy Lee also found himself out of favour, replaced by Stevie Nicol. The re-shuffle did nothing to halt the slide and Spurs won 1–0.

Joe was frustrated but resolute in his belief that we would turn things around, and he kept his sense of humour and wit. During the post-match press conference a reporter asked if he regretted having changed the side.

'Change is inevitable,' replied Joe. 'Except when you're standing in front of a vending machine or a phone box.'

The following Saturday I managed to get through another ninety minutes against Stoke City reserves. This time I didn't score, though Craig Johnston did.

I'd done some huffing and puffing to get through the game against Stoke, but wasn't too concerned about this. When a player had been sidelined for some months the sheer adrenalin rush of being able to play again, coupled with the realisation that his injury has not affected his pace, ability to turn quickly and so on, will get him through the game. The second game he will find a little harder, the third harder still, as he is not getting the adrenalin boost he felt in his first match. Only with four to five games under his belt will he more or less have regained match fitness and be firing again.

I felt I needed another couple of games with the reserves to get back to full fitness but was keen to play some role in Liverpool's next game, the Merseyside derby against Everton. I thought if I was made a substitute against Everton and Joe brought me on for the last twenty minutes I would make a contribution while at the same time easing myself back into the swing of things. So I went to see Joe and put my proposition to him.

'Do you think you're fit enough?' he asked.

I told him I would be OK for a twenty-minute run-out should I be called upon.

At first Joe agreed, but no sooner had I left his office than he came out and caught up with me.

'I've changed my mind,' he said. 'I don't think I'd better give you a shirt.'

I spent the next couple of hours working in the gym, but the more I thought about it his retraction the more I disagreed, so I went back to see him.

'What's with the change of mind?' I asked somewhat irritated. 'Why won't you give me a shirt?'

'You might as well not be included at all as be on the bench,' said Joe. 'If you're fit enough to be sub then you're fit enough to play.'

I didn't think I was quite up to ninety minutes against Everton, but against my better judgement I found myself saying, 'All right then, I'm fit enough.'

'That's all right, then. You're playing – from the start.'

I may have started against Everton but I never truly got going. I never coped with the pace and tempo of the game, which was hectic and frenetic from kick-off to final whistle. There was only one goal in the game, and it was scored by Graeme Sharp to give Everton their first win at Anfield since 1970. As if that wasn't bad enough, defeat saw Liverpool slip to fifth from bottom, the lowest position the club had occupied in Division One since 1954.

Once again the Job's comforters in the national press went to work. The consensus was that Liverpool had reached the end of an era. 'Dark clouds have replaced the once golden sky,' wrote the *Daily Mail*.

Having guided us to three trophies the previous season, amazingly Joe found his credentials as a manager under question. Those who should have known better were writing that Liverpool could soon be looking for a new manager. It was ludicrous. I was having none of it and neither was any other player. No one could deny we'd had a bad start to the season but, given the loss of key players and the fact that players such as Kenny and Alan Hansen were experiencing a dip in form, it was little wonder results had not been good. But not for one moment did I or anyone else in the club believe the glory days of Anfield were a thing of the past, or that Joe could not hack it as manager.

In 2007–8, Rafael Benitez found himself the subject of similar scurrilous articles in the press because he had not guided Liverpool to a trophy success. The fact a team does not win a trophy does not make a manager who has previously enjoyed success a bad manager. Far from it. Bill Shankly and Bob Paisley are regarded as the greatest managers Liverpool has ever had. Shanks is rightly held up as being one of the greatest managers in the history of the game, to this day enjoying true legendary status. Yet, under Shankly, Liverpool did not win a major trophy for seven years, from 1966 to 1973. Talk to Tommy Smith or Ian Callaghan and they will tell you that during that period no one ever questioned Shankly's credentials as a manager, suggested that his job was under threat or penned articles saying Liverpool were a spent force. It was different back then. In 1984 we were beginning to see the scenario we are all too familiar with today, that of the media creating pressure for managers. Following a run (however short) of poor results for a team, certain elements of the media will suggest the manager's job is in jeopardy, often fuelling the situation they have contrived with the use of emotive adjectives, such as referring the manager as being 'beleaguered'.

Tell people something often enough and they will believe it to be true. Chairmen read this stuff. Not wanting the club portrayed as being in decline, nine times out of ten they will resort to a knee-jerk reaction. Time, not money, is the greatest asset a manager can be given by his chairman.

Throughout the difficult set of results, Joe remained resolute and enjoyed the full support of everyone at the club. To the best of my knowledge, the chairman, John Smith, and his co-directors paid no heed to what was being written. I never heard any mutterings from the boardroom regarding their disappointment at our poor start to the season. The attitude that prevailed throughout the club and amongst our supporters was, 'We'll show them.'

On the Wednesday following the derby defeat we entertained Benfica in the second round of the European Cup. Aware we had been struggling to rediscover form Benfica must have really fancied their chances of getting a result at Anfield but we had other ideas.

Joe recalled Kenny and Sammy Lee, while I continued in the role of striker. The first half, played in incessant rain, was open and evenly contested, then, just before halftime, Mark Lawrenson made a strong run that took him to the by-line. Lawro's cross was helped on by John Wark and I struck from close range. A wave of relief passed over me. With a goal to my name in only my second game back, my pores seemed to ooze confidence.

The goal, just before halftime, lifted us, and in the second half we set about Benfica in no uncertain fashion, like the Liverpool of old. Only six minutes after the break, however, Gary Gillespie, starting only his fourth game in eighteen months, lost his footing and Diamantino raced away, drew Grob and scored from an acute angle. I felt it tough on Gary who, up to that point, had not put a foot wrong.

Even with Benfica having equalised, I still felt we had the beating of them. On seventy-one minutes, Sammy made ground on the right and floated a cross into the penalty area. For once Ronnie Whelan failed to connect cleanly with the ball and when his miss-hit shot came my way, I despatched it into the net. I jogged over to the Kop, raising a finger in response to the applause, and cheers rained down from the terrace. It felt great to be back.

Five minutes later, Craig Johnston, who had come on for the injured John Wark, hit a long ball into the Benfica box. Ronnie rose to help the ball on with his head and I applied to finishing touch. A hat-trick against Benfica. I had exceeded all my expectations, and the adrenalin coursed through my body.

Still we kept the pressure on. In the remaining quarter chances came and went. I hit the base of the post with an angled drive but, in the end, we were more than happy to settle for 3–1.

To score a hat-trick in only my second game back in the first team and against such quality opposition erased any doubts I had that my operation may have affected my speed and sharpness. My work outside the box hadn't best pleased me, though I had worked hard in tracking back, but any misgivings I had were more than compensated by the fact that I was back on the goals trail. I knew I was still a little off full-match fitness but I also knew my predatory instincts and speed had not deserted me and that delighted me. All I ever wanted to do was score goals.

We were very happy with the result against Benfica but, just as we never believed the run of poor results made us a poor team, we didn't think one excellent result meant we had turned the corner, a feeling seemingly shared by Joe who, after the game, exuded relief rather than joy.

'Thank God for that,' he told the press. 'We really needed a good win for the fans and the players. It has been gloom and doom, but this win should do the lads good. I won't have a sleepless night tonight, and I'll need it as we still have work to do.'

Yet again Joe had proved himself a wily manager.

'I had to convince you that you could get through ninety minutes against Everton,' he told me. 'OK, so you didn't pull up any trees, but that didn't concern me. If you hadn't played against Everton you wouldn't have got that hat-trick against Benfica because you wouldn't have had the sharpness.'

In our following match we beat Nottingham Forest 2–0 at the City Ground in a game in which I managed to add to Ronnie Whelan's opener. Though we lost 1–0 against Benfica in the return in Lisbon, the job we had done on them at Anfield was good enough to see us safely through to the quarter-finals. The defeat in Lisbon was to prove something of a rarity from thereon, as we hit a rich vein of form that saw us rise steadily up the First Division table.

The excellent results we subsequently posted in the League had much to do with every player appearing to find optimum form again, not least Kenny, who, having suffered the ignominy of being dropped against Spurs, was once again firing on all cylinders. It took me some time to get back to what I would call my best. The knee was fine, but I was hampered by niggling injuries that made me aware I was not completely 100 per cent. This apart, I continued to find my touch in front of goal and finished the season with fourteen League goals to my name from twenty-eight appearances, in addition to which I scored seven in the FA Cup and two in the European Cup. I was happy with the return, also happy to be playing upfront alongside Paul Walsh. Given I am six feet tall, in all my time at Liverpool I never played along-side a big man upfront, though I often wondered how I would have fared should I have had such a foil. Kevin Keegan, for instance, benefited greatly from having John Toshack alongside him. Apart from John's sharp football brain, his sheer physical presence was problematic for defenders and his aerial prowess created many chances for Kevin. I never had a strike partner of similar height to knock down balls for me, take the brunt of the physical stuff or act as a target man. I was always paired with a striker of medium build with skill and pace.

At Liverpool we always played to our strengths, one of which, as far as I was concerned, was getting the ball into space to take advantage of my speed and sharpness rather than my height. If there was any heading to be done, I got up and did my best. I never considered myself a great header of the ball, yet I did surprise myself by scoring quite a number of goals this way. It wasn't so much a case of me being able to out-jump defenders as losing them and getting into space whereby I had a more-or-less free header. As Joe once told me, 'It's not your height that gets you headed goals, it's what's in that head of yours, awareness and vision.'

In the second half of the season we lost only three of twenty-one League matches, the last defeat in our final game of the season in the Merseyside derby at Goodison Park, with Everton having already tied up the Championship. Our resurgence in the New Year saw us rise to second in the League but Everton's lead was such that they could not be overhauled and they finished thirteen points ahead.

Credit to them – Everton were superb. They also won the European Cup Winners Cup and were beaten FA Cup finalists, achieving their success by playing fluid, attacking football. We were left to rue our poor start to the season. On the plus side I think our results in the New Year proved Liverpool were far from a spent force. Following the departure of Graeme, the team had undergone something of a transitional period as new players such as John Wark, Paul Walsh and Jan Molby bedded in. Unfortunately, this period had also coincided with a loss of form from some key players while others, such as myself and Sammy Lee, had been sidelined through injury. I think Liverpool could have coped with one of those facts, but the combination of them all at the same time severely affected the cohesion and balance of the team.

Our return to form in the New Year saw us make progress not only in the League but also the FA and European Cups. Our FA Cup run began with a convincing 3–0 win over Aston Villa at Anfield in which I helped myself to a couple of goals. I scored the only goal of the game against Spurs in round four, a victory which earned us a potentially tricky tie at York City in round five.

The tie against York took place towards the end of February. It was bitterly cold. Mounds of straw, which had been used to cover the pitch to protect it from frost, were piled high on the perimeter track. The straw did its job of protecting the pitch from the worst of the frost but, even so, conditions underfoot were treacherous. The same for both sides, I know, but it is on such tricky surfaces that cup shocks are more liable to happen and I don't think I was alone in welcoming the final whistle with both teams locked at 1–1. I managed to score in the second half, as did Ricky Sbragia for York, the signal for hundreds of young supporters who were sitting on the straw on the perimeter track to escape the crush on the terraces, to gleefully throw mounds of straw into the air. When the game re-started I glanced across to one of the touchlines and it was as if a hundred or so scarecows had been placed down the side of the pitch. For all those young supporters saw the game at closer quarters than the rest of the crowd, they never at any time ventured on to the pitch. Nowadays if a supporter so much as much as set foot on a perimeter track he or she might well be arrested. While I fully understand the reasons for not having supporters encroach on to the field of play, I do think some of the safety measures currently in place are draconian.

A crowd of over 43,000 turned up at Anfield for the replay. It was another cold night but from the moment Ronnie Whelan gave us the lead York felt the heat, and the result was never in doubt. We rattled in seven goals without reply, but I picked up a niggling ankle injury, which resulted in me being substituted by Paul Walsh.

Come round six, however, I was fit to face Barnsley at Oakwell. A crowd of 20,000 was treated to an enthralling but goalless first half. The Barnsley central defensive paring of Eddie May and Paul Futcher (his brother, Ron, was also in the side) gave me very little, if any, leeway in the first period, but when Ronnie Whelan opened our account in the second half the game changed dramatically. Barnsley had to come out of their shell and, with their midfield pushing on, I capitalised on the fact I was finding more space. I went on to notch another hat-trick, though the final scoreline of 4–0 belied the fact that the tie had been entertaining and finely balanced in the first period.

The draw for the semi-finals was broadcast live on television and, as with all subsequent televised semi-final draws, proved something of a non-event. Once the first two teams had been drawn from what was then a velvet bag, there was little point in carrying as there is no longer an element of drama, but carry on they did. Luton were first out of the bag and Everton second, which meant we were to play Manchester United. Having established this, the draw continued, almost as if the plummy-voiced FA officials expected two teams other than Liverpool and United sensationally to emerge from the bag.

I do think the element of excitement surrounding the draws for the FA Cup has been greatly diminished by live broadcast on television. In the days when the draw was broadcast on radio only, incongruously it was both a major and minor event, one that separated the true supporter from the passive fan. The only visual representation was tangential; the newspapers of the following day would carry photographs of a group of long-haired, long-sideburned players of a lower division or non-league club, their ears cocked to the radio.

As a boy I would listen to the draw and imagine it taking place in a dusty, wood-panelled room, the little wooden balls drawn from the velvet bag by octogenarian FA officials wearing dated three-piece suits and wing-collared shirts. I would listen avidly as fingers silently disappeared into the velvet bag, followed by the pronouncement of the number. Try as I might I could never work out the rationale behind those numbered balls. Exeter might come out as number nine which led me to believe, logically, Everton would be number eight, but it never worked out that way. There didn't seem to any reason behind the numbers given to each team, and, as such, one never knew when the number was announced which team it related to. Nowadays, we are told which numbers relate to which teams before the draw takes place. To my mind, it serves to dilute the drama of the occasion still further.

The wooden balls have been replaced by garish plastic balls, like those used in the National Lottery, and bounce around in glass box, like balls in a bingo hall. The draw is no longer made by anonymous denizens of the game but by former players who always come across as being self-conscious, even somewhat embarrassed, and at a loss as to whether they should say something funny or not. The mystery of the FA Cup draw, once a small, but exciting lesser-spotted ritual of football that was once a highlight for fans of whatever hue, has been lost to us for ever. I can't help but feel the FA Cup draw is now puffed up with self-regard. Thanks to television, the draw now has lights, graphics, gaudy colours and, worst of all, an audience who, when asked who they hope their team might be drawn against, predictably reply, 'Manchester United'. Cheap showmanship has replaced intrigue, mystery and entertainment as every last drop of what the draw once offered to fans has been sacrificed in the name of commercialism and TV ratings.

As you might expect, our semi-final against Manchester United at Goodison Park was billed in the press as 'classic Cup encounter' and, for once, the meeting of the two clubs lived up to expectation. The game was full of cut-and-thrust cup-tie football with neither side giving an inch. At the end of ninety minutes the teams could not be separated, a Bryan Robson goal for United in the second half having been cancelled out by one from Ronnie Whelan three minutes from time and so we went into extra time.

During the game I picked up a thigh strain, but, with Paul Walsh having replaced John Wark, had little option but to carry on. Further goals from Frank Stapleton for United and Paul Walsh for us resolved not a thing and so both teams travelled to Maine Road four days later for the replay.

The time element was such that I was not fit for the replay, so I watched what proved to be another absorbing game from the stands. For the first time in the tie we took the lead when, in the first half, United's Paul McGrath diverted an effort from John Wark past Gary Bailey. United, however, refused to be bowed by such a setback. In the second half, with Gary Gillespie on for Kenny, ominously United began to regain the upper hand and eventually their efforts were rewarded. Bryan Robson equalised and then Mark Hughes pounced to give United a lead that, in truth, I never felt they looked like relinquishing.

It was hugely disappointing to exit from the FA Cup at the semi-final stage, particularly as Everton had beaten Luton, so there had been the prospect of an all-Merseyside final. Everton were by then way out in front in the race for the League title but our season was far from over. We had success in the European Cup very much on our minds.

Having disposed of Lech Poznañ and Benfica, we beat FK Austria 5–2 on aggregate to progress to the semi-finals of the European Cup where our opponents were Greek champions Panathinaikos.

Panathinaikos were a very skilful team whose technique was widely admired, but we felt they would not relish a night out at Anfield with the Kop in full cry. So it proved. The first half-hour saw us take the game to Panathinaikos who, for all their skill and guile on the ball, seemingly thought nothing of stopping us any way they could. Those first thirty minutes were littered with fiery fouls committed by the Greek champions, a symphony of whistling from the referee and resultant free-kicks. Yet all this proved merely to be the crucible. Out of the fire came something to remember. I combined with Kenny to create an opening for John Wark, who hit a searing drive past the flailing arms of Laftsis. From that moment on I felt the game was never in doubt.

In the second half I scored twice in the space of ninety seconds, then late in the game Jim Beglin rifled home his first ever goal for the club to make it 4–0. If the looks on the faces of the Greek lads as they left the field were anything to go by, another European Cup final appearance for Liverpool appeared to be a foregone conclusion.

During the game I had been the subject of, let me say, some very close attention from defenders Kyrastas and Antoniou. That in itself didn't bother me as I regarded niggly fouls – shirt-pulling, pushing, jabbing fingers and jibes – as something I had to cope with when playing in Europe. The attention was incessant and went largely unpunished by the referee, but when I was held back by the shirt for the umpteenth time when trying to make a run into space, frustration got the better of me. I made my views known to the referee in no uncertain terms, seemingly too strongly, because rather than cautioning Kyrastas he wrote my name into his book. I was gutted to have been cautioned. Throughout my entire career I was never sent off and only picked up two book-ings, both for dissent. This one stuck in the craw as I had been the constant subject of petty fouls both on and off the ball but had never retaliated.

At the time the rules were such that should I receive another booking in the second leg I would miss the subsequent European tie which, to all intents and purposes, was going to be the final. As a result, before the second leg in Athens, Joe took me to one side and told me he felt the tie was 'nailed' and that he didn't want to run the risk of me receiving another caution which would rule me out of the final. So he had decided to rest me and play Paul Walsh.

I was happy with Joe's decision. I felt he was acting in my best interests as well as those of the team. Having experienced one European Cup final I was eager to play in another.

In the event the lads did a highly professional job out in Athens. They took control of the game from the start and even before Lawro put the issue beyond doubt on the hour with the only goal of the game, I knew another European final was beckoning.

As runners-up in the League and beaten FA Cup semi-finalists, the European Cup represented an opportunity for further glory. Injuries apart, and the fact we had failed to lift a domestic trophy, I'd enjoyed the season up to this point. On the international front I was now an established member of the Wales team and our performances in our World Cup qualifying group had given us a real chance of making it to the 1986 finals in Mexico. With just one game remaining, against Scotland in September 1985, Wales were leading our group by two points from Scotland and Spain, both of whom had two games remaining. The pick of our performances had been a 3–0 win over Spain at the Racecourse Ground. I scored twice on the night, but the pick of our goals was our second, a spectacular scissors volley from Mark Hughes from twenty yards, which beat Spanish keeper Arconada all ends up. This goal, effectively, earned Mark a transfer to Barcelona.

Writing this book has involved a lot of research, as it is difficult for me to recall in detail events of more than twenty years ago. In so doing my memory has been refreshed and, having checked certain facts, I have found I am able to recall stories and incidents that, over the years, have slipped from my memory. There is, however, one story about which, at the time, I was completely unaware. According to records, on the 28 January 1985, Liverpool received an offer of £4.5 million for me from Roma. At the time I had no knowledge of this whatsoever. No one at the club informed me of Roma's bid. Again, I have no idea why. I can only assume the club didn't want to sell me, or that the bones of the proposed deal were unacceptable. Whatever the reason, the interest from Roma was seemingly buried. I'm guessing, but I should imagine Joe wasn't made aware of Roma's bid either, as he was upfront with every player, a man of unyielding integrity. It feels very strange. All these years on I can't imagine what my reaction would have been should I have been made aware of the bid. I was very happy at Liverpool, and in all probability would not have moved at the time, but I would have liked to have known about this offer. It was, after all, my career. Perhaps having made the bid, Roma then had second thoughts and withdrew.

For all the excellent and exciting football played, attendances at League games in 1984–5 continued to fall, though the First Division bucked the trend, as in excess of a million more spectators attended games than in the previous season. It was the lower division clubs that were suffering at the turnstiles, but such concerns paled into insignificance on 11 May when fifty-six fans perished as a result of fire sweeping through the main stand at Bradford City's ground during a game with Lincoln City.

Bradford City were celebrating promotion to Division Two and the tragic scenes were captured on television. It was truly terrifying and, when the death toll was announced, my heart was heavy. There were demands by fire chiefs for significant improvements in standards of safety at grounds, the fire having been deemed to have been started by a discarded cigarette which set fire to rubbish which, over the years, had accumulated under the largely wooden stand which dated back to 1909.

The Bradford fire was terrible and shocking, but it was an accident, albeit one waiting to happen. I had never known such tragedy to inflict itself upon football. My heart went out to all those who had died and their families, little knowing that a fortnight later another tragedy would befall our beautiful game. One that would have a deeply profound effect on me and everyone connected with Liverpool football club and our European Cup opponents, Juventus.

CHAPTER EIGHT

The Boy With the Thorn in His Side

Liverpool's success over the years had been such that it was almost expected we would contest a European final of one sort or another. Certainly the players felt that way. For all expectation was high, I was really looking forward to the European Cup final against Juventus. The Italian champions, who had never won the European Cup, had a star-studded team, which included Italian internationals Tacconi, Bonini, Cabrini, Scirea, Tardelli, Rossi (the hero of their 1982 World Cup success), Polish superstar Boniek and one of my all-time heroes, Michel Platini, who had just been awarded the Ballon d'Or (European Footballer of the Year) for a third successive year. While having the utmost respect for Juventus, I was relishing the thought of pitting my wits against such world-class players, confident that I would give a good account of myself on the night.

Three days before we were due to fly out to Belgium, Joe gathered the players together to talk about the final. What we were not aware of at the time was that Joe had decided to retire. Not wanting to disrupt our preparations he kept the news to himself, though I believe he had made his decision known to the board.

Like Bob, Joe had been a reluctant manager and had taken on the role because of his love of the club and the fact the players had wanted him to do it. He was an emotional guy, and perhaps, at his age, he felt his heart and nerves simply weren't up to the stress and strain of another season of top-flight football.

So, unaware of Joe's pending departure, we were in great spirits when we flew out to Brussels. I couldn't wait for the game, though I wasn't exactly 100 per cent. In our final League game of the season the previous week against Everton, my pal Kevin Ratcliffe caught me on my right shin. I had been unable to take part in training until the day before we set off from Liverpool. The shin was still sore but it was nothing that would prevent me from lining up against Juventus. Then, in that final training session, Kenny drove a ball against my right hand. The ball bent back my thumb (which was very painful), but worse still, the impact broke a bone in my wrist.

There was no way I was going to hospital where I might have the wrist put in plaster which could mean missing the final, so we did running repairs down at Melwood. My wrist was heavily bandaged and I pronounced myself fit to play.

On the night of the game, as our coach travelled through Brussels towards the Heysel Stadium, we passed thousands of Liverpool supporters who appeared to me to be in fine spirit and voice. They gave us a rousing welcome, which made us all the more determined to win the European Cup, so they would have something to crow about back home when they met up with Evertonian friends.

But when we arrived at the stadium and went out to inspect the pitch I was a little taken aback. The stadium looked tired and run-down and I remember thinking it was an unfitting venue for European football's most prestigious occasion. In fact, concerns had already been expressed as to the suitability of the Heysel Stadium for a European Cup final. The question of safety had been raised and Liverpool's secretary, Peter Robinson, had urged UEFA to stage the final at another venue. Apparently, his request had fallen on deaf ears.

What surprised us as we walked around the pitch was that rival groups of fans appeared to be in close proximity to one another on the terraces. There seemed to have been no efforts to segregate the supporters of the two teams but, at this stage, there appeared to be no cause for concern, as the mood among fans came across as being good-humoured. That said, I felt faintly disturbed about what might happen once the game got underway and one team scored.

We didn't spend too long out on the pitch as there was a pre-match game between Belgian youngsters due to take place, so, having looked at the ground and decided what sort of boots to wear, we headed back to the dressing-room.

Our dressing-room was the one situated nearest to the terracing where I had seen both Liverpool and Juventus fans congregating. The room itself was small and very stuffy – again, not in keeping with what one would expect from a top European game – so we opened the windows to let in some fresh air. This was some three-quarters of an hour before the scheduled kick-off. With the windows open we could hear the chanting of the two sets of supporters getting louder by the minute – then, suddenly, there was a loud bang, like that of cannon firing.

On hearing this almighty bang someone, I think it may have been Lawro, said, 'What the fucking hell was that?' The bang was followed by what sounded like distant thunder, only for this sound to be consumed by one of general consternation as all manner of panicking voices found their way through the open windows.

The atmosphere in the dressing-room immediately changed from chirpiness to one of fear and concern. We realised something bad had happened but, at this stage, no one could hazard a guess as to what. Tracy and my dad were in the crowd. Having seen the crumbling nature of the stadium for myself, my first fear was that the floor of one of the stands had collapsed under sheer weight of numbers. I was gripped by fear and, along with the other lads, dashed outside to see what had happened, my mind in a tizzy and my body shaking with nerves.

I knew the tickets I had given to Tracy and my dad were for the main stand so, naturally, that was where I first looked. Mercifully, it was all in one piece. It was only when I looked to the terracing at the far end of the ground, where I had seen both sets of fans mingling, that I was struck by the enormity of what had happened.

The terrace was in pandemonium. The corner to my left was a jumble of human chaos. I could see that part of the wall bordering the side of the terrace had collapsed, which, I assumed, was the source of the loud bang we had heard in the dressing-room.

I was so shocked I just stood looking up at that terrace, as mayhem unfolding before my eyes. I saw what I took to be injured people being carried forward and laid down on the perimeter track. I was struggling to come terms with it all when, eventually, someone took hold of my arm and guided me back towards the dressing-room. My mind was so much in turmoil I had no idea who this 'someone' was.

Minutes before the adrenalin had been pumping furiously as I began to prepare myself for one of the biggest games of my career. Now I was just numbed by shock. No one spoke in the dressing-room. We just sat in silence, each of us totally alone with our thoughts.

Through the open windows came the noise of sirens. I was longing for the sound to fade, but it never did. It just kept coming.

A far more distressing sound then penetrated the room through the open windows, the screams of fans being taken from the stadium on stretchers and the anguished cries of their friends accompanying them. It was a living nightmare. People came in and out of our dressing-room with various accounts of what had supposedly happened. At this stage, though we knew a stadium wall had given way, I was not aware of anyone having died.

For a tortuous hour we sat in that cramped dressing-room and simply waited, only occasionally speculating on what may have caused this disaster and what the immediate outcome was going to be. Chillingly, word came that hundreds of supporters had been badly injured. On hearing this I can vividly recall sitting there as if in a vacuum, as if this really couldn't be happening. We all appeared to be in a state of shock. I know I was. Having looked forward to the final with such relish and anticipation, the last thing I wanted to do now was play a game of football.

Joe left the room only to return some minutes later. He told us UEFA officials were debating what to do: to play the game or cancel it.

Eventually we received word the match was to go ahead. It was felt that to play the game would prevent a further escalation of trouble. Seemingly, officials had little confidence in the police being able to prevent further clashes between the rival set of fans. We all harboured great reservations but the consensus was the officials had probably made the right decision.

We took to the field but I doubt if twenty-two players have ever been less prepared to play football. From harbouring high hopes that this would be a night of nights for Liverpool and myself, my mindset was that I was now participating in the most meaningless game of football of my career. I was still not aware of people having perished, but knowing many people had suffered serious injury I figured there was a likelihood of there having been fatalities. With such a notion in my mind, like the rest of my teammates, I began the game without any conviction whatsoever.

Generally speaking I felt the Juventus players were up for the game. I don't know if some of their players seemed ready for a vendetta, as if they were determined to take it out on us for what had happened, but they applied themselves in way we were unable and unwilling to do.

The game had been underway for only three minutes when Lawro was injured and had to be replaced by Gary Gillespie. In normal circumstances I would have felt for Lawro, but on this occasion I rather envied him for being able to leave the field. Whenever I was in close proximity of Tardelli, he grasped my bandaged wrist and squeezed it. Such was my state of mind I couldn't bring myself to remonstrate with him or the referee, Andre Daina from Switzerland.

I can't recall the actual game in any detail. I am sure that because of the tragic events my mind never committed the football to memory in the first place.

Juventus won 1–0, their goal scored by Michel Platini from the penalty spot. I do remember that Gary Gillespie up-ended Boniek a good yard outside the penalty area. The referee was some twenty-five yards away from the incident but had no hesitation in awarding the penalty. Normally we would have contested such a decision but there was not even a muted protest. Likewise towards the end of the game when Ronnie Whelan was brought down by Bonini inside the Juventus box and the referee, having glanced across to his linesman, waved 'play on'.

When the final whistle sounded I offered the briefest of hand-shakes to the Juventus players and the match officials. I couldn't wait to get off that pitch but we had to endure the presentation ceremony, which, again, seemed wholly incongruous and inappropriate to me, as were the subsequent celebrations of the Juventus players. All I wanted to do was to see Tracy, who I knew would be waiting for me at the reception arranged for after the game. It was then that I was made aware of the full horror of the night.

I have never been to a post-match reception with such a black atmosphere. Players, wives and girlfriends just sat around in small groups, trying to grasp the full sickening story of what had happened.

We heard conflicting stories of what had caused the mayhem. Seemingly Liverpool and Juventus fans in sections Y and Z of the ground were merely yards apart, both sets of fans separated by chicken wire fencing and a thinly policed section of terracing deemed to be 'no-man's-land'. Even to this day it is not clear who first started to throw missiles, but missiles were soon being exchanged. Eyewitness accounts later said that one of the sources of missiles was the crumbling stadium itself; those intent on trouble could literally prise stones from out of the terracing beneath their feet.

As the exchanges became more heated (where were the police during all of this?), a group of so-called Liverpool supporters apparently charged across the terracing, through and over the chicken-wire divide, causing Juventus fans to fall back. The Juventus fans were massed against the side perimeter wall, near to the corner flag. Some attempted to escape the mayhem by scaling the ageing wall, but the wall could not withstand the weight and pressure and it collapsed, sending many fans plummeting forty feet to the ground.

A total of thirty-nine people lost their lives: thirty-two Italian fans, four Belgians, two French and one Irishman. Some six hundred other supporters were injured, many badly. Bodies were taken out of the ground and laid out in rows outside. Others were placed on the perimeter track.

As police, emergency services and officials dealt with the unfolding disaster, a number of Juventus fans in section Z rioted at their end of the stadium. They marched down the perimeter track towards Liverpool supporters, seemingly intent on more trouble, but the police marshalled the numbers and fortunately halted their advance, though these fans and the police were then involved in a series of violent confrontations.

Days later I was still numbed by the suffering and the memory of what I had seen. That this should happen at a football match left me struggling to come to terms with the horror of it all. Everyone connected with the club felt the same way. My heart went out to those who had lost loved ones and friends. I also felt sorry for Joe. That such a thing should have happened in his last game in charge of the club to which he had devoted much of his life was heart-rending.

The aftermath to the Heysel tragedy was predictable. Officially the blame was directed towards Liverpool fans. On 30 May, an official UEFA observer at the game, Gunter Schneider, endorsed this view when he said, 'Only the English fans were responsible. Of that there is no doubt.' UEFA, the owners of the Heysel Stadium, the Belgian FA and Belgian police were never the subject of an enquiry as to their possible culpability. Somewhat unbelievably, there was no official inquiry as to the causes of the disaster.

On 2 June UEFA banned all English clubs from European competition for 'an indeterminate period of time'. In the event

English clubs were banned from playing in Europe for five years. In the case of Liverpool, this was to be six years.

A month later, on 6 July, a Belgian parliamentary investigation into the causes of the disaster stated politicians, police and football administrators must all take part of the blame for what had happened.

The British police launched an investigation to bring the perpetrators of the trouble to justice. As a result of this investigation there were twenty-seven arrests on suspicion of manslaughter, the only extraditable offence applicable to the horrific events at the stadium. Just over half of those arrested were from the Liverpool area; the remainder were from all over England and Scotland. Some of those arrested had previous convictions for violence, in most cases football-related.

Four years later, after a five-month trial in Belgium, fourteen so-called Liverpool fans were given three-year sentences for involuntary manslaughter. Around half of those convicted had their sentences suspended.

To this day I find it curious that Liverpool supporters were involved in the horrific events of that night. In an era when hooliganism blighted the game, our supporters enjoyed a reputation for not causing trouble. On the contrary, they were widely known for their friendliness and sporting behaviour. I do wonder how many of those who threw missiles and were involved in the troubles of that night were actually genuine Liverpool fans. In researching this book, I came across a photograph of a section of the crowd on the terraces. It shows a section of the Liverpool support, most of whom appear to be minding their own business and looking towards the pitch. A small section of fans are near the fencing divide, on the other side of which are Belgian police in riot gear. Some two yards from the fencing, on the Liverpool side, is a young man wearing an Arsenal shirt. The colour image is so clear you can even see the 'Gunners' badge on his breast. I'm not suggesting the young man in question was a source of trouble but, I ask you, what genuine supporter would attend a European Cup final involving Liverpool wearing an Arsenal shirt?

CHAPTER NINE

A Kind of Magic

The Heysel disaster affected everyone connected with football. There was a noticeable depression hanging over the English game as we prepared for 1985–6. Nowhere was this more marked than in the city of Liverpool. As players all we could do was apply ourselves fully to the season ahead, uphold the high standards and proud traditions of the club as set in place by Bill Shankly, and hope that in some way we could restore some self-esteem.

In the aftermath of Heysel, Joe announced his retirement. I was sad to see him go. I owed him so much. When he finally told the players he said, 'I love this club and this game, but feel if I carry on any longer they might not love me any more. There's a perfectly good reason for my decision which I'll make up later.'

The newspapers were full of speculation as to who the next Liverpool manager would be. The general feeling among the players was Phil Neal would get the nod. Phil was a vastly experienced player who had the respect of everyone in the dressing-room. Although not the most outgoing person, he was popular with the lads and his knowledge of the game was considerable. The other name mentioned in the dressing-room was

Kenny. The players felt either would be a popular choice as we knew the tried and trusted ways of Liverpool would continue.

In the end Kenny got the job and opted to become player-manager. One of his first decisions was to appoint Phil as captain. In his dual role Kenny was taking a lot on his shoulders and he sensibly turned to Ronnie Moran, Roy Evans and other members of the Anfield boot room for advice and assistance. In what was an inspirational move on his part, Kenny also managed to persuade Bob to come out of retirement and act in an advisory capacity.

When we reported back for training and Kenny held his first meeting I sensed he was rather uneasy in his new role – and with the change in relationship he now had with the players. Gone was the mischievous, bubbly Kenny I knew so well. He seemed self-conscious as he talked of his hopes for the season ahead, the work ethic and so on. As time went by he reverted to the affable Kenny I knew, though, in so doing, keeping his own counsel. I suspect this was not easy for him as he was still very much a player himself. In those first few days we continued to call him Kenny and he never took issue with that. It was Ronnie Moran who told us things were now different.

'You have to call him "boss" or "gaffer",' said Ronnie. 'He's the manager now and we don't want to compromise his position. As Tommy Steele said, "Things ain't what they used to be".'

So Kenny became 'boss', except during games where it was still thought appropriate to refer to him as Kenny. Then he had to take the complaints, curses and cajoling just like the rest of us.

When Ronnie left the dressing-room, young Brian Mooney asked, 'Who's Tommy Steele?'

'You've heard of Tommy Steele, Brian. He used to be leader of Liberal party,' joked Lawro, and we all took this as our cue to expand the theme.

'Nah, that's Dan Steele.'

'No, no, Dan Steele is that American rock singer.'

'That's Steely Dan.'

'Steely Dan's a band. Bruce Springsteen's the American rock singer.'

'That's right. Known as "the boss".'

'I thought Kenny was the boss.'

'He is.'

'Kenny's a rock singer now?'

'Must be, he's the boss.'

'Bloody hell, things ain't what they used to be.'

'That's what Tommy Steele said.'

Young players like Brian Mooney would sit perplexed by this surreal banter among the senior players, just as I had done when I first joined the club.

It was this sort of comic interchange that helped make our dressing-room a happy one. Though I wasn't conscious of this at the time, this witty repartee also served to establish some sort of hierarchy in the dressing-room. The senior pros would compete with one another to come up with the funniest or cleverest line. We all had fun seeing how long we could continue a joke, and woe betide anyone who came up with a below-par line. This sort of comic banter had been started by Graeme and Kenny and somehow had become a part of our dressing-room culture.

Bill Shankly begat Bob who begat Joe who, in turn, was succeeded by Kenny, and so the traditions and culture of Liverpool football club remained in place. Kenny, presumably adhering to the old dictum 'If it isn't broke don't try and mend it', hardly changed a thing. Pre-season training was typically hard, geared to building strength, stamina and fitness levels, with ball work thereafter. It could have been Joe running the show, or even Bob. We continued the daily routine of meeting and changing at Anfield then travelling to Melwood by coach for training. Even Shanks' policy of players showering back at Anfield rather than at Melwood remained in situ.

During the summer, FIFA lifted the worldwide ban on English clubs, though the European ban remained in place. In those days there were not the enormous commercial benefits to playing in the Far East or the USA, so all our pre-season friendlies took place at home, a backhanded benefit of our European ban for the likes of Oldham Athletic, Crewe Alexandra and Bristol City.

Our first outing was at Burnley. A friendly it may have been, but the attendance at Turf Moor was over 18,000, the highest Burnley had enjoyed for some time. As matches go it was somewhat one-sided, we dominated the game from start to finish and could have won by more than the final scoreline of 5–1. Though it was a friendly I was pleased to score a hat-trick. I felt sharp, confident and I couldn't wait for the real stuff to start. A new, vibrant confidence was sweeping through the ranks, almost as if the disappointment and tragic events of the previous season had further galvanised us as a team.

Our season opened with the visit of Arsenal. After a hesitant thirty minutes we settled down and began to play with purpose and style. Goals from Ronnie and Stevie Nicol gave us the perfect start to the new campaign. The Kop was in good voice, Bruce made two superb saves but also caused a few hearts to thump when, instead of clearing his lines, he decided to dribble the ball past Graham Rix and only just got away with it. It was business as usual.

After such a promising start we then proceeded to be out of sorts in our following two matches. The first, a 2–2 draw at Aston Villa, was something of a disappointment for me. I'd scored in the first half, Jan added a second five minutes from time and, with only three minutes to go, I had the chance of wrapping up all three points when we were awarded a penalty. Goalkeepers usually bounced on their toes ready for take-off when facing a penalty, but Nigel Spinx simply stood rooted to his line, shoulders slightly hunched, and never took his eyes off the stationary ball. When I addressed the ball, in a split-second I glanced-up and he hadn't moved a muscle. But when I made contact with the ball, he moved all right, flinging himself through the air to his left to palm the ball away to safety. Penalties usually fell to Phil Neal or myself, and when we were awarded this one, I had had no hesitation in saying I'd take it. I was hugely disappointed not to have scored, as it would given us the win, but put it down to being just 'one of those things'.

Back in the dressing-room Phil Neal, tongue in cheek, said, 'Next time we get a pen, I'll show you how to put them away.'

'Like hell you will.' I told him, and I meant it. My success rate with penalties was, like Phil's, very good. The fact I'd missed one didn't rock my confidence in the slightest. I was out to enjoy another season of doing what I loved – scoring goals – and I didn't mind how they came about.

I may have been disappointed following the Villa result but the whole team was greatly disappointed when, in our next game, we lost 1–0 at Newcastle United. No player was on song that day and, to compound our problems, Kenny sustained a knee injury that required eight stitches. During the post-match press conference the reporter from the *Liverpool Daily Post* asked, 'Are there any other players injured?'

'Every one of them,' replied Kenny,' but in each case it's their pride.'

Kenny's injury ruled him out of our next game, against Ipswich Town at Anfield. Craig Johnston replaced him in midfield, while

Sammy Lee was recalled in place of Jim Beglin, who, to be fair, had played in midfield against Newcastle when really his best position was at full-back.

Before the match Kenny held a meeting and told us all he was 'very disappointed' with our performance at Newcastle and that 'nothing less than a big improvement' would be acceptable.

'I received a video of the game at Newcastle,' he said. 'I taped *Neighbours* over it.' Then he turned to Ronnie Moran and asked if he wanted to say a few words.

'We've got to go out there and do these, and do them good and proper,' said Ronnie, 'You know that Rudyard Kipling poem, "If", where he says, it isn't whether you win but how you play the game that matters? Great poem, except for that part, which is bollocks. As far as this club is concerned, winning is all that matters – and if we win in style, which all you lot can do, then all the better. So let's do it!'

From the start we had Ipswich on the back foot. Stevie Nicol was making some tremendous runs down the right flank and it was he who gave us the lead after a quarter of an hour. Little over five minutes later, Stevie made progress down the right again, his cross was headed on by Ronnie and I swept the ball past Paul Cooper for number two. Four minutes later Stevie set up Jan Molby, who side-footed home from a yard out.

You can always tell when things are going well for a team. Players make jokes at the expense of others, which doesn't happen when a team isn't performing well. During the halftime interval Jan took some good-humoured stick about his goal.

'Good job it was no further out than a yard; you might have put it wide,' ribbed Craig Johnston.

'And it is a good job it didn't fall to you; you would have been offside,' chimed Jan.

To their credit, Ipswich rallied in the second half but we were never really in danger. The nearest they came to pulling a goal back was when Grob went down smartly to collect a low drive from Alan Sunderland. Just after the hour mark, Stevie and Craig Johnston combined to create an opening for me at the far post and I had the simple task of guiding the ball home. We were so dominant we could have had another three or four instead of the one Craig Johnston volleyed home in the dying embers of the game, but we came off more than happy with the scoreline and our overall performance.

We drew one and won two of our following three matches. I felt we had started to play really well, but Kenny thought we were missing a little bite in midfield, the sort of fire Graeme had once provided. Jan Molby had now settled into the side, and his nous, guile and ability to spray the ball around the park were great assets. Jan was a very gifted and creative midfield player but, with the best will in the world, wasn't the greatest at winning the ball and battling for midfield dominance. Kenny felt Jan needed someone alongside him with a bigger engine, someone who was highly combative and a good ball-winner, so he bought Steve McMahon from Aston Villa.

Steve is a Liverpool lad who'd started his career at Everton before joining Villa. I thought his signing was a masterstroke on the part of Kenny. He turned out to be the final piece in the jigsaw and joined a select band of players – including Kevin Sheedy, Johnny Morrissey and Dave Hickson – who had the honour of playing for both Liverpool and Everton. Joe had actually tried to sign Steve, but he had opted to go to Villa Park as he felt a direct move across Stanley Park would be too insensitive.

Steve made his league debut in a 2–2 draw at Oxford United in mid-September and, barring injuries, was to remain a mainstay of the team throughout the season as we contested the title with Everton and West Ham United, with Sheffield Wednesday and Manchester United hanging on to our coat-tails.

The mark of how good a team Everton had at the time was that although we enjoyed a run-up to Christmas of seventeen games of which we only lost one (at QPR), we had been unable to dislodge Howard Kendall's side from the top of the League. We felt we had proved we had the edge on Everton when goals from Kenny, Steve McMahon and myself helped us gain a 3–2 win at Goodison in September, but Everton's form thereafter had been such we entered the festive period in second place.

Phil Neal had given way at right-back to Stevie Nicol, and Jim Beglin had established himself in the other full-back position at the expense of Alan Kennedy. The idea was for Stevie and Jim to play forward as much as they could, with Lawro forming a central back three along with Alan Hansen and Ronnie. Jan was the playmaker who also proved something of a goal-taker, Steve McMahon was ball-winner, with Craig Johnston happy to operate in something of a free role. Kenny's appearances were intermittent and I found myself playing much of the time alongside Paul Walsh who operated just behind me and in front of the midfield.

Having enjoyed a super run in December we began to stutter. It started with a 2–0 defeat Arsenal in mid-December which was followed by three draws and another defeat, at Manchester City. When the New Year dawned we found ourselves in fourth place.

I didn't think our dip in form called for wholesale changes. We'd enjoyed a good run but the league was so tight and competitive three draws and two defeats had seen us slip down the table. Kenny didn't panic. He kept with the same team and it paid dividends. On New Year's Day we drew 2–2 with fellow title contenders Sheffield Wednesday at Anfield and followed this with a battling win down at Watford.

If you are going to win a Championship, then you have to go to the Watfords of this world, roll your sleeves up and be prepared to battle, which is what we did. Watford played a long-ball game, which they mixed with no-nonsense physical approach. Rarely had I played in a game where the styles of two teams were so contrasted. We preferred to play the possession game, keeping hold of the ball, passing it around to one another, looking for an opening. Watford, on the other hand, seemed to think, 'Why make a dozen passes to get the ball deep into the opponents' half of the field when you can do it with one.'

It might be too much of a simplification to say the pattern of the game was us interchanging passes and, when our attack broke down, Watford simply resorting to lofting a route-one ball down the field to Colin West but, basically, that's what happened. It wasn't pretty.

Lawro, Alan and Ronnie spent so much time in the air against Watford, they could have qualified for a pilot's licence. They were tremendous, as was Steve McMahon in midfield. Two goals from Paul Walsh and one from yours truly enabled us to leave with a 3–2 win from Vicarage Road.

It's funny how seemingly minor things can stick in your mind. I remember travelling back to Liverpool from Watford and our team coach joining the M6 from the M1. Just at this point an item came on the radio to the effect that the Football League, frustrated by the lack of constructive ideas with regard to the ills that beset the game, and annoyed by talk of a plan to revolutionise English football by the creation of a break-away league of First Division teams, had cancelled a proposed meeting with club chairmen. At the time I gave little, if any, thought to this news item, as it seemed the

Football League was doing what it traditionally did when confronted with a major problem: burying its head in the sand. No one on the coach made any comment whatsoever about the suggestion of a new league being created, but it stuck in my mind. Looking back, it goes to show how slow the game's governing bodies were in reacting to new, innovative ideas. It would be another six years before the Premiership came into being.

The Watford result proved the beginning of another great run of results for us which gathered momentum as the New Year unfolded. I was continuing to find the back of the net with some regularity, benefiting from the exquisite passing of Jan Molby, whose presence afforded us extra creativity. What helped Jan was the contribution, combative qualities and work rate of Steve McMahon. Relieved of much of the responsibility for winning the ball in midfield, Jan was now able to give full vent to his considerable talent for creating openings, which, in turn, benefited me. Jan also showed he was a fine taker of a chance himself, and was to end the season with thirteen league goals to his name, one of four Liverpool players to hit double figures, the others being Paul Walsh, Ronnie Whelan and myself.

The hard-fought win at Watford was part of a nineteen-game run during which we suffered but two defeats – at Ipswich and, somewhat worryingly given our Championship aspirations, against fellow challengers Everton. On that day goals from Kevin Ratcliffe and the new Goodison golden boy, Gary Lineker, gave our neighbours bragging rights in the derby match and put a dent in our hopes of overtaking them in the race for the title.

Again, it was so tight at the top that one defeat against Everton saw West Ham leapfrog over us into second place. Everton were three points clear of the Hammers, who led us by a single point. Disappointing as it was, following the Everton defeat we still felt we were in with a good chance of winning the Championship. Everton had some very tough games coming up, including Luton Town, and the general feeling in our dressing-room was that they would come unstuck at some point. The bugbear to visiting Luton was the plastic pitch at Kenilworth Road, which no team liked, not least because it didn't lend itself to sliding tackles, and the bounce of the ball was so different to that of grass you could never judge it. We couldn't play our normal game and we felt the same would be true of Everton.

On the other hand, we felt all our remaining twelve matches were winnable. It would be a tough ask for us to win all twelve, while at the same time hoping Everton dropped at least five points, but that's what we set out to do.

Though we had previously suffered defeats at the hands of Ipswich and Everton, generally speaking our performances had shown a marked improvement since the wobble at Christmas. We bounced back from the disappointment of the derby day defeat with a 2–1 win at Spurs and continued our resurgence. QPR were beaten 4–1, Southampton 2–1 at the Dell which, due to the tight confines of the ground and, relatively speaking, small pitch, was always a difficult place for visiting teams to get a result. In our next game we thrashed Oxford United 6–0 and I added to my goals tally for the season by scoring a hat-trick. The day proved a very good one for Liverpool. Not only did we win convincingly against Oxford but, as we had hoped, Everton came unstuck on Luton's plastic pitch. We were beginning to close the gap on our neighbours.

On the final day of March we avenged our Boxing Day defeat at Maine Road by beating Manchester City 2–0 at Anfield, whereas Everton could do no more than a goalless draw at Manchester United. Having previously drawn with Chelsea, the hope we had of Everton dropping points in their difficult fixtures had became reality and, for the first time, our win against Manchester City saw us assume top spot in Division One.

As the saying goes, our destiny was now in our own hands – all we had to do was to keep on winning. Such was the confidence flowing through the team now that we believed we could keep the run going right to the end. Kenny brought himself back into the side and his presence in the team had a marked effect. He didn't possess the pace of old but he was still a world-class player and what he may have lacked in speed he more than made up for with his guile and experience. He knew how to take control of a game, up the tempo or slow it down as the situation demanded and, of course, he still played those delightful balls into space for me to run on to, and was no slouch when it came to taking a chance himself.

With Everton breathing down our necks and West Ham also in with a shout, we didn't let up. We won six consecutive games which took us to the final day of the season against Chelsea at Stamford Bridge.

To provide Kenny with a fairy-tale end to his first season in charge, we had to win at Chelsea. West Ham were playing their sixth game in sixteen days at West Brom and Everton were at home to Southampton. A draw at Stamford Bridge would be enough for us to win the title should Everton and West Ham lose, but we weren't in the mood to leave anything to chance. We travelled down to London on the Friday with one thing on our minds: the win that would seal the Championship for Liverpool, our great supporters – and Kenny.

We were not without support. As our bus made its way through SW6 towards Stamford Bridge we passed hundreds of Liverpool supporters en route to the ground. The game was a sell-out and among the 44,000 crowd were some 6,000 of our fans, which was a fillip to us. I always felt buoyed at seeing lots of Liverpool supporters when our coach approached a ground for an away fixture. Their presence made me feel we weren't out there on our own, as playing away from home can make you feel a little alienated.

The traffic was heavy in the approach to Stamford Bridge, which slowed us down somewhat. The card game I'd been involved in had wound down, so I sat and took in the sights, trying to commit them to memory, as I hoped, and believed, this was to be a momentous day in my career and for Liverpool.

As our coach turned off North End Road we were caught in a human avalanche rolling down the Fulham Road in cars, coaches, mini-buses and white vans. The nearer we got the round the more supporters were on foot. Groups of Liverpool fans, seemingly drawing confidence from their numbers, sang loudly of their eternal devotion to the club. The Chelsea fans seemed to be doing their best to ignore them, as one might the irritation of someone playing music too loudly on a train when you're due to get off at the next stop.

I'd travelled to enough away matches to recognise certain 'types' amongst the supporters: the optimists who never expect defeat, full of animated talk, hands gesticulating wildly; the ones who travel in hope rather than expectation, experience having taught them the folly of being blindly optimistic, talking quietly and cautiously, heads slightly bowed; the 'experts' who look serious and debate the wisdom of having a right-footed player play on the left, or how Kenny could be better employed if he played 'deeper in the hole' or anything else Jimmy Hill might have said. Children, excited beyond belief, skip as they try to keep up with adults. Clean-cut men in their twenties, not sporting the colours of any club, marching down the pavement with a chip on their shoulder, as if they are looking for trouble. Young and not-so-young women, always bedecked in scarves of the bar variety, and happy, as if going out for a night out on the town. The elderly supporters who, at the time, were quickly becoming an endangered species at games, still incongruously wearing shirt and tie to the match, shoes polished like glass, as if they were off to church.

A football crowd is always going to be more beer and fags than champagne and Chanel, but it is no less appealing for that. Differing personalities will congeal in a moment of high drama into a single voice. For some the key moments of the game will be imprinted into the memory for ever.

Jan Molby failed a fitness test which meant a recall for Lawro, who had been omitted for our two previous games, the wins against Birmingham and Leicester City. Stevie Nicol and Jim Beglin continued at full-back, with Lawro forming a central back three with Alan Hansen and Gary Gillespie. Kenny, Ronnie, Craig Johnston and Kevin MacDonald formed the midfield. As usual, I was to plough a lone furrow upfront.

When the game got underway the atmosphere inside the Bridge was highly charged. Chelsea began in determined mood and in those opening minutes we struggled to get possession of the ball but, once we did, we settled down to play our trademark football. After eight minutes we mounted our first attack of note and nearly took an early lead. Nigel Spackman slipped as he went to meet a cross from Stevie Nicol, and the ball ran through to Kevin MacDonald, whose first-time effort was pushed around the post by Tony Godden. From the resultant corner Stevie had a shot blocked and, with the ball flying about the box, Craig Johnston managed to latch on to it long enough to test Godden again. Just when I thought we had Chelsea under the cosh they broke, and it

A KIND OF MAGIC

needed a smart save from Grob to prevent us going one down. A little reminder that this afternoon was not going to be a jolly.

Stevie Nicol and Jim Beglin were very good at getting forward and did so to excellent effect. On twenty-three minutes Stevie won a corner on the right and when the ball came over, Gary Gillespie beat everyone except Tony Godden, who scrambled his firm header away for yet another corner.

I'd noticed the Chelsea players seemed to want too much time to mark-up from set-pieces and that we'd rather played into their hands by not quickly taking a corner or free-kick. So when Godden turned Gary Gillespie's effort for a corner, I turned to Craig and said, 'Hurry, quick one.'

Craig duly obliged. He ran with the ball to the corner, placed it on the 'D' and wasted no time in floating it back into the box. Jim Beglin flicked it inside. With the Chelsea defence caught unawares, there was Kenny to chest the ball down then hit a volley off the outside of his right foot past Godden.

I can still vividly see, in my mind's eye, Kenny running past Godden's right-hand post, arms outstretched, his face grinning like a Cheshire cat. With the ball in the net, our considerable support offered ample evidence of their location in the ground. Amidst a cacophony of cheers form our supporters the players mobbed Kenny, genuinely delighted that he, of all people, had made the breakthrough.

The first half ended with Chelsea giving it real go but, for all their pressure, I never felt they made any impression on our defence. During the interval I can't recall anyone asking, or anyone telling us, how Everton and West Ham were doing. We just wanted to win the match and the Championship.

Chelsea began the second half in much the same way they ended the first, working very hard and keeping us penned into our own

261

half of the field without every truly testing Grob. I felt I should have had a penalty when Doug Rougvie brought me down after I'd made a decent run into the Chelsea penalty area, but the referee, Mr Shapter, waved 'play on'. Rougvie looked across at me and said, 'Bit lucky to get away with that.'

Minutes later someone, I didn't see who, caught me in the face with a flying elbow when a knot of us challenged for a high ball. Again, to my bemusement, the referee kept play moving. With challenges becoming more heated, Mr Shapter eventually had to intervene when Craig took exception to a wayward tackle from John Millar and the pair of them tried to swap shirts by wrenching them off one another. No bookings though, just a word from Mr Shaper that both should concentrate on their football. These days both would probably have been sent off.

With fifteen minutes remaining Kenny could have put the issue beyond doubt; that he didn't being down to a moment of uncharacteristic profligacy on his part when he fired over from the edge of the box with Godden scrambling across his goal.

It didn't matter. In an effort to salvage something from the game Chelsea gave it one more go but when Mr Shapter blew for time it was all red-shirted embraces.

Delighted to have regained the title from Everton, our large following of travelling fans aired their tonsils and were still singing when we were called upon to pose for an 'official' title-winning photograph. We were so excited, happy and energised we couldn't comply with the photographers' request to remain still. We were jumping up and down, dancing jigs, hugging one another. Eventually the photographer gave up asking us to pose and took his shot.

During the post-match interview, which seemed to go on for ever, a *People* journalist intimated Kenny's peach of a goal was a great one to have clinched the Championship.

'Ach, it could have just easily gone in the enclosure,' replied Kenny, decrying his goal and thus his part in the win that brought the Championship to Anfield for the sixteenth time, a League record.

'Everyone else contributed more than me. I was a bit player,' added Kenny. 'Like Rushy with his goals, Jan Molby, who really came into his own, Steve McMahon, Bruce, the back four, everyone, including Bob Paisley and the backroom staff.'

Kenny might have fooled some, but not the record books. He was the first player-manager to win the Championship and, more to the point, was on the brink of achieving the 'double' in his first season as a manager, because we had also made it to the final of the FA Cup where were due to play Everton.

We were very disappointed not to be competing in Europe, the first time this had happened to Liverpool for twenty-one years. Though, of course, fully understanding the reasons as to why, I couldn't help feeling that European football was also missing out because I firmly believed, at the time, that Liverpool and Everton were the best two teams in Europe. That season's European Cup final between Barcelona and Steau Bucharest confirmed my view. It was a travesty of a game and stunningly boring. From the start Steau seemed intent on smothering football and taking the game to penalties, which they succeeded in doing. Barca made a hash of the shoot-out and Steau were crowned as European Champions.

I'd go as far as to say that the side of 1985–6 was one of the best Liverpool teams I had the privilege of playing in. We played open, attacking football, though we were far from being alone in that respect. Everton, West Ham, Manchester United, Sheffield

Wednesday, Spurs and Chelsea were all given to playing enterprising and entertaining football and yet, due to circumstances over which we players had no control, attendances at First Division matches and Football League games in general had slumped to an all-time low.

In 1985–6, just over 9 million spectators attended First Division matches, almost 5 million fewer than in 1976–7. The total number of spectators attending games was less than 16.5 million, half of what it is today. The Heysel tragedy, the Bradford fire and the inability of the game's ruling bodies and the authorities to rid our game of the criminal element, had all combined to make football a far less attractive proposition than once it had been.

In September I had played in Wales's crucial World Cup qualifying game against Scotland, a game we had to win. We didn't. A draw put Scotland above us on goal difference. Spain were still favourites to qualify, but the draw against Wales meant that Scotland, with the not too arduous task of winning a play-off against the winner of the Oceania qualifying group, were set fair for Mexico. Scotland achieved the draw against Wales courtesy of a highly disputed penalty, but our chagrin and the joy of the Scots was shattered on the night with the news that the Scotland manager, Jock Stein, had died of a heart attack.

Jock Stein's death was a tragic end to what had been a pulsating game of football. Everyone was shocked and everyone mourned. It somehow contrived to further beset football with more negativity. Stories of death relating to football were understandably given precedence in the media and, however unwittingly, served to make football unpalatable in the eyes of much of the nation.

In 1986 English football was in dire need of a good news story, a high profile occasion where two teams played cavalier football, in which both sets of fans openly displayed impeccable behaviour, friendliness and sportsmanship. The first ever all-Merseyside FA Cup final was to provide all that and more.

Our route to Wembley took us via Norwich City, Chelsea, York City (again we survived a scare at Bootham Crescent only to progress at Anfield with something to spare), Watford (more altitude-testing for Hansen and co.) and Southampton in the semi-finals.

Our semi-final against Southampton took place at White Hart Lane and went to extra time. There hadn't been a fag paper's width between the two teams, Southampton doing well to overcome the loss of Mark Wright, who, sadly, broke his leg in the thirty-ninth minute of the game. Just when it appeared the teams could not be separated, nine minutes into the extra period, I managed to break the deadlock.

Kevin Bond played the ball back to goalkeeper Peter Shilton. As soon as I saw what Kevin was going to do I closed in, more in hope than expectation, but you never know.

I soon did know. Kevin hadn't put enough behind the back pass and, having manoeuvred myself into a position whereby I could nip in and intercept any pass back to Shilton that didn't have enough purchase on it, I did just that. As soon as they saw me take to my toes, Shilts and Kevin Bond took to theirs, but with the benefit of having anticipated what might happen I reached the ball first. Shilts, as he always did, came rushing out to cut down my angle of vision but I had a second or so advantage over him, saw the gap and fired low into the corner. Shilts was furious with Kevin. We were ecstatic.

Southampton then threw caution to the wind. The old Liverpool war horse, Jimmy Case, and Andy Townsend gave it all they had, working hard to take the game to us, but our midfield were more than their equal. Five minutes later Kenny played yet another wonderfully timed pass behind the Southampton backline. I sprinted into the space where the ball now was, and fired across Shilts to ensure we would be coming back to London for the final.

In the week that separated our clinching of the League title and the FA Cup final we felt the tension and expectation. Both teams had it all to play for. The tabloid press billed the match as a shoot-out between myself and Gary Lineker. I didn't pay any heed to that (I doubt if Gary did, either), and approached Wembley brimming with confidence. I was on song goal-wise, and felt we were the better team.

For much of my childhood the FA Cup final had been the only domestic club game broadcast live on television. The whole nation seemed to settle down to watch it and I lapped up all the pre-match items on television, even the often excruciatingly embarrassing strand featuring celebrity supporters, and the 'It's a Knockout' competition between the rival fans. In the late 1960s and 1970s it was a novelty for there to be television coverage of football at eleven-thirty in the morning. I'd watch the players of the respective finalists at their team hotel and try to imagine what it must be like, not only to prepare to play in an FA Cup final but to stay in a hotel. I'd avidly watch the 'How They Got There' feature, not least because, due to the restrictions placed upon tele-vised football by the FA and Football League, we hadn't seen some of the games the teams had won on their route to Wembley. I also would enjoy seeing footage of past finals, particularly those grainy black-and-white images from the 1950s and early 1960s accom-panied by the reserved tones of commentator Kenneth Wolstenholme who, unlike commentators of today, seemed solely intent on describing the action.

Back then, the FA Cup final was the most important and

exciting day in the football calendar, not least due to the rare treat of televised coverage. Nowadays there is live football on television every day of the week, sometimes three games in one day. You don't have to watch them, of course, but the saturation coverage has served to dilute the impact and attraction of the FA Cup final. It is in danger of coming across as being just another televised game, particularly as, the 2008 final excepted, it invariably features at least one of the big four Premiership clubs.

Quite a bit of the boyhood enthusiasm I had for the FA Cup final remained with me as we prepared to meet Everton. In fact, I was so excited I had trouble sleeping the night before the game. I lay in bed thinking I must be the only player whose boyhood dream was proving more powerful than the need to adopt a totally professional attitude and get some sleep! At the time I thought I was being a little silly. All these years on, I'm rather happy I thought that way.

The teams for what was to be an historic FA Cup final lined up as follows:

LIVERPOOL: Bruce Grobbelaar; Mark Lawrenson, Jim Beglin, Stevie Nicol, Ronnie Whelan, Alan Hansen, Kenny Dalglish, Craig Johnston, Ian Rush, Jan Molby and Kevin McDonald.

EVERTON: Bobby Mimms, Gary Stevens, Pat van den Hauwe, Kevin Ratcliffe, Derek Mountfield, Peter Reid, Trevor Steven, Gary Lineker, Graeme Sharp, Paul Bracewell and Kevin Sheedy.

Referee: Alan Robinson (Portsmouth)

There were notable absentees from the line-ups. Steve McMahon had broken his leg, hence the inclusion of Kevin MacDonald, who didn't even feature in the Liverpool squad named in the match programme. For Everton, Neville Southall was injured – he had missed the last quarter of the season – and Bobby Mimms had taken over in goal. Southall's omission led to a unique piece of FA Cup history. Pat Jennings had retired from the game, but had been signed by Spurs in case of emergency. Pat had been eligible to play for Spurs in the FA Cup, but his services had not been called upon. Everton, in need of cover for Bobby Mimms, had received special dispensation from the FA to sign Pat, even though he was already registered to play for Spurs. In the event Pat played for neither club but, to the best of my knowledge, remains the only player registered to play for two clubs in the FA Cup in the same season.

I still have the match programme from the final. It contains a heartfelt message from FA chairman Bert Millichip, who, no doubt reacting to the negative headlines the game had been receiving, made a plea for MPs, potential sponsors, players, stars of entertainment, and parents to lend their support to the FA's 'Friends of Football' initiative. All very laudable, but there was an indication as to how outmoded was the thinking of the FA when Bert asked all parents to encourage their children to take an interest in football, adding, 'not just Dad who takes son to the match, but also Mum who washes the kit'.

Everton began the final in determined mood and dominated the early stages. We just couldn't get going and fell behind after twenty-eight minutes. The Everton goal came, uncharacteristically, as the result of a mistake on the part of Kenny, who dwelt too long on the ball and was caught in possession. Peter Reid capitalised and hit a terrific thirty-yard pass through our defence that saw Gary Lineker outpace Alan Hansen to go clear. I thought Grob did well to block Gary's initial shot, but the ball fell kindly and he rounded a still-prostrate Grob to score what was his fortieth goal of the season.

During the interval the first thing Kenny did was apologise for having lost possession which led to the Everton goal. That said, he told us we hadn't started to play anywhere near to our potential, and had allowed Everton to boss it. We had to seize the initiative in the second half.

That was easier said than done against a side the calibre of Everton. Ten minutes into the second half, there were two moments when I thought we were all but done for when Kevin Sheedy, then Trevor Steven, both fired narrowly wide with Grob beaten. Having had two golden chances and not taken them, I felt Everton had missed their opportunity to kill us off. Having survived those two scares we began to play with much more purpose and, for the first time in the game, Everton found themselves under pressure. We turned the screw and eventually our pressure told.

Ronnie intercepted a pass from Gary Stevens, slipped the ball to Jan, who sent me clear. I sidestepped the onrushing Bobby Mimms, glanced up to get my bearings and stroked the ball home.

Minutes later we took the lead. I played the ball to Jan, whose cross narrowly evaded Kenny, only for Craig Johnston to arrive at the far post and unerringly despatch the ball into the net. Craig jumped into the air with glee, his legs crossing like a pair of scissors as we all made beeline for him.

With our supporters roaring us on we continued to take the game to Everton who, knowing they had to be more adventurous, brought on Adrian Heath for Stevens and resorted to playing just three across the back.

With little over five minutes remaining Jan and Ronnie combined to open up the Everton defence and I ran through to fire the ball into the far corner of the net, in so doing dislodging an automated camera that had been placed there. That piece of film was subsequently shown countless times on television. Curiously, I never got tired of seeing it.

It had been a thrilling final. At one point, things did look decidedly dodgy from our point of view but, not for the first time, we had galvanised as a team to assert ourselves on a game. A turning point had been Grob making a superb save from Graeme Sharp when we were trailing. If that had gone in, or the subsequent efforts from Sheedy and Steven, our task would have been monumental. As it was we rode our luck, then worked hard to play ourselves back into the game. If you were to ask me the telling difference between us and Everton on the day, I'd say we took our chances, whereas Everton didn't.

We were all delighted for Kenny. To win the 'double' in his first season as a manager was an extraordinary achievement. Needless to say I was delighted to have scored twice in my first FA Cup final, exceeding even my childhood dreams.

I was especially pleased when Alan Hansen led us up to the Royal Box to receive the FA Cup from the Duchess of Kent. Before the final Alan received the news that he had been omitted from the Scotland squad for the World Cup finals in Mexico (they had managed to win their play-off against Australia). His omission hurt him deeply and, for the life of me, I couldn't understand why such a top-class defender had been overlooked by Scotland. Alan was one of the best defenders of his time, and to my mind it was little short of criminal that Scotland had thought to embark upon the finals of a World Cup without him.

As we celebrated our success at Wembley and, of course, the magical 'double', I did spare a thought for Everton. Fierce local rivals they might be, but their performances that season had merited a trophy. They played attractive and entertaining football. At Wembley, they would probably have triumphed against any other team, but all the 'rules' that seemed to apply to other sides didn't work on us. We had the all-round quality, work ethic, grit and determination to win games when it appeared we might be down and out. We had so much quality in the ranks I firmly believed we were, at the time, the best team in Europe, if not the world. But of course we were never going to have the opportunity to prove that.

It had been another memorable season for me. In addition to having scored twenty-three goals in the League I had scored six in the FA Cup and three in the League Cup (in which we had reached the semi-finals only to beaten by QPR). Yet again I had topped thirty-plus goals and continued the record of Liverpool never having lost a game in which I managed to score.

These days one often hears complaints about the number of foreign players in our game and concerns that it is hindering the progress of home-grown talent. I think such views are valid, particularly when I see certain Premiership clubs fielding teams without a single British player in their ranks. However, it is worth noting that the Liverpool side that won the 'double' in 1985–6 did not contain a single English player, either. The only player born in England was Mark Lawrenson who, though he was born in Preston, played for the Republic of Ireland. I happened to mention this fact not so long ago to a friend who is an ardent Liverpool fan and something of a club historian.

'You're absolutely right, Ian, but even in 1986 that was nothing new,' he told me, 'When Liverpool played their first ever match in the Football League in 1893, the team contained only one Englishman, the goalkeeper, and he had a Scottish name, McOwen. The rest of the team were Scots, Irish and Welsh.'

Following our success at Wembley, the newspapers were full of stories that I was high on the wanted list of several top

Continental clubs, including Terry Venables' Barcelona. According to the press, Juventus were favourites to sign me. Other than reports in the newspapers I hadn't heard anything to this effect, so paid little heed to what I believed to be speculation. Apart from anything else, following the tragic events of Heysel, I didn't for one moment believe that Juventus would want to sign a Liverpool player, as it would invoke the ire of their supporters.

However, when I reported back to Liverpool following a summer holiday with Tracy, Kenny asked if I would call in to his office. Seemingly there was something urgent he needed to discuss with me.

(Right) The headline reads 'The Lady in Rose Also Celebrates Rush'. Note the crumbling state of the terracing at the much-vaunted Delle Alpi stadium.

© Steve Hale

© Bob Thomas/Getty Images

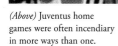

(Above) Juventus home games were often incendiary in more ways than one.

(Right) In action for Juve against Sampdoria. As the lone striker there was a distinct lack of service and support so I often had to go it alone.

© PA Photos

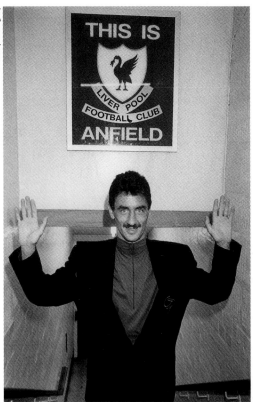

(Left) On my return to Anfield from Juventus. The marks on the base of the sign show where the paint has been worn away by Liverpool players tapping the sign for good luck when taking to the field.

(Below) Liverpool fans display their delight on my return, though I don't think it equalled mine. My year at Juventus was not so much an 'Italian Job', more a case of 'The Self-Preservation Society'.

(Below) Things got a little lax during Graeme Souness's time as manager, particularly the dress code on match days. Only kidding. We always made the most of the club Christmas party.

(Above) From left to right: Ronnie Rosenthal, me, Ronnie Whelan, Alan Hansen and John Barnes with a trophy we got to know rather well – the League Championship.

(Below) How Kenny managed to get through an FA Cup final at Wembley wearing that hat I'll never know. When I first joined Liverpool I didn't warm to Kenny but he was a tremendous influence on me and my career, and we became the best of friends.

(Below) Playing for Wales against Albania in a European Championship qualifier in 1994.

(Above) OK, Mark, say you fulfilled your dream of being a manager, and Manchester City offered you a job, what would you do?' Mark Hughes and I take time out from a Wales training session before playing Belgium in 1991.

(Below) At home with some of my trophies. On the left is the FWA Footballer of the Year award.

(Left) With Robbie Fowler following Liverpool's victory over Bolton Wanderers in the 1995 League (then Coca-Cola) Cup. From the first moment I saw him I knew Robbie had the potential to be a great player.

(Below) Following my final game for Liverpool at Anfield I throw my shirt to the Kop and those fans who mean so very much to me.

(Right) Playing for Leeds United against Liverpool. Jason McAteer had been repeatedly pulling at my shirt. I tell him, 'If you want it that bad, wait till the end of the game and I'll give it to you.'

(Below) I enjoyed my seven months at Newcastle, standing in for an injured Alan Shearer. Irrespective of what some might say, the holding I am subjected to here is part and parcel of professional football – you just have to get on with the game.

© PA Photos

(Above) John Barnes and I share a joke with the media at a Newcastle press conference.

© PA Photos

© Getty Images

(Right) Celebrating a goal during my spell with Sydney Olympic against Marconi. The standard of football in the Australian National League was very good, though most of the best Australian players leave to ply their trade overseas, such as my then Sydney team-mate Brett Emerton.

(Right) Sharing a joke with Kenny after my testimonial game at Anfield.

(Below) In addition to being Elite Coach for the Welsh FA Trust and coaching duties abroad, I manage to fit in media work, here commentating on a Liverpool game with John Aldridge.

(Above) Chester manager, November 2004. I look bemused as Northampton score, though we came away from Sixfields with a 1–1 draw.

(Above) It is a tradition that Liverpool players get together to raise money for charity. Here at a dinner, on the front row with Kenny and I, are club director David Moores and Roy Evans. Third from right, standing, is Ray Houghton look-alike, the actor Vince Earl (formerly of *Brookside*).

(Left) With Her Majesty the Queen at Buckingham Palace on receiving my MBE for services to football.

(Right) My family mean everything to me: with Daniel, Tracy, Jonathan and Alfie the dog at home.

CHAPTER TEN

Say Hello, Wave Goodbye

It had been some time since I had been in the manager's office. The flock wallpaper had gone, as had the plaster ducks and the picture of the scrambling pigs. 'Fings' weren't what they used to be. Sitting alongside Kenny was our secretary, Peter Robinson.

'The stories in the newspapers about you moving,' said Peter.

'Well, that's the newspapers for you,' I said dismissively. 'It's the close season. You know how it is, Peter; it's the silly season for newspapers. They haven't got any news to write about.'

'That's as maybe, Ian, but those stories, they're true.'

I literally flopped back in my chair. I was totally flabbergasted. I was being moved on? My mind went blank with the shock of the news.

Peter went on to say that, reluctantly, the club were prepared to sell me. The European ban was having a severe effect on club finances and, after much deliberation, the club had agreed so sell me as a solution to a cash-flow problem that would only get worse unless a sizeable injection of capital was generated.

I was struggling to get my head around the situation but noticed how carefully Peter had phrased his words. His words implied it wasn't himself, the chairman, the board or Kenny who was prepared to sell me, but 'the club'. As if no one was assuming responsibility for my sale, or, more likely, didn't want to be seen as being responsible.

'How'd you feel?' he asked.

'How do you think I feel?'

Right then, I didn't know how I felt about the situation. My initial reaction was mixed. I loved it at Liverpool. There were no problems in my private life. Things were great with Tracy and me. I had just helped Liverpool to the 'double'. I was scoring in excess of thirty goals a season. Why on earth would I want to leave this club?

On the other hand, I reasoned that if the club didn't want me to stay I might as well go. I didn't want to hang around like an unwanted guest at a party. Seemingly, I had no value to 'the club' other than the transfer fee to be received for my services. Out of curiosity, I asked if any of the stories in the press about Italian clubs making offers for me were true.

'We've had several enquires from European clubs,' Peter informed me. 'Two serious offers: one from Barcelona, the other from Juventus.'

Another thought then entered my mind. If the club had received several enquiries about me, it stood to reason that someone within the club had circulated the news that Liverpool were willing to sell me. I was in my mid-twenties but was streetwise enough not to believe in such a coincidence as several clubs simultaneously making an unsolicited enquiry about me on the off-chance Liverpool might be willing to sell.

Kenny suggested I give the matter considered thought, discuss the situation with Tracy, and perhaps speak to the clubs as it might help me make up my mind.

I first talked the matter over with Tracy. We eventually concluded that it was no good arriving at a decision until I had spoken to Barcelona and Juventus and heard what was on the table. I didn't have an agent at that time, so I dealt with the matter myself.

I first spoke to Terry Venables at Barcelona. He didn't have to sell the club to me. I knew plenty about Barcelona. The deal was very tempting. The financial package on offer would set me up for life. Mark Hughes, one of my good pals from the Wales team, was already with Barcelona and telephoned me several times, on each occasion encouraging me to join him at the Nou Camp. Barcelona were willing to play £4.3 million. It transpired Juventus were willing to offer somewhat less for my services, £3.2 million. Either way, Liverpool's perceived cash flow problem would be eased by more than just a bit.

I went back to see Kenny.

'Don't worry about the size of the fee, or getting the most for the club,' he said. 'Just go to where you feel you would enjoy your game more. And if you don't want to go at all, we'll be only delighted to keep you.'

I sensed, however, that Liverpool did want to sell me and, although Kenny's words were undoubtedly sincere, no one else with any authority within the club was telling me they wanted me to stay.

I had a really tough decision to make. I truly loved playing for Liverpool and had no reason to believe I would continue to be anything other than very happy if I stayed. But financially, it was the optimum time for me to seek pastures new. With Tracy and I getting married the following summer, I felt I had a future family to think of now.

There was another issue I had to take into consideration.

Because I had been at Liverpool from my teenage years I was not one of the club's big earners. It's a fact of football life that you get a much better deal from a club when you join them as an established player in your mid-twenties, as opposed to a player who joined in his teens and has been given pay rises on a gradual basis, which is why some agents are keen to secure a move for a player who is in his twenties, even though the player may be settled at his current club. In addition to which, the agent will earn a much bigger commission when he does move a player, rather than just taking a percentage of a wage from a player who stays with the same club for a number of seasons.

Juventus came across as being very keen to sign me. Liverpool granted me permission to speak to them so I travelled down to London to meet officials from the club, their President Mr Boniperti and the money-man, Gianni Agnelli. I took a solicitor to listen to the legal aspects and advise me accordingly.

On the journey down a thought suddenly occurred to me. I didn't speak Italian and neither did my solicitor. What's more, I'd heard Boniperti and Agnelli didn't speak any English. I thought, 'This is going to be some meeting.' Happily, when I arrived at the hotel in which the meeting was to take place, I discovered the Juventus party had had the foresight to engage an interpreter.

In meetings, as in life, you have to face your demons. The first question I asked was: in light of the tragic events at Heysel, if I did sign for Juventus, what sort of reaction could I expect from their supporters and Italian people in general? I was assured by all that the welcome I would receive would be nothing less than warm and friendly. Nobody in Turin held Liverpool players, or British people as a whole, responsible for the tragic events of that fateful night. Mr Boniperti was at pains to emphasise my coming from Liverpool would not pose a problem for me or anyone else, that it was a good thing as it would help repair relations between the two clubs.

Mr Boniperti was keen to sign a 'big name' from British football and told me he was pleased I was a Welshman. In his own days as a player, in the 1950s, he had played alongside the great John Charles at Juventus. He hoped my impact at the club would be similar to that of the 'Gentle Giant'.

The talk eventually turned to money. The terms on offer did not quite match those of Barcelona. However, I quickly worked out that the three-year contract on the table would earn me over eight times as much as I could earn with Liverpool.

I returned home and endured a couple of restless nights as I turned the matter over and over in my mind. Deep down I didn't want to leave Liverpool. I was still living at home with my parents, and had a wonderful relationship with Tracy. I wouldn't exactly go as far as to say I was living in a comfort zone, but I was more than comfortable with my life. OK, I was in my mid-twenties, but uprooting and going to live in Italy, or Spain, would be one hell of a wrench, not least because it would be the first time I had ever left home.

With my impending marriage to Tracy I felt the time was right to start a new chapter in my life and career. After some deliberation I decided to opt for Juventus, basically because I felt Serie A was the biggest stage in the football world and I wanted to pit myself against the best week in and week out. Tracy and I were also quite taken with the thought of the Italian lifestyle. But there was also another reason.

The events of that tragic night in Brussels had remained with me. By joining Juventus I thought I could give the people of Turin something back, not anything that would erase the pain they felt, but something, I didn't know what, that was positive.

I'm not trying come across as some sort of saint. If there had been a significant discrepancy in the two deals I was offered, I would almost certainly have opted for Barcelona. The tipping moment came when I was invited over to Turin to have a look around the city and the club itself.

It was arranged that I should travel with Peter Robinson and the club's lawyer. As I had still to make my final decision and the Barcelona offer was still on the table, it was agreed our visit should be kept secret. Some secret. When we arrived at Turin airport some 8,000 Juventus fans were there to greet me.

As we walked across the tarmac to the airport terminal and Peter Robinson saw the thousands of supporters awaiting us, he turned to me. 'I'm very annoyed at this,' he said. 'Your visit here was supposedly to be kept secret.'

'They're not here for me,' I said tongue in cheek. 'They've come to see you. Surely you know you're one of the most popular club secretaries in Europe.'

The meeting with the Juventus officials was very amicable, but just when I thought everything was going well, there was a caveat. I was informed that the rules in Italy at that time limited foreign players to two per club. Juventus already had Michel Platini and the Danish international Michael Laudrup, which proved something of a spanner in the works. So where, I asked, did that leave me?

I was told there was 'no problem', which, to me, there obviously was. Mr Boniperti went on to say Juventus were so keen to have me they were willing to sign me there and then. Apparently, Michel Platini had planned to retire at the end of 1985–6 but had been persuaded to stay on at the club for one more season.

'When Platini retires at the end of 1986–7, we will recall you,' Mr Boniperti concluded.

'From where?' I asked, becoming confused and not a little concerned.

'Lazio,' replied Mr Boniperti much to my surprise. 'We will sign you now and loan you out to Lazio for the season, then, when Platini retires, you come back here.'

'With all due respect, no,' I said, and I meant it.

I was having none of it. Joining Juventus was a massive decision for me but I was on the brink of making that decision because I considered them to be one of the greatest clubs in the world. I was on the point of committing myself to Juventus, not Lazio who, at the time, were in Serie B. To me such a move would be akin to me leaving Liverpool to spend a season at Sheffield United or Sunderland.

At first there was an awkward silence, then Juve's lawyer said something to Mr Boniperti who then spoke to the interpreter who, in turn, spoke to the Liverpool club lawyer and Peter Robinson. I sat sipping water and wondering what the hell was going on.

The group got together, there was a huddled conversation, but no one appeared to be smiling, which told me nothing could be agreed.

Eventually I gestured to Peter and the Liverpool lawyer.

'OK, if I have to go on loan, what about this,' I suggested. 'I sign for Juventus and I go back to Liverpool on loan for the season.'

The lawyer raised his eyebrows, but I could tell by the slight sideways nod of his head he thought this a possible solution to the impasse. Peter Robinson practically grazed his lower jaw on his shirt buttons at the thought of Liverpool receiving over £3 million but still having me for another season.

My suggestion sparked another huddled conversation only, this time, it ended with nodding heads and smiles all round.

For all the considered thought you give to a certain matter, often, in arriving at your decision, rather than being convinced, you convince yourself you have made the right choice. There's a difference between the two and, more often than not, we are left with little option but to follow the latter because, in truth, we know we are incapable of being absolutely certain. That's how it was for me regarding my decision to join Juventus. When I was a boy I thought everyone – teachers, doctors, nurses, politicians, parents even – were so self-assured, that they always made the right decision. There was no grey area, no variables. As an adult I knew that not to be true. In life, no matter how much thought you give to an issue, often, you are left thinking you have done little more than take a punt.

Sometimes you're right and it turns out for the good, sometimes not. *C'est la vie.*

I signed on the dotted line.

As I prepared for 1986–7 I was acutely aware that I was not so much on loan as on trial that season as far as our supporters – and, I sensed, some of my Liverpool teammates – were concerned. I was aware that when Kevin Keegan left Liverpool for Hamburg on a similar kind of delayed deal in 1977, he had evoked the ire of many of our supporters. Nobody could ever accuse Kevin of giving anything less than 100 per cent in any game he ever played in, but a core of our supporters took his departure badly. That said, I think what evoked anger in a number of fans was Kevin saying he was leaving Liverpool to 'further his career'.

I think if Kevin had said his decision to join Hamburg was down to him wanting to ensure the financial security of his family, Liverpool fans would have understood. What they didn't under-stand was how leaving a club as successful as Liverpool, the

European champions, could possibly enhance his career as a player. Many fans felt Kevin had not been straight with them, hence the bad feeling.

I did not want that sort of thing happening to me. I felt I enjoyed a special relationship with Liverpool supporters ever since I broke into the team, and I didn't want to my Anfield career to end in misunderstanding or, heaven forbid, acrimony. So I was straight with our supporters. I told the media that my decision to leave Liverpool had initially not been mine, but once the ball was rolling, I'd made the decision to join Juventus for the financial security of my family. To the best of my knowledge, no one took umbrage with that.

I wasn't the only striker to leave Merseyside. Having failed to sign me, Terry Venables didn't look too far from Anfield for an option. He signed Gary Lineker from Everton. The fee was £4,262,000, a record for a Spanish club. It was reported Gary would bank some £1.5 million if he saw out his contract at Barcelona – excluding wages and bonuses. Somehow I couldn't help but think Gary would be certain he had made the right decision.

I wanted to give Liverpool supporters a final season to really remember me by, and the only way I could think of doing that was to score as many goals as I could. Of course, my impending move to Italy did not go without comment in the dressing-room. Previously the lads had referred to me as Ian or Rushy. I was now to be known as Luigi.

During the summer of 1986, England returned from Mexico having been eliminated from the World Cup following defeat against Argentina in the quarter-finals, a game Diego Maradona had a hand in (quite literally). As for Scotland, they came home a little earlier having finished bottom of their group.

The season started well for Liverpool and me. We opened with a 2–0 win at Newcastle United and I scored both goals. Nottingham Forest were early leaders in Division One but we were cosily tucked in behind them in second place. It looked as if the job of the lady who looked after the silverware in the Anfield trophy room was going to be secure for another year, at least.

Up to December we played seventeen league games of which we lost four. It was good enough to get us to the top of the table. We had also made good progress in the League Cup, in which the most sensational result was a 10–0 demolition of Fulham at Anfield in which I helped myself to a couple of goals and Steve McMahon to four. The heady days seemed to be continuing unabated.

A new recruit was Barry Venison, whom Kenny had signed from Sunderland. Barry initially started at right-back but later switched across to the left where he proved himself to be equally effective. Otherwise, at this stage of the season, it was the usual suspects. Kenny began the season in midfield but, come October, left himself out of the side. I never gained the impression the pressure and demands of combining both roles were beginning to tell on him. Kenny was still a great player, but he was now coming up to thirty-six. A player never loses skill, it's his legs that go, and Kenny was beginning to sense he had reached the stage in his career that befalls every player. He was to make an occasional appearance throughout the season but, wisely to my mind, felt the demands of playing in midfield were better suited to a younger pair of legs.

On Boxing Day we suffered a 1–0 defeat against Manchester United at Anfield. Having at one stage been bottom of the League in September, new United manager Alex Ferguson had since improved matters, though only slightly. United's victory came as something of a wake-up call for us.

In our next game away at Sheffield Wednesday, I scored the only goal of the game, which was the start of an unbeaten run of twelve matches which included ten victories. During this run I scored eleven goals. I was fizzing, enjoying myself, confident that my last season at Anfield was going to be a memorable one. Come the end of March we were top of the League, another Championship beckoned, then it all went pear-shaped.

Of our nine remaining matches we contrived to win but three. Grob sustained an injury which meant he missed the final four matches of the season, his place going to Mike Hooper. Lawro was also sidelined and new signing Nigel Spackman came into the back four. We were also missing Paul Walsh and Jan Molby in the final run-in. I'm not saying the players that replaced the regulars did not do a good job, but so many changes to personnel did have an effect. It takes time for new players to adjust, to get to know their teammates and, with Everton on a great run as the season reached its climax, time was what we did not have.

While we faltered down the final straight, Everton won eleven of their remaining twelve games, eventually winning the title by nine points. I was extremely disappointed that, in my final season at Anfield, we had not won the Championship. It would have been a perfect way for me to exit.

It was also great disappointment to me when we exited the FA Cup at the first time of asking, beaten by Luton Town after a second replay.

In January, we drew 0–0 at Luton and, as was the norm in those days, the replay was arranged for the following Wednesday night. Before a mid-week home game the players spent the best part of the day resting at the Holiday Inn before travelling to Anfield for the game. I remember this day particularly well, and for good reason.

After a light lunch we took to our rooms to sleep, the routine being we would be roused at around 5pm then assemble in the hotel lobby ready for the short trip to Anfield.

Before turning in I looked out of my bedroom window. The sky was battleship grey but there was no sign of snow. This came as something of a relief because there had been reports of blizzards sweeping the south and Midlands. As I took to bed, I hoped the snow would continue to avoid the north-west.

A little after 5pm the players assembled in the hotel lobby. Kenny arrived and asked us to gather around; he'd received some disappointing news. Our tie against Luton had been postponed because the Luton team coach was stuck some thirty miles north of the town on the M1. Apparently the blizzards had caused chaos.

No sooner had Kenny delivered this news when he noticed there was a player missing. The player in question was Alan Irvine, a striker who had been signed from Falkirk and who'd yet to make an appearance for the first team.

Ronnie Moran was sent to find Alan who, it turned out, was rooming alone and had not heard Ronnie's knock on his door.

Before Alan and Ronnie arrived in the lobby Kenny told us no one was to make any mention of the fact the game has been postponed. He was going to have some fun. Kenny loved to play pranks. He never did anything juvenile, such as cutting someone's socks in half, but took great pleasure in coming up with protracted jokes.

Alan Irvine eventually came down to the lobby, bleary-eyed, flustered and full of apologies. Kenny gave him a mild rebuke for having kept us waiting, after which we boarded the coach for Anfield.

Kenny sat at the front, as he had taken to doing. No sooner had we left the hotel grounds when he asked Alan to come and sit next to him. Alan did as he was asked, while the rest of us tried to cock an ear to hear what Kenny was about to say.

'I'm playing you tonight, Alan,' Kenny said.

Heads dipped. There were broad smiles. I could see the one on Alan's face was as broad as a melon.

'You up for it?' asked Kenny.

Alan was indeed.

'Lawro has a knock, I'm playing you at the back alongside Alan Hansen.'

Alan's mouth plopped wide open. 'Centre-half?' he queried, as if Kenny had taken leave of his senses. 'I've never played there in my life.'

Suppressed giggles all around.

'That's as maybe,' continued Kenny, 'but I've been watching you in training. I think centre-half is your natural position. I think you can do a job there for us.'

Their conversation continued, with Kenny telling Alan he was not to mention any of this to the rest of us, as he wanted to reveal the news once we arrived at Anfield.

It was all the rest of us could do to stifle our laughter.

Alan returned to his seat at the rear of the coach. I asked him what the boss had to say to him. He was really coy, muttering something about us all being told later.

John Wark said something to the effect that it must be very important news.

'Perhaps the boss is thinking of making a change,' suggested Grob.

'Yeah, that must be it. What's his plan?' I asked.

'I can't tell you. You'll find out soon enough,' ventured Alan.

We made as if trying to work out what the change to the side could possibly be while Alan sat in smug silence.

Liverpool supporters travel to Anfield from all over the country.

As our coach pulled up outside the ground there was quite a number of fans milling about. Seemingly, news of the postponement had reached them too late to stop them travelling. The presence of so many supporters was a godsend to Kenny's wind-up as so many fans milling around the main entrance offered the impression that the game was still on.

When we gathered in the dressing-room, Kenny took to the floor and informed us Alan was to make his debut at centre-half. He then proceeded to draw diagrams on a white board (which, invariably, he never used) of how he supposedly wanted the two Alans to play in the heart of defence, indicating how Barry Venison and Gary Gillespie should provide cover.

We all made as if we were listening intently while, really, we are all manically struggling not to laugh.

When Kenny finished with the whiteboard he told Alan to get changed and the rest of us to go down to the foyer to issue our complimentary tickets to family and friends.

I joined the rest of the lads in heading for car park and home, leaving Alan to get changed alone in the dressing-room.

About half an hour later, Anfield was deserted. Everyone had gone home but Alan, and the dressing-room attendant who came down the corridor to lock up.

The attendant was surprised to hear the sound of a ball being kicked against a wall in the home dressing-room and decided to go and investigate. He opened the door and was confronted with Alan, in full kit, warming-up with one of the practice balls.

'What're you doing here, son?' asked the attendant.

'Waiting for the rest,' replied Alan, by now all psyched-up and ready for action. 'How long they gonna be?'

'Oh, I'd say about five feet ten,' replied the attendant, realising a wind-up was on the go.

Alan didn't laugh. 'Sorry, not in the mood for jokes right now.'
'Well, now, that is a pity.' The attendant told him.

Failure in the FA Cup was compensated by an excellent run in the League Cup. We reached the final where our opponents were Arsenal. The omens at Wembley seemed good when I gave us the lead. I say that because, at the risk of repeating myself, Liverpool had never lost a game in which I had scored, by now a total of 144 games.

In the twenty-fifth minute, I managed to finish a move put together by Jan and Steve McMahon by sliding the ball past Arsenal keeper John Lukic. Such was our dominance at this stage of the game that I thought we would go on to take Arsenal apart. They had come into the final off the back of nine league games without a win, having scored just one goal. I just couldn't see them scoring against us.

Part of the attraction of football is its unpredictability, as we were to find to our cost. Charlie Nicholas equalised following a goalmouth melee that resembled a scramble to catch the last bus home. Thereafter the pattern of the game changed. Kenny brought himself on after seventy-two minutes but even he couldn't make an impression on the control that Paul Davis, David Roscastle and Steve Williams had exerted in midfield. Perry Groves came on for Niall Quinn and, within minutes, raced into our penalty area and cut the ball back to Charlie Nicholas. Our luck wasn't in. Nicholas miss-hit his shot, which cannoned off Ronnie, past the flaying arms of Grob and into the net. The record books now give the goal to Charlie, but it's irrelevant. The League Cup went to Arsenal.

That season I scored thirty goals in the League and four in the League Cup, a total of thirty-four, to which could be added eight in friendly matches. Officially, I may have been a Juventus player, but no one could accuse me of not giving my all for Liverpool.

In my final game at Anfield, at home to Watford, I scored the only goal. The game over, few supporters seemed to be leaving the ground. Alan Hansen said, 'They're waiting for you to say goodbye.' With the ground still jam-packed I did a lap of honour, all around the pitch and all alone. The noise was deafening. I couldn't believe the supporters were displaying so much emotion for me. It was all too much for me. About halfway round I started crying, too. I took off my shirt and threw it into the crowd, then continued my 'goodbye' to further tears and rapturous applause.

Unbelievably, there were still thousands of supporters milling outside the main entrance after the game. I wanted to go outside, say hello and wave goodbye. But the police were concerned that there might be a crush when fans surged forward to offer their best wishes. Reluctantly, on police advice, I agreed to leave the ground by another exit.

I was planning to go out for meal with Tracy, but Kenny had other ideas. He had organised a surprise farewell party for me at which wives and girlfriends were also in attendance. It was a great night and, I must admit, I drank a little too much. So much that I fell foul of Kenny's impishness.

There was a table buffet and towards the end of the night, a rather sumptuous cream scone was left sitting on the table. For the life of me, I don't know why, but I suggested to Kenny the cream scone would make a great hat for his wife, Marina. I asked if I could put it on her head and my understanding was that it was OK to do that. Worse for the drink, I smacked the cream cake on to Marina's head. Needless to say, she was not amused. Hell hath no fury like a woman 'sconned'. As Marina turned on me, I wimpishly told her Kenny had said it was OK. When

Marina then turned on her husband to ask if this was true, Kenny, brave as a lion, told her, 'I never said a word. What would I be doing asking him to do a thing like that?' Tracy was equally furious with me. 'What on earth possessed you to do that?' she asked. To this day, I don't know.

Women, like the taxman, never forget. A year later, when I had returned from Italy to play in Alan Hansen's testimonial game, Marina came up behind me during the post-match buffet as I sat chatting, and planted a large gâteaux over my head.

'Now we're quits,' she said, obviously delighted by the cream and chocolate sauce running down my cheeks and the back of my neck. As the old football axiom goes, if you dish it out, then you also have to take it.

The one crushing disappointment to the season was that Liverpool didn't win a trophy. Midway through the season we had been nine points clear at the top of the League, to let that lead slip and then to end nine points behind eventual champions Everton was, to say the least, very depressing. Looking back, I think complacency crept into the play of certain players, which was not like Liverpool at all. I also felt some of the players Kenny brought into the side were good First Division players, but not of the standard to help us win a Championship. The fact we also blew a 1–0 lead in the League Cup final to a team who had not won for nine games was also upsetting.

I knew Liverpool would bounce back and win the Championship again. Performances and results had indicated things weren't right but, as I prepared to leave, I knew Kenny had it in him to make the signings to put things right. He had already brought in John Aldridge from Oxford United to replace me when I left. John and I had played together towards the end of the season, enough to convince me he was a natural goal-scorer who would take over my mantle without any problems. Liverpool would be back at the forefront of English football, of that I was sure, and a part of me regretted I would not be playing my part in any future success.

Tracy and I were married that summer. It was a great day that we shared with our respective families, friends and a number of Liverpool players, Kenny included. We honeymooned on the island of Aruba in the Dutch Antilles and, within two days of our return, were Turin-bound.

Occasionally one hears of current Premiership footballers complaining about the scrutiny they are placed under by certain elements of the media. They should try plying their trade in Italy.

Tracy and I arrived at Turin airport to be greeted by thousands of Juventus fans and a press contingent that appeared to be only marginally less in number. Once inside the terminal building we were taken to a room that had been set aside for a press conference. I was fine with that, but the first question rocked me.

'Mr Rush, would you have fought in the Falklands should you have been called up?'

I said something on the lines that the question was irrelevant because I had not been called up, nor had there been any likelihood of UK civilians being conscripted to the armed services.

'What do you think of the marital problems of Prince Charles and Princess Diana?'

'I can't comment. It's been some time since I have spoken to either.'

'How do you assess Margaret Thatcher as a Prime Minister?'

'With difficulty.'

'Which do you prefer – English, American or Italian literature?'

'Are you sure you've got the right person? I'm Ian Rush the footballer, not Gore Vidal.'

Irrelevant questions apart, I was soon to discover that when it came to concocting wild stories the Italian press make Jeffrey Archer sound like George Washington.

Tracy was sitting alongside me as I did my best to field what I saw as being a bizarre set of questions for a footballer. It was a very hot day and Tracy sat sipping a glass of Coca-Cola. The following day some newspapers carried a photograph of Tracy with the glass to her lips, and the story that she had sat alongside me drinking a succession of Camparis.

The one saving grace of this first confrontation with the Italian media was that Tracy answered the questions that were put to her in Italian. (She speaks very good French and is sufficiently conversant in Italian to conduct meaningful conversation.) At this stage of proceedings I didn't speak a word of Italian. That was my first mistake.

Life with Juventus began with a ten-day training programme in Switzerland. The trip involved a friendly against Lucerne and I marked my debut by scoring our first goal in what was a 2–0 victory. I have to say this came as some relief to me as almost 10,000 Juve fans had made the four-hour trip to Switzerland and I was keen to impress. I thought I did OK in this game. The Juve fans certainly seemed to think so and gave me a generous applause as I left the field, but I noticed my new teammates were somewhat less accommodating.

Back in the dressing-room no one spoke to me. I was unable to join in the post-match banter because I didn't speak Italian. I knew quite a few of the Juve players spoke English, but the fact no one engaged me in any sort of conversation made me feel rather out of things. Seeing as this was our first game, I didn't worry about it too much, believing that once my face became familiar I would be welcomed into the fold.

My sense of unease, however, was to be later compounded when we journeyed back to Italy. I sat down on the coach and no one came to sit next to me. These were pre-iPod days but most players, myself included, owned a Walkman tape machine. No sooner was our coach on its way than my ears were assailed by the 'tin-tin-tin' of various forms of rock and pop music coming from individual Walkmans. It suddenly occurred to me that not only had the Juve players not spoken to me, they'd hardly said a word to one another and seemed prepared to spend the entire journey in their own little worlds. When in Rome (OK, Turin) and all that. I retrieved my own Walkman along with one of the 'Teach Yourself Italian' cassettes I had brought with me from England.

'*Mi chiamo Ian.*'

'My name is Ian,' I muttered.

'*Vengo dalla* Liverpool.'

'I come from Liverpool.'

Not that any of my new teammates seemed bothered.

Throughout the pre-season training few players spoke to me unless it was out on the training pitch, a situation not helped, of course, by my lack of Italian. Nowadays, overseas players benefit from the help of a players' liaison officer and an interpreter if needed. At the time, I had no such assistance.

Before the start of the new season we were joined in training by Michel Platini, who was on business in Turin and joined in our training to keep himself fit. Though contact had been intermittent over the years, Michel and I had remained pals since Wales's victory in Toulouse. One day after training we sat down for a chat.

I told Michel of my experience of Juve to date, how I had found the line of questioning by the Italian press bewildering.

'If they ask you about literature, tell them you read Shakespeare. If they ask what music you listen to, tell them Mozart, or Verdi's opera,' he advised. 'In Italy, Ian, you tell the press what they want to hear – and tell them in Italian. Remember this, Italians will always believe what they read or hear, rather than what they see.'

At one point in our conversation I tried to persuade him to change his mind about retirement and play another season with Juventus.

Michel is an extremely bright guy. He had deduced I was not settling at the club and would have loved him to be there as a teammate and friend. He told me, however, that his mind was made up. There was no way he would play again – for any club. He then gave me a long, serious look.

'Ian, I must tell you this,' he said. 'I retired when I did because I saw the team for what it is. You've come to the right place but at the wrong time.'

This didn't make me feel any better.

'Juve . . . they are not a team,' he continued. 'They are a collection of individuals. Gifted individuals, but no team. You understand what I am saying?'

I did. I hadn't exactly enjoyed my first few weeks at the club and, from what Michel was telling me, had the uneasy feeling they might not turn out to be unusual.

Michel went on to tell me the balance of the team was all wrong, that it lacked quality, inspiration and imagination in midfield, that there was little cohesion and spirit, and, off the field, little camaraderie. The latter I had already sussed for myself.

'I am your friend, so it hurts me to say this,' Michel said as we parted. 'I wish you luck, because I fear you will need it.'

Tracy and I were living in a sumptuous villa on the outskirts of Turin. It was a fabulous iced-cake place with a terracotta roof from which, on one side, tumbled a burgundy bougainvillea as wide as a decent-sized waterfall. The villa was flanked by manicured lawns, the front lawn boasting two white acacias that were worth seeing. At the rear there was an elevated garden accessed by half a dozen or so stone steps. Here there was another bowling-green lawn, lemon and peach trees, an ancient grapevine and a fabulous flowerbed ringed by an ornamental stone balustrade that, in England, would have been a prized asset of the National Trust. As first homes go, it was the stuff of dreams.

I stepped inside the relative cool of the villa that night, my head still reeling with what Michel had told me. Suddenly, Tracy appeared at the top of the wrought-iron banister staircase.

'Oh, you're back early,' she said. 'The last of our stuff has arrived from home. I haven't finished unpacking it yet.'

'Well, I wouldn't be in any hurry if I were you.'

I got on well with the Juve manager, Rino Marchesi. I liked him. He was a warm man, a very good coach, who had previously been at Napoli and Inter Milan. He was into the second year of a two-year contract but the knives were already out for him. The press and supporters were not pleased that Juve had endured, by their own high standards, a mediocre season. I gathered that if the current season did not see the club at the top of Serie A, Marchesi would be on his way.

Most of the power at the club seemed to lie with Mr Boniperti, though the club itself was owned by Gianni Agnelli, who also enjoyed a controlling interest in the Fiat company which had had close links with the club since the 1930s. Every fortnight I joined the rest of the players at Mr Agnelli's sumptuous mansion that straddled Villa Perosa, where he would give us a pep talk. At Liverpool I'd had very little contact with the chairman and his co-directors. The Liverpool board never interfered with team affairs. At Juve it was different. While my teammates spoke little to me, Mr Agnelli appeared to have a lot of time for me. When the other players had departed he would ask me to stay behind and offer me advice and encouragement, saying he understood how difficult the transition had been for me. While it was a real lift to have the support of a man of his stature, I did wonder whether this caused any resentment among my teammates. I sensed that it did.

After a few months I had picked up enough Italian to get by in basic conversation with people and had learned the Italian for the majority of football terms I need to know. But I was still left feeling very much an outsider in the dressing-room and sensed hostility towards me from some of the squad. I did make friends with some players, including goalkeeper Stefano Tacconi, defender Pasquale Bruno, who, like me, was a recent recruit, and Sergio Brio, who lived up to his name by being full of it. Pasquale Bruno lived quite close to us, so we often went out together and became good friends. I gained the impression he too found it difficult to make friends with many of the squad.

Many of the other players said little to me. When I entered the dressing-room conversation would suddenly stop, which led me to believe they may have been talking about me. When social-ising after a game, on more than one occasion players would turn their backs on me when I entered the room. I found it increasingly difficult to relax, never mind assimilate, in that kind of atmosphere.

A few days before the season was to get underway, I damaged my right thigh muscle in training. I missed the first three weeks of the season and, even when I did return to action, I could still feel the injury.

Juventus did not enjoy the best of starts and when I was eventually fit enough to play it was apparent the rot had set in. Results were not good and the team was just above mid-table. Within two months the Italian press were writing me off as a multi-million-lire flop. While I shrugged aside such press comment, I sensed the appearance of such stories seemed to be welcomed by one or two players in the dressing-room, almost as if their view of me had been vindicated.

Come Christmas, when Italian football takes a mid-season break, we were already too far adrift of the likes of AC Milan, Napoli, Roma and Sampdoria to have any chance of winning the league. We were going to be pushed even to qualify for a place in the UEFA Cup. Talking of which, we'd also been knocked out of that competition by Panathinaikos. The press and the supporters turned on Rino Marchesi with such venom it was obvious to me, even at this stage of the season, that his days at Juve were numbered.

At the midway point in the season I had five goals to my name, and what worried me most was that I had created all five goals by myself. For someone who had been used to the midfield creating chances for me, the distinct lack of service from the Juventus midfield left me in no doubt that I was in for a tough season in front of goal.

I was never a George Best, Ryan Giggs or Cristiano Ronaldo, the type of player who can run with the ball and destroy defenders. I was more in the mode of Jimmy Greaves, a clinical finisher who depends on teammates to make the openings for me. At Liverpool I had thrived on the creative work of Kenny, Graeme and latterly Jan Molby. Juventus didn't possess a single player with the nous to open up defences with a telling pass.

I became very frustrated, and Tracy bore the brunt of it. Back home in the villa I would mull over the events of the day, withdraw into myself and subject myself to moods of depression. It takes a lot to get me riled or upset, but during this period of my life I found I had an uncharacteristically low tolerance level. I would become agitated very easily over small things; for example, I remember once having difficulty removing the plastic packaging from a new toothbrush and found myself manically tearing into it. It was the little things which made me realise that the move to Turin was having a bad effect on me.

Thank heavens Tracy was around. It wasn't the best of starts to our marriage but she possessed the strength of character and understanding to cope with my sometimes irrational behaviour and dark moods.

Curiously, while the Italian media gave me a right old slaughtering, the Juventus supporters were wonderful towards me. I can't recall ever being given a bad time from the terraces, or ever hearing of a less than complimentary word around the city. When I first arrived in Turin I was a little apprehensive that locals might somehow blame me for what had happened at Heysel, but this never proved to be the case. The only people who ever referred to that tragic night were the members of the British media who came over to see me.

I believe one of the reasons for the warmth I enjoyed from the Juventus fans was that I mixed with them. Many of the Juventus players, as with most of the top players in Italy, were afforded star status and behaved as such. They were aloof from the fans who paid their wages. I sensed that amongst these players there was a general mistrust of the ordinary fan. That was not me. After training, Pasquale Bruno and I would often call at an open air café patronised by Juventus fans. We enjoyed chatting with the supporters, hearing what they had to say on certain matters, and I think they enjoyed what we had to say, too. Those chats at the café were amongst the few occasions when I did feel happy. Talking with the supporters helped me with the language, as they would often explain certain words or phrases to me. They would correct my Italian, but in a very warm and friendly way so as not to make me feel embarrassed. I honestly felt much more relaxed sipping an espresso with the fans than I ever did in the Juventus dressing-room.

It was a good job I was on a decent wage because our phone bill had as many digits as our number. Tracy and I both called our families regularly, while I also rang the lads at Liverpool to see how they were getting on. They weren't missing me too much – they were top of the league and heading for the FA Cup final. I also rang Graeme, now manager of Rangers, who had just won the Scottish League Cup. Having played in Italy, he offered me advice on how I might better adjust. I told him it was not Italy, nor the lifestyle that I found difficult, but the football, playing in a team that had little spirit and camaraderie. His advice to me was to be even more selfish on the field, to get as many goals as I could. Given the lack of openings created for me that was going to be tough.

When I returned after the Christmas break I decided I would be much more forceful – more greedy and selfish on the field. In games, whenever I received the ball, I did my best to create an opening for myself. I shouted and screamed for the ball when teammates had it and, let them know in uncertain terms (and in Italian) what I thought of them when they didn't play me in. It worked, to a point. After the mid-season break I scored nine league and cup goals to finish the season with fourteen to my name: seven in the league and seven in cup competitions. To put this tally into some sort of perspective, the total number of league goals scored by Juventus that season was a miserly 35. If I also tell you we conceded 30 you can tell how dull many of the matches were.

Of the seven cup goals I scored, I scored four in one game, against Ascoli. We were really playing well that day and I fancied myself to go on and notch five or six, so was very disappointed to be substituted. I was told the reason for my substitution was to 'keep me fresh for the next game'. I couldn't see the logic in this. Having scored four goals I was giving Ascoli all manner of problems and wanted to stay on the field. I felt more goals would boost my confidence enormously. When I reluctantly left the field, I felt it a mark of how well I had played when one of the Ascoli players ran up to me, shook me by the hand and said, '*Complementi*.'

Juventus finished the season in sixth place, ahead of local rivals Torino on goal difference, but well adrift of champions AC Milan and runners-up Napoli. The one saving grace was that we qualified for the UEFA Cup via a play-off against Torino. The game ended goalless after extra time so went to a penalty shoot-out. I hadn't been selected to take a penalty but, with us having one penalty remaining which would decide the game, no Juventus player seemed to want to assume responsibility, so I stepped up to put it away and Juventus into Europe.

We managed just one victory in the League away from home, 2–1 at Pisa, who avoided relegation to Serie B by a single point. (The new away kit included a pink shirt. Needless to say, this resulted in much cat-calling from opposition fans.) There was the occasional good result at home, 4–0 against Empoli, 3–0 against Avellino and, by far our best performance, a 3–1 victory over Napoli. But, as our final league position suggests, in the history of Juventus the season had been hugely disappointing.

In terms of technical ability I had no doubt I was playing in the best league in the world. Most of the world's top players were plying their trade in Serie A, and playing against such quality week in and week out proved a real education. Of all the top players on show, the two that stood out for me were Diego Maradona, who was with Napoli, and Ruud Gullit, who, along with Marco van Basten, had helped AC Milan win the league title.

I'm 6ft but next to Gullit I felt small. He was a huge, powerful player with wonderful balance and an incredible turn of speed. He was practically unstoppable when he made surging runs into the penalty areas, and any defender who did manage to get near him had to time his tackle to perfection, otherwise he would be away or there would be a penalty. I also noticed how hard Gullit worked, on and off the ball. He seemed tireless.

With all due respect to Gullit, I would say Diego Maradona was the best player in the world at that time. When we played against Napoli I was surprised at how small he was. He also appeared as broad as he was tall and his thighs were like bags of concrete. For such a small guy he was incredibly strong, and when I challenged him he used every muscle in his body, including his backside, to fend me off or shield the ball. Like Stanley Matthews, Maradona's control of the ball was impeccable, almost as if he had a sixth sense. He always knew where that ball was and could exercise complete control over it without ever looking down. Having played alongside Kenny Dalglish I thought I'd seen the player with the most remarkable vision I'd ever seen, but I have to say, Maradona displayed a vision that no other player could match. He was a spartan player, too, never wasting a pass or a chance to score. In addition he was a natural leader on the pitch, possessing absolute authority. For such a stocky guy he was so nimble that he found extra agility and turning capacity.

Against Napoli he and I chased the ball when it was running towards a corner flag. He got there just ahead of me. I thought I had him boxed in, only for Maradona to suddenly turn, flicking the ball in the air with the outside of his left boot as he did so. The ball flashed past my right knee, followed quickly by him. In a split second he was behind me, the ball at his feet, and accelerating away.

He was the hub of that Napoli team. Every move stemmed from him and, when a teammate was in trouble, he was always there to help out. He was a genius of a footballer, so much so I feel it disingenuous of me to suggest he had a weakness, but he was all left foot. That said, what a left foot it was. He could turn defenders both ways with it and it was also strong enough to resist all the ferocious tackling that was launched at him. He was also, by the way, very adept at falling over an outstretched leg, and must have won more penalties than any other player that season. But my view was I too got kicked black and blue by defenders who got away with it most of the time. One of the many things I learned from my season in Italian football was that if you had the chance to turn the tables on defenders, you took it. Maradona went to ground as easily as a lead balloon but you sort of forgave him for that because he was such a brilliant footballer. In fact, I would go as far as to say Maradona had the arts and crafts of the game in greater measure than any other player I ever played with or against – and that's saying something.

Towards the end of the season speculation had already started that clubs back in England had monitored my situation and were on the point of enquiring as to my availability. I took all such speculation with a pinch of salt. I had, by now, begun to adapt to the Italian way of life and, remembering how unsettled I had been when first joining Liverpool, was of the mind I probably had put the worst days at Juventus behind me.

In April 1988 I travelled back to England to play in a testimonial for John Charles and Bobby Collins at Leeds United. I was guesting for Leeds whose opponents were Everton, and was delighted to learn that Michel Platini and Kenny Dalglish had also accepted invitations to turn out on the night.

For a testimonial game the match was very competitive. At one point I found myself dropping deep in search of the ball, just as I had been doing at Juventus. Kenny yelled at me to get back upfront. Later in the game I drifted out wide.

'You don't score from out there!' Michel called out. 'Go in their area and we'll make goals for you. You're not playing with Juve!'

I wasn't and I had been made very conscious of that fact – because I was enjoying myself and the service I was receiving, which enabled me to score twice. The game was shown live on Italian television, so I was pleased to show them that, given the right service, I would score goals.

After the game I had a long chat with John Charles.

'I had my problems too when I played for Juventus,' he told me. 'People wanted to run my life. Just be your own man, Ian. Keep your head up and keep battling away.'

I intended to do just that.

I flew back to Italy with Michel in his private jet, a symbol of his star status which, in later years, would be afforded to some players with not a tenth of his ability. When I returned I learned that qualification for the UEFA Cup courtesy of the play-off penalty shoot-out against Torino hadn't been enough to save Rino Marchesi's job. His contract with Juventus was not being renewed. I felt genuinely sad for him.

I had one more game to play in Italy, for Wales against the national team in Brescia. I would be up against some of my Juventus teammates and before I set off to join the Wales party, those Juventus lads gave me a fine send-off, each raising five fingers to indicate how many goals Italy were going to score against Wales.

Before the Italy game Wales were to play Malta. Regular skipper Kevin Ratlcliffe was absent due to injury and when I joined the Wales party, newly appointed manager Terry Yorath took me aside and said he was making me captain. I was never one of those players who pulls out of the international squad claiming injury but is always fit for his club's next league match the following Saturday. To be selected for Wales was always a great source of pride to me, and to be made captain thrilled me to bits. It was the fulfilment of a lifelong ambition and I was determined to carry out my duties both on and off the pitch to the best of my ability.

Wales beat Malta 3–2 on a pitch that, if it had a blade of grass on it, I didn't see it. The baked-earth pitch and the sweltering heat took its toll and we struggled to get the win, but win we did. I was on a natural high as I walked off the pitch, having led Wales to victory in my first game as captain.

I felt I had a lot of things to prove to a lot of people in the game against Italy. I was as wound up before the game as I have ever been. After Terry had said his piece in the dressing-room, I took to my feet to offer words of encouragement. I didn't refer to me and Italy or the send-off I had received from the Juventus players, I simply spoke of the pride we had in being Welsh, that no one expected us to win because no one rated us as a team or individual players.

'Let's get out and show them, hey?' I urged my teammates. 'Let's do something today so that when we're old and have grandkids, we'll have something we're proud to tell them.'

Italy, urged on by a very volatile home crowd, took the game to us from the start, but they dallied too long on the ball and we were never made to feel uneasy. Having coped with their opening attacks, confidence grew in the ranks and we began to put the home side on the back foot. There was some ten minutes of frantic activity then, after half an hour, I managed to get ahead of Baresi to a cross from Mark Hughes to head past Zenga.

The goal only served to increase the frenzy of the game. Frustrated, Italy began to kick and hack and generally resort to the rough-house stuff, so we got stuck in too. By no stretch of the imagination was the match a shining example of the beautiful game, but we held on to our lead to emerge with a victory that, for me, was the sweetest of that entire season. When the final whistle blew, the stadium rang with boos, jeers and, I noticed, some tears of frustration. There was more emotion on those terraces than in a whole series of *Little House on the Prairie*.

The Italy players did not take defeat well, either. On hearing the final whistle I turned to the nearest player to me, Giannini, and offered to shake his hand. He brushed it away saying, 'Wait till you play against Roma next season, see what I'll do to you.'

Two days later, on 7 June, I met with Mr Boniperti and Mr Agnelli. We had a long, frank meeting during which I told them how disappointed I had been with the season that had just passed. I told them I felt a number of Juventus players had not warmed to me, even though I had made an effort to befriend them, that I even felt animosity towards me on the part of some players. I told them how I felt about the team, that it lacked the quality, particularly in midfield, to launch a serious challenge for the league championship in the coming season. I concluded by saying I was prepared to see out my contract but would understand should they want to sell me and bring in someone new.

'But we still have total confidence in you, Ian,' Mr Agnelli told me. 'We want you to stay. You tell me which British players you would like me to bring in alongside you. You tell me, I will get them.'

I mentioned Mark Hughes, Peter Beardsley and John Barnes. 'Any one of those,' I suggested.

I had always had a great deal of respect for Mr Agnelli – and still do. He was a man of his word. Within a week Juventus made offers for both Mark Hughes and Peter Beardsley but received the knock-back on both counts.

A few days later, it was announced the legendary Italy goal-keeper, Dino Zoff was to take over as the new manager. This was a fillip to me. I knew Zoff and felt he would have Juventus playing attacking football. He was also a strong character who knew what he wanted from players. I felt if anyone was going to clear out the bad apples it was he.

All in all I felt things were looking up when Tracy and I set off for a summer holiday in the Cayman Islands. How wrong I was. Towards the end of the holiday I developed what I thought were heat bumps. I wasn't feeling brilliant when we flew back for a break at Tracy's parents' house, so she called a doctor.

The doctor was in no doubt. I had contracted chicken pox. This was an ailment I associated with childhood, so wasn't too concerned when I heard the doctor say this, but I was feeling really poorly and asked if chicken pox in adulthood had a more severe effect.

'It can do,' said the doctor. 'The fact you're feeling so bad, however, isn't simply down to chicken pox. You also have hepatitis, shingles and, from the colour of your skin, I'm almost certain you also have a liver infection.'

Four illnesses in one go. I felt about ninety.

Having been diagnosed, I thought I would make a quick return to full health, but I didn't. I had no appetite, had trouble sleeping and the pain was intense. I endured a miserable three weeks at the end of which I had lost a lot of weight. When I started to feel better, a specialist told me I would need a good deal of rest before I could even think about returning to Italy and training again.

I duly rested and eventually joined my teammates for the preseason trip to Switzerland, but I was in no fit state for training. At the end of the first session I felt exhausted and began to fear there was no way I was going to be fit for the start of the new campaign.

Michael Laudrup was still at the club, but during the close season Juventus had also signed Portugal's Rui Barros and the Russian international Zavarov. Although the Italians had relaxed their rules regarding foreign players, and each club was now allowed three players from overseas, one of us had to go and, as Barros and Zavarov were new recruits, that meant either Laudrup or me.

Juventus agreed terms with PSV Eindhoven for the transfer of Michael Laudrup, which didn't please him. He thought it a big step backwards in his career – but more probably, in financial terms. So I was not altogether surprised when he rejected the move.

At the time I had an adviser, a chap named Paul Dean. On 13 August, Paul rang me from England.

'Would you be interested in returning to Liverpool?' he asked.

As soon as I heard those words, my heart lifted. I was thrilled at the very prospect of pulling on the famous red shirt again.

'Is the Pope's hat over the top?' I replied.

The ball began to roll as if coming down Everest. Within a week I was a Liverpool player again. It all happened so quickly. Tracy had to stay on in Turin to supervise the transport of all our stuff back to England. I flew over to Liverpool, signed the contracts, then flew back to Turin for two days to help Tracy pack and say my goodbyes.

I thanked Boniperti and Agnelli, wished Dino Zoff good luck, said goodbye to those Juve players I got on with and paid one last visit to the open air café to say thank you and farewell to those friendly supporters. They were fantastic to me. They told me they were sad to see me go but wished me every success. One fan, a man in his sixties, told me, 'I don't think we shall be seeing any more Juve players here again'. Sadly, I felt he was right. The Italian press, true to form, said Juventus would be better off without me. But the heart-warming farewell I received from those fans at the café more than made up for the bad press. If only I had known such friendship in the dressing-room.

I was told the reason for Juventus wanting to sell me was that, should I remain at the club, they would exceed the limit for overseas players. The club obviously felt they had better options and, to be honest, so did I. Liverpool, meanwhile, wanted me back for the simple reason that I was a proven goalscorer at the club and still very much in my prime. I knew the culture and ways of the club, was familiar with the style of play and knew just about everybody. In short, I would be a low maintenance player. The fact I was returning for slightly less than Liverpool had paid for me also meant the club had realised a profit on my move and return.

On my last day, I gave a press conference in which I told the media I was happy to be going back to Liverpool, but also sad to leave the people of Turin who had made me so welcome. I was diplomatic enough not to refer to the Juventus players.

'Apart from your football, what will you be most looking forward to doing when you return to England?' one reporter asked.

'Reading Shakespeare and listening to Verdi,' I told him.

What's more, I told him in Italian.

CHAPTER ELEVEN

Nothing Could Ever Be The Same Again

Just about every article I have read concerning my season at Juventus infers I was a flop, had trouble adapting to the Italian way of life, and didn't learn the language.

All these years on I am still glad I went there. As for me being a flop, the Juventus fans didn't think so. By my own standards fourteen goals in a season was a poor return, but given the lack of service and the fact the team scored only thirty-five league goals that season, I felt it respectable enough.

True, I struggled to learn the language but, within a year, had learned enough Italian to get by in conversation. As for the lifestyle, to say I didn't adapt is nonsense. Initially I did find it hard to settle but, in time, both Tracy and I enjoyed Italian life, though we never did become accustomed to the ways of the press.

What I didn't like, and never did adapt to, was playing in a team where just about every player was playing for himself. I could create opportunities for myself but in order to hit thirty goals a season I needed good service from midfield and that was never forthcoming at Juventus. Before setting off for Italy I had been an

Artful Dodger pickpocket of the penalty area. On my return I was still that type of striker but with a lot more besides.

A number of things were attributed to me which were either not true or else an over-simplification of the truth. When I decided to write this book, I contacted my friend, the writer, Les Scott. At one of our get-togethers, Les referred to what is arguably the most repeated quote attributed to me: 'Playing in Italy was like playing in a foreign country.'

'I came across the quote countless times in books, but when did you say this?' asked Les, 'because I've not been able to find an interview or a direct source for that quote from you.'

'That's because I never said it,' I told him.

It was Thursday, 18 August 1988 when I rejoined Liverpool. Kenny met me at Manchester airport and drove me to Anfield for a press conference. My move had been kept such a closely-guarded secret that even the most experienced football reporters were taken aback when I walked into the room.

After the press conference a reporter cornered Kenny, hoping, I suppose, to get some sort of story or quote that had been denied to everyone else, and asked him what I had said in private about my time in Italy.

'He said, "Playing in Italy was like playing in a foreign country,"' replied Kenny, tongue in cheek.

It was another of Kenny's impish wind-ups. The reporter, of course, took Kenny's words as gospel.

Regarding my year with Juventus, it was never written that I came back a better player, which I did. My technique improved immensely. When some strikers have a shot at goal, they think the job is done. Playing for Juventus meant that I fulfilled other roles, which made me an all-round better player.

Due to the fact I was on my own upfront and received very little support, once I had created a chance I continued to work my socks off. As soon as the shot had been saved or blocked, I began to chase. Invariably the ball would be fed by the goalkeeper to either full-back or the sweeper. I saw it as my job to close them down and put them under pressure. I realised, once I had scored or had a shot saved, that it was all about going to the next level rather than jogging back thinking, 'Well, that's me done, time for you lads to do a bit.'

Before going to Italy I'd worked to close down defenders, but during my second spell with Liverpool this part of my game had greatly improved. So much so that goalkeepers were reluctant to feed the ball to their full-backs or central defenders. This meant their only other options was to throw the ball to their midfield, or kick it to their own front men, putting their possession of the ball at risk.

The extra work I was putting in did not go unnoticed at the club. Sammy Lee was once asked by football writer Bryon Butler, 'Who would you say is your best defender at Liverpool: Hansen, Lawrenson, Beglin?' Sammy's reply was 'Ian Rush', much to Butler's surprise.

I had picked up or worked out for myself certain little moves that I would try. I was always looking to exploit the space behind the full-backs with the aim of getting the opposition defence back-peddling. As a striker this increases your options for shooting, crossing the ball or laying it back for one of your midfield players. As a striker you run into that area and your marker has to go with you, but even if you get the ball, space is limited. So I had started to encourage the wide midfield players to drop deeper to receive the ball, hoping the full-back would advance accordingly. For example, if I was playing alongside Peter Beardsley, whichever one of us was on that side of the pitch would show for the ball. One of the opposing centre-backs had to go across and mark whoever was wide. The other central defender would then have to step up into the space left by his fellow centre-back. If I had been left in the middle, I would then call for the ball to be played quickly into this channel and I'd be away, in space in one of the most dangerous areas of the pitch.

Due to the lack of service at Juventus, I had to do such things off my own back otherwise I wouldn't have been creating openings at all. I was working harder but thinking more, which is what I mean when I say I was a better technical player on my return from Italy. It is just one simple example of how I began to organise myself and my teammates. Looking back, I suppose it was the first sign of the coach in me.

Another move I put into operation in Italy which, on my return, Peter Beardsley and I often executed, was almost a set play. If the ball was around the halfway line on one side of the pitch and I was the furthest striker from the ball, Peter would 'show', moving some ten yards or so up to the player with the ball, consequently taking one of the opposing centre-backs with him. As soon as Peter made this run, our midfield player in possession of the ball would by-pass him and play a cross-field ball in the air to me. As soon as that ball was played, Peter would spin off his marker and sprint towards goal. The aim was for him to arrive just outside the penalty box ahead of his marker in time to receive the ball from me. Peter then had the option of going for goal himself or playing the ball square to me, because I would have taken to my toes to get wide of him with a view to having a go myself.

We didn't have to tell teammates what we were doing because, as Bob Stokoe said, you don't have to tell good players what to do, they know. Of course, you play off the cuff a lot of the time, but introducing little moves such as these paid dividends.

The hardest thing about playing as a striker is not scoring goals, but finding the space that allows you an opportunity on goal. Defences are so well organised, particularly those I came up against in Italy, I had to be constantly thinking of ways of creating space.

When I had someone alongside me, we would play one up and one off, i.e. one of us would push right up on the central defence pairing, the other dropping into what is now commonly referred to as 'the hole'. When a team loses possession, invariably they try to ensure their back-line and midfield are as close to one another as possible. This made life difficult for me because there was no space for me to work in. So when we didn't have the ball, I'd get Peter, or whoever, to drop behind the midfield. When we regained possession he would then be in space to run at the opposition defence or open it up by either playing a through ball or stage an attack by passing the ball into dangerous areas for our wide players to run on to. This is why you often found Peter, or sometimes me, around the centre circle when the opposing defence was tightly formed, available to pick the ball and get things moving. Eric Cantona spent most of his time at Manchester United playing this way.

Defenders don't like players running at them with the ball, which is what the player in 'the hole' must do. Kenny and Peter Beardsley were great at this, as is, of course, Cristiano Ronaldo. There was no point in putting Graeme or Steve McMahon in the hole because their strengths lay elsewhere. It has to be a player with great vision, whose passing is top class, who can run at defences and hit a decent shot.

Ploughing a lone furrow upfront, as I did in Italy, is hard graft. You need to have midfield players who are going to support the attack very quickly. While Liverpool players were ready to do this, it didn't happen with the Juventus players, who slowly and methodically came out of defence. Playing as a lone striker I was always calling for teammates to play the ball through midfield. There was no point in launching a long ball up to me as I wasn't that sort of target man. Besides, even if I held it up long enough for support to arrive, the opposition would be in place behind the ball. At Liverpool we liked to pass the ball, which suited me. With Juventus we didn't have the players capable of the support play crucial to making the system of playing one upfront work.

Playing on my own upfront made me more of a creator around the edge of the box. The circumstances I found myself in when playing for Juventus, however irksome I felt them to be at the time, resulted in me improving my all-round play but were to the detriment of me as a goal-scorer. I spent a lot of time receiving the ball, trying to hold it, then laying it off to teammates coming from deep. I found I had become so focused on being a build-up player that I wasn't always looking for space in which to score goals myself. In short, I felt Juventus had signed a goal-scorer proven at the top level, but had wasted me.

My time in Italy was not the best year of my career, or life, but it was far from the disaster some have made it out to be.

My summer illness had weakened me to such a degree I only managed a couple of days of light pre-season training at Juventus. The Liverpool squad had been hard at it for weeks. I wasn't fit and I still didn't feel 100 per cent, but was so overjoyed at the thought of playing for Liverpool again that I let my heart rule my head.

Liverpool were due to play Wimbledon in the Charity Shield at Wembley. I knew I would not be fit to play in that game. What was more, the way I was feeling I suspected it would be months before I was back to my old self.

I did try to temper expectations. I gave an interview to the *Daily Mirror* during which I said, 'It'll take some time for me to regain full fitness. Judge me then, when I've had time to get myself put right.'

I was on the bench for the opening league game at Charlton Athletic. John Aldridge was on fire that day, scoring a hat-trick in a 3–0 victory. Twenty minutes from time, Kenny brought me on. If you have ever jumped into a swimming pool and the change in temperature has taken your breath away, that's what it was like for me coming on against Charlton. Once a game gets underway players will get what we call a second breath, adjusting to the speed and tempo of the game. When I was introduced at Selhurst Park (Charlton were homeless at the time and tenants of Crystal Palace) the speed of the game was such I just couldn't get into the swing of it.

I had another run-out as a substitute in our second match, at home to Manchester United. The game was very tight, decided by a penalty from Jan Molby, but I did feel a little better and thought I made more of a contribution to proceedings. Even so, I was surprised when Kenny named me in the side for our next game at Aston Villa.

Against Villa, Peter Beardsley dropped to the bench, and Steve McMahon was also left out, Nigel Spackman coming in to give us a little more cover. A goal from Ray Houghton earned us a 1–1 draw. Again, I did OK, but knew I was far from sharp.

I felt I could play myself back to fitness. But the effects of my illness still lingered, not enough to sideline me but enough to make me realise I was never completely well.

I played in the following game against Spurs then missed a

couple of games only to be recalled for the game at Luton with their plastic pitch. Liverpool never enjoyed playing there and it showed. We lost 1–0.

Kenny continued with me. I scored my first goal in a League Cup tie against Walsall, which came as some relief, as did the fact I netted in a 2–1 defeat at Nottingham Forest. I scored in the next two matches – a 2–0 win at West Ham and a 3–0 home win over Middlesbrough – but this did little to convince me I was firing on all cylinders. Against Middlesbrough, just when I was on the point of convincing myself I was going to be fine, I pulled up with muscle strain and had to be replaced by Steve McMahon. Against Luton I'd picked up a slight hamstring strain but with treatment had managed to shake it off. My body was sending me messages.

So it went on. I was in and out of the side as I struggled to find fitness and overcome the lingering effects of what had been a quadruple illness. I lacked that yard of pace which had previously served me so well. I was just twenty-six, so I knew it hadn't deserted me for ever, but I just couldn't re-discover my sharpness and was beset by niggling injuries.

Football League chairmen had accepted an £11 million a year deal from ITV to broadcast matches and, with more and more live games on television, the press were beginning to change the way they covered football. People no longer relied on newspapers to find out what happened in games, so football pages contained more emotive analysis and comment.

I was the subject of some of this emotive writing and there were occasions when I was slaughtered in the press. 'HAS RUSHY LOST IT?' and 'RUSH'S BEST DAYS NOW BEHIND HIM' were two such head-lines that irked.

Kenny was a great source of comfort and support. 'Pay no atten-tion, it's all bollocks,' he said. 'It's what we think at Liverpool that matters. They all think they're bloody experts. I have total belief in you. Get yourself fit again and the goals will come.'

The players were also fully behind me. John Aldridge, who had assumed the role of main striker when I was in Italy, came up to me one day at Melwood as I sat reading a particularly biting piece about me in a tabloid. He must have read the same piece himself because he said, 'Don't read that shit. You're the greatest striker I've seen. There's loads more goals in you yet.'

That was big of Aldo, because the papers were continually speculating that, following my return, his days at the club were numbered.

Though John and I were in competition to lead the line, we got on very well, which is often the case when two players are competing for one place. It's strange, but you never see the other person as a threat. There seems to be an invisible buffer between you that prevents resentment or animosity. The actual decision of who plays rests with the manager, not the other player, and if you are truthful with yourself, you will know why you've been left out of the side. When Bill Shankly was manager he left centre-half, Larry Lloyd, on the sidelines for a spell. After playing a number of matches for the reserves and not having regained his place in the first team, Larry let his feelings be known to Shankly. 'If you want to get in the team, get in!' Shankly told Larry. 'I'm not stopping you getting in the team – you are!'

Peter Beardsley and John Barnes had also slotted into the team while I'd been in Italy. Peter was a quiet lad off the field, but assertive on it. He possessed an array of quicksilver skills and, for a man of his size, was extremely strong. He seemed almost to bounce around defenders. John, on the other hand, was a livewire in the dressing-room and saw himself as a snappy dresser. I had the peg next to him and, just as Kenny, Graeme and Alan Hansen had done when I first arrived at the club wearing crap clothes, I used to slaughter John for what he wore. But compared to what I had donned in my early days at Anfield, John was a model of sartorial elegance. He would arrive for training wearing a vivid yellow or orange jacket and black or lime green shirt. To say the clothes John wore were loud would be an understatement. I used to say to him, 'Any more of this and I'll have to wear sunglasses.'

John had superlative skills and I have often been asked why he never seemed to replicate his performances for Liverpool when playing for England. John won seventy-nine caps and during his ninth game for England scored a quite brilliant individual goal against Brazil in a 2–0 win in Rio. But it makes life difficult when you produce a sublime performance so early in a career. Although you may subsequently produce consistently good performances, everything thereafter will appear as something of an anti-climax. John was also asked to fulfil a variety of roles when playing for England and I don't think he enjoyed the sort of service he received when playing for Liverpool. But he was an outstanding player and possessed dazzling skills which he was able to demonstrate even in the heat of battle. I would go as far as to say that John was the most skilful player Liverpool possessed at this time. Despite this tremendous talent he was always battling to keep his weight down; he only had to look at a Jaffa Cake to put on half a pound. He gave his all for Liverpool and was always keen to improve as a player. I was now a senior player at Anfield and, on one occasion, John asked for my advice.

'Stay out of McDonald's,' I told him.

On Boxing Day I played, and scored, in the 1–0 victory over Derby County but sustained yet another injury, a groin strain, which meant I missed most of the rest of the season. To say I was frustrated would be an understatement. I had wanted my first season back to be a memorable one, but ill health, injury and the fact I had never regained optimum fitness had dogged me throughout.

There were six games remaining when I returned to the fold in mid-April. For all it had been a stop-start season for me, the upside was that Liverpool were in contention for the League and Cup 'double'. The quest for the First Division Championship had evolved into a two-horse race between ourselves and George Graham's Arsenal. In the FA Cup, Liverpool had reached the semi-finals. All was going well for the team and the club.

Kenny had seamlessly created a new Liverpool side. Some of the old guard such as Lawro and Craig Johnston had gone. The likes of Grob, Ronnie Whelan, Stevie Nicol, Steve McMahon and, I suppose, myself, were now old hands. Jan and Gary Gillespie were still there but, like me and Alan Hansen, had been plagued by injury throughout the season. Peter Beardsley, John Aldridge, John Barnes and Ray Houghton had been mainstays of the team, and Gary Ablett, David Burrows and Steve Staunton had been introduced during the second half of the season and done extremely well. Alan Hansen returned to action the same time as me. We felt we had the ideal mix of experience and youth to enable us to achieve another season of glory for Liverpool. Confidence was very high in mid-April as we prepared for final run-in, with the 'double' firmly in our sights.

I had sufficiently recovered from injury to be included in the squad for our FA Cup semi-final against Nottingham Forest at Hillsborough. I was still some way off being match-fit and didn't expect to be named in the starting line-up, so was not surprised when Kenny told me I was to be on the bench.

Saturday, 15 April 1989, Hillsborough

I am about to take my place on the bench, track-suited, ready to be called upon if need be. Our FA Cup semi-final against Nottingham

Forest is about to start. As I take my seat, I glance across to the Leppings Lane end. It is packed with Liverpool supporters. I have seen packed terraces before, but not like this. The central area behind the goal is particularly congested. The sun is shining. It's a warm day for mid-April. I think how hot those supporters must be.

I look out across the pitch. The teams are lined up ready for action. My eyes go back to the Leppings Lane end. There's a perimeter fence, which looks to be about 18 feet high, beyond which the terrace appears to be divided up with fencing into pens. I think this a curious arrangement but nothing more than that. The Kop is a massive terrace but, once you're on it, you're free to stroll anywhere and chose your spot. This doesn't appear to be the case with the Leppings Lane terrace.

The game gets underway and I focus on the action on the field. From the off we gain the upper hand. After two minutes Peter Beardsley hits the Forest crossbar. I'm watching the ball rebound and, suddenly, through my peripheral vision I see the Liverpool supporters immediately behind the goal haven't responded. It's strange because it's as if I am aware of this lack of response, yet it doesn't register in my brain as a conscious thought, not then.

John Aldridge has the ball. I'm watching him but, for a split second, I divert my eyes to the Leppings Lane end. Is that someone trying to climb over the perimeter fencing, or is he just trying to elevate himself to obtain a better view?

Play unfolds. We are on the attack again. Another split-second thought: 'Our fans are a bit quiet.' No sooner does this thought enter my head then it is gone.

I see one of our supporters on the pitch.

'Fan on the pitch. Bloody hell,' says a voice in the dugout.

The fan is saying something to John Aldridge.

'Get off. You'll get us all in trouble,' I hear Aldo say.

The fan seems to be pleading with Aldo. What's going on?

There's a policeman on the pitch, but he is not heading towards the fan. He's jogging towards referee Ray Lewis.

Someone nudges my arm. I turn to see who it is but no one is looking at me. Everyone on the bench is staring down the pitch towards the Leppings Lane terrace.

There are some supporters on the grass and the perimeter track to the left of the goal. Some are on their knees. One looks as if he is vomiting. Other fans are lying on the grass. A number of supporters are trying to scale the perimeter fence. I see one pushed back by a policeman, only for the fan to force his way past the officer and fall on to the perimeter track. Kenny and I stand up. Out of the corner of my eye I see the players coming off the pitch. They are jogging towards the tunnel. Ray Lewis follows carrying the ball in one hand, flanked by his linesmen.

Kenny makes to follow the lads down the tunnel. I fall into step behind him. As I turn to go down the tunnel I look back down the pitch.

A supporter is tugging at an advertising hoarding. There are more fans on the grass. It's chaotic.

I head for the dressing-room. Officials, stewards, policemen are running up and down the corridor, bumping into one another.

In the dressing-room Kenny tells us we must keep focused on the game. Everyone does their own thing to keep their mind focused on the game. Some do stretches, some breathing exercises. I jog on the spot and desperately try to concentrate on nothing but the game.

'Keep focused,' he repeats. 'Keep your minds on the game.'

There's a knock on the dressing-room door. Ray Lewis enters.

'Five minutes, lads,' says Ray and then leaves, presumably to tell the Forest lads the same.

'Can't see this being five minutes,' says Alan Hansen *sotto voce*.

Neither can I.

'Stay focused.'

I am. Once I am in game mindset, I stay there. I'm not thinking about what I've seen.

Somewhere someone is shouting. There is no anger in his voice, but what is it? Panic?

Now I *am* thinking about what I've seen. It's a crush. Fans spilling on to the pitch. It'll take time but they'll sort it out and then we'll be back out.

Kenny is pacing up and down, up and down.

I hear shouting again, from the corridor outside.

'Get that! Take it! Where's Mick?'

I don't know what or who the voice is referring to, but everyone has looked up.

Kenny opens the door, goes out into the corridor and closes the door behind him.

Three, four people are shouting?

'People are dying!' I hear a voice call out.

Kenny returns. His face is ashen.

Everyone is looking very concerned. No one is talking. The silence is uncommon, full of dread. I suddenly feel very anxious.

There's a knock on the door. Ray Lewis steps into the room again.

'That's it, abandoned,' he says.

'What the hell's happened?' asks Aldo.

'Hey, whatever it is, it's bad,' says Alan Hansen, his voice full of foreboding.

I'm back in my civvies, making my way along the corridor up towards the players' lounge. There are Liverpool supporters by a pay phone at the bottom of the stairs. One is trying to get through to someone.

'What's happened?' I ask a lad in his twenties.

'People are dead,' he says, the words croaking out of his mouth.

Is it the whole ground? What has happened? I am desperate to see Tracy, to see for myself she is OK.

A great wave of relief sweeps through my being when I enter the lounge and see her there.

'It's awful. Terrible,' Tracy says, her eyes welling with tears.

Instinctively I reach out and hug her.

The rest of the lads have headed for their loved ones, too. For a few minutes we are all separated from one another.

There is a television mounted on a wall but it's showing a horse race.

Kenny is frantic. Seemingly, his son, Paul, had a ticket for the opposite side of the ground, the big cantilever stand, and hasn't shown as yet. I've never seen him like this before. Then Paul appears. Kenny makes his way towards his son and hugs him.

'It's awful. I think some people are dead,' he says.

The room suddenly goes quiet. The television is relaying news.

'We are receiving reports that the FA Cup semi-final at Hillsborough between Liverpool and Nottingham Forest has been abandoned due to a serious incident at the Leppings Lane end of the ground, where many of the Liverpool supporters are congregated. Worryingly, it appears a tragedy may be unfolding. We are receiving unconfirmed reports of fatalities and of many injured. We go over now to Hillsborough . . . '

I hear this but it's as if I am in a state of suspended animation. I'm not moving. All I can do is stare numbly at the TV screen.

There are tragedies that happen in your life which you never forget. All these years on the memories of Hillsborough remain so horrific I find it very difficult to talk about them. It is impossible to convey my feelings on that fateful day and in the days that followed. I just can't describe the grief I felt. Countless words have since been written about the terrible events that caused the death of ninety-six Liverpool supporters. All I can say is, things were never to be the same again – for those who lost loved ones, for everybody.

For all those present that day, and for those who weren't but had loved ones or friends present, Hillsborough was a nightmare, the second such nightmare to strike at the heart of Liverpool football club. Many times I have wondered why, 'Why us? Why did people have to suffer so, at Heysel, at Hillsborough?' In such tragic and terrible circumstances I discovered why my faith is so important to me.

I don't wish to go into the ins and outs of who was responsible for the tragic events of Hillsborough. This has been well documented elsewhere, and by people far more qualified to pass judgement than me.

The whole of Merseyside was plunged into mourning for weeks – many mourn still. Everyone connected with the club was devastated. Yet such numbing tragedy can pull people together in a way nothing else can. This proved to be the case. Everyone on Merseyside felt pain and grief. We all tried to support one another. Players were present at every funeral; we visited the families of every poor soul who had perished, and spent countless hours just talking to people but, in the main, just listening.

Kenny assumed responsibility for everything the club did to try and help people through the ordeal. He faced the world's media. He attended virtually every sad event – one day he and Marina went to four funerals – met bereaved families and comforted players. How much all this took out of him I can't say, but it did have a great effect on the man. He, like everyone else, was never quite the same again.

Every year, on the anniversary of the disaster, a memorial service for the victims has been held. Families come to Anfield and after the service we have tea and talk. It is a sad and poignant occasion but I have noticed how, over the years, the small talk is of how the club and team are doing, if we will win a trophy or not. Hillsborough is rarely mentioned in conversation. It's not that people have forgotten, or that the passing of years has eased pain. Nobody will ever forget, nor would they want to. I believe it is still just too painful.

Even in the aftermath of such an awful tragedy, life had to go on. At the time there was much debate as to whether the FA Cup should be continued that season, or whether it should be abandoned as a mark of respect to those who died. It was a heart-wrenching decision for all concerned, particularly the FA. Eventually it was decided the competition should continue. At Liverpool we were prepared to accept whatever decision was made but, at the time, football was the furthest thing from our minds. Despite this, I think it was right for us to carry on. I felt continuing to play games was an indication of the collective strength of the city, and displayed the respect we had for all those who had lost their lives. We wanted to show the world we grieved but also that we were strong. I also felt should we go on to win the Cup it would be a fitting tribute to the memory of those who had perished.

By the time the replay against Nottingham Forest was arranged – at Old Trafford – it had become nothing short of a crusade for Liverpool football club. I sensed the whole of the nation wished us to win. No disrespect to Nottingham Forest but I believe the sheer intensity of the occasion overwhelmed them. I didn't make the starting line-up on the night but from the start I felt the result was never in doubt. In the event two goals from Aldo and an own goal from Brian Laws took us to Wembley, where, fittingly, our opponents were to be Everton. Merseyside was to be united at Wembley in every sense of the word and we saw the final as being an opportunity to show the world the city was united in grief.

We had been forced to postpone a number of League games but were still up there with Arsenal in the race for the title. As we approached the FA Cup final we had two League games remaining, against West Ham United and, our final game, against of all clubs, Arsenal. At one stage, George Graham's side had looked favourites to land the title but, before the FA Cup final, had slipped up, losing at home to Derby County then doing no better than a goalless draw against Wimbledon. Suddenly we were right back with a real chance of the League Championship – and the 'double'.

Our schedule in May was hectic. Six League matches, the rearranged FA Cup semi-final against Forest and the Wembley final against Everton; eight games in the space of twenty-six days. Emotionally energised, the team set about the schedule desperately wanting to achieve glory. Not for ourselves or the football club, but for the people of Liverpool and the memory of those who had lost their lives at Hillsborough. I had never been so emotionally bound up in a cause. Peter Beardsley made a good effort to sum it all up by saying, 'Win or lose, let's make sure the real winner is football.'

I had four League games as a substitute under my belt when we set off for Wembley, one of these games being a goalless draw against Everton, a game which understandably took place amidst an atmosphere of great emotion from start to finish.

I was still far from fully fit and thought I wouldn't be taking any part in proceedings at Wembley. This in mind, I went to see Kenny. I told him my ambition was to work to regain fitness for the beginning of the following season. In order to help me do this, I asked if I could be excused training in the weeks preceding and following the final as I wanted to book myself in for a fortnight at the FA training centre at Lilleshall with a view to building strength and stamina.

'Aye, that's good idea and I think you need it,' Kenny told me, adding, 'but I need you, too. I want you to be on the subs' bench at Wembley.'

Kenny went on to say he felt my goal-scoring exploits over the years against Everton had made them fearful of me. We also had the League games against West Ham and Arsenal that were crucial to the destiny of the title and he wanted me around for my experience. The Lilleshall trip was put on hold.

With the possible exception of the 1958 final between Manchester United and Bolton Wanderers following the Munich air disaster, I doubt there has ever been such an emotional Wembley final as the all-Merseyside FA Cup final that year. Certainly there hasn't been since.

The game was played on a tidal wave of public sympathy. Of course we were desperate to win, but deep down I knew, whatever the outcome, the result was not important. In keeping with the family occasion everyone wanted it to be, both clubs invited former players as guests on the day. The former Everton captain, Brian Labone, told me a wonderful story about the 1966 Cup final when he had skippered the Everton team against Sheffield Wednesday.

In the time-honoured way, Brian was in the process of introducing Princess Margaret to his teammates before the kick-off when she suddenly turned to him.

'Where exactly is Everton, Mr Labone?' asked Her Royal Highness.

'We're from Liverpool, ma'am,' replied Brian.

'Ah, yes,' replied the Princess, seemingly suddenly to recall that Liverpool had defeated Leeds in the previous season's final. 'How forgetful of me. We had your first team here last year.'

How Bill Shankly would have loved that one.

We played well and were leading through a fourth-minute goal from Aldo when I replaced him in the seventy-second minute. With us one goal to the good the last thing I'd expected was to be called into action, particularly in place of our goal-scorer. But Aldo had run himself into the ground in our cause. Coming on as I did was a tremendous boost to my confidence. I realised Kenny still had an unshaken belief in my ability, even though I had done precious little to justify it since my return from Italy.

Though not fully fit, such was the emotion of the occasion I was getting through the game on adrenalin. Just when we appeared to be heading for victory on the strength of Aldo's goal, Everton seized a dramatic last-minute equaliser through Stuart McCall, who'd also come on as a substitute.

McCall's goal sent the final into extra time. As we gathered on the pitch to prepare for another thirty minutes of play, I sensed McCall's late equaliser had knocked the stuffing out of some of the lads, so I seized the moment.

'Hey, come on, this is a test of what sort of players we really are. Don't let anybody feel sorry for themselves. Let me tell you, the mark of a great side is how it responds to setbacks. This game hasn't been snatched from us. We've been given thirty more minutes to win it. So come on, let's do that.'

Kenny clapped his hands together, I would like to think because I had said the right thing. When play resumed, we got stuck into Everton.

Only four minutes had passed when Stevie Nicol centred the ball from wide. I managed to get the ball under control with one touch, turned Kevin Ratcliffe and, on seeing a gap, fired the ball low past Neville Southall and into the corner of the net. Another automated camera behind the goal took a tumble.

Everton would not lie down. They came back at us and, on what was turning out to be a memorable day for substitutes, Stuart McCall latched on to a headed clearance from Alan Hansen to volley an equaliser from twenty-five yards for his second goal of the game.

Everton's elation lasted but two minutes. The mercurial John Barnes twisted and turned to find space enough for him to float the ball into a gap between Kevin Ratcliffe and Dave Watson. The ball arrived at around shoulder height. There was no way I was going to pull that ball down with my boot, so I bent my head to meet it. Rather than go for power, I flicked the ball, directing it towards the far corner. It was my fourth goal in two finals against Everton and it was enough to help us win the Cup.

The sense of achievement we all felt on hearing the final whistle was clearly evident for all to see. It had been one of the most dramatic finals in the long history of the Cup and my elation at having scored twice was, of course, tinged with great sadness. The feeling I had was a very curious one which I can only describe as being ecstasy and sorrow in equal amounts. I had never experienced such a mix of confusing emotions in my life and never have since.

The Everton players were, as ever, generous in defeat. Neville Southall offered his congratulations to me, then said, 'Will you do me a favour, Rushy?'

'Sure. What?'

'Just fuck off! I'm sick of the sight of you,' he said with a smile of frustration as he tousled my hair before throwing an arm around me.

Then Kenny came over, put both arms around me and said, 'Don't tell me now that you didn't want to be sub.'

I joined my teammates as we celebrated. We gazed up at the alp-like terraces that were a sea of red and blue. It was a day no one present would ever forget, but to my mind it was far more than that. It was the day a smile returned to the faces of our supporters, Liverpool football club and English football as a whole.

Three days later I returned to the starting line-up for our game against West Ham United and scored in a 5–1 victory to set-up a dramatic denouement to the League season.

Will there ever be a Championship finale to rival the night we entertained Arsenal at Anfield? We were in the driving seat. A draw would give us the title. Even a single goal defeat would mean Liverpool would be champions by virtue of goal difference.

Arsenal had to win by two clear goals and we had not lost at home by such a margin for over three years. Added to which we had only conceded eight goals all season at Anfield. It was the closest ever race to the Championship in the history of the Football League and we were confident of victory.

As a gesture of Arsenal's support in the wake of Hillsborough, every member of the Arsenal team took to the pitch bearing a bouquet of flowers, which they proceeded to present to our supporters, a gesture that was much appreciated by all who had gathered for this game of games.

We should have gone out and played our normal game, attacked Arsenal and placed them under pressure, kept possession of the ball as we always did. Instead we played an overly cautious game. The first half was unworthy of the occasion. No team carved out a meaningful chance on goal. There was too much nervous play. With thirty-two minutes gone, I pulled up with a groin strain. In previous weeks I knew I had been riding my luck. My body just couldn't cope with the rigours of another game and had let me know. I was deeply disappointed and not a little angry with myself when I had to make way for Peter Beardsley.

From my position on the bench I watched the title slip from our grasp. We seemed content to play for a draw and seven minutes into the second half were made to pay.

Arsenal won a free-kick just outside our penalty area and both Tony Adams and Steve Bould went forward. Nigel Winterburn floated the ball behind a knot of our defenders who were crowding Adams and Bould. Adams went for the ball, didn't connect and it ran through to Alan Smith, who may, or may not, have applied the faintest of a touch. The ball evaded Grob and nestled into the corner of the net.

Our lads surrounded the referee, convinced Smithy had not made contact with the ball. Should that have been the case the goal should have been disallowed as it had been indirect free-kick. The referee, however, waved aside our protests and we found ourselves chasing the game. 'Still,' I thought to myself, 'if it stays like this, we're home and dry.'

But, having scored, Arsenal remained calm and patient, and continued to probe for the goal that would land them the title in the most dramatic circumstances imaginable.

We continued to plug away honestly but without inspiration. Though we had not played well, with a few minutes of the game remaining, I thought we were going to be OK. Someone on the bench said the game was about to go into time added on. Surely there was no way Arsenal could nick it?

Lee Dixon played a long ball up to Alan Smith who helped it on, I sensed, in the hope someone was making a run. That someone turned out to be Michael Thomas, who suddenly found himself with a one-on-one with Grob. Thomas was not of the doubting variety. He calmly flicked the ball over Grob and into the net. My heart sank into my boots. I looked across the benches. Kenny had suddenly become hollow-cheeked next to his exuberant neighbour, George Graham.

We only had time enough to kick-off when the referee's whistle blew to end the game and confirm Arsenal as Champions. With the obvious exception of the Arsenal contingent, the disappointment around Anfield was palpable. I felt totally drained of emotion, as did the rest of the lads. I couldn't quite believe what had happened, let alone come to terms with it.

Credit to Arsenal, they had a mighty task to undertake and they did it. I don't think I have ever seen two sets of players with such contrasting emotions as I did that night. Our dressing-room was depressingly solemn, an atmosphere not helped by the rejoicing we could hear coming down the corridor. Deeply disappointed as we were we upheld the Liverpool maxim set in place by Bill Shankly, that of being dignified in victory and gracious in defeat. As painful as it was, to a man we went into the Arsenal dressing-room and offered their players our congrat-ulations.

After the game Kenny referred to the manner in which Arsenal had played. 'It wasn't the Liverpool way,' he said. I don't think Kenny was being ungracious, just stating a fact. It was not the Liverpool way but, to be honest, on the night we ourselves had not played 'the Liverpool way'. There had been an unnatural caution about us from the very start.

I don't wish to make excuses or take anything from Arsenal but, looking back now, I feel the whole trauma of the preceding weeks finally caught up with us. Physically and emotionally we were drained. I felt for Kenny. As I said goodbye to him that night he looked washed-out, his normally rosy cheeks colourless. Body posture tells you a lot about a person. As Kenny made his way to his car, his shoulders were hunched, his step like that of a man more than twice his age.

I drove back to the house on the Wirral that Tracy and I had bought and were in the process of turning into a home. I had two weeks of hard labour at Lilleshall to look forward to and a lot more work on the training field besides.

More importantly, though, Tracy was expecting. On 13 June 1989, she gave birth to our first son, Jonathan. It was to have a profound effect on us both. We no longer saw ourselves as a couple, but as a family and we were gloriously happy in that notion. I found myself doing things I had never imagined myself doing, such as listening to the World Service at 2am when it was 'my turn', singing nursery rhymes at seven in the morning and taking an inordinate interest in the moisture absorption qualities of nappies.

CHAPTER TWELVE

Step On

Spiritually, English football seemed to be at rock bottom at the start of the 1989–90 season. And yet, from grass roots level to the First Division, the new shoots of recovery were beginning to show.

At Liverpool we had one aim: to win the Championship. We hoped it would be the first step towards establishing a new era in the history of the club. There was also the hope we could win the title in some style and help to restore some of the game's credibility.

There was a new face in the camp. Swedish centre-back Glenn Hysen had joined from Fiorentina and was to make his presence felt along with the emerging talents of Steve Staunton, David Burrows and the versatile Barry Venison. Alan Hansen was back in the fold and I knew I would be contesting the main striker's role with Aldo.

On that opening day I received the nod for our game against Manchester City. We won 3–1 and though I didn't score I knew I was back to full fitness and, more importantly, had lost none of my sharpness.

We remained unbeaten in our first eight League matches and I finally got off the mark in a 3–0 win against Derby County, but the most memorable team performance was the night we crushed Crystal Palace 9–0 at Anfield.

The result was a club record win in the First Division and was notable for the fact that eight different players managed to feature on the score-sheet, the first time this had happened in the history of the Football League. For the record those scorers were: Stevie Nicol (two), Steve McMahon, myself, Gary Gillespie, Peter Beardsley, Aldo, John Barnes and Glenn Hysen.

The victory over Palace also marked Aldo's 'farewell party'. He was a superb striker and wanted to stay at Liverpool, but he also wanted regular first-team football and so had agreed to join Real Sociedad. I was sorry to see him go – as were the rest of the lads – but understood his reasons. Aldo was named as substitute against Palace but was desperate to play an important role in the game and, hopefully, score so that he could bid a suitable farewell to our supporters.

We were 5–0 up when Ronnie Whelan was tripped in the Palace penalty area. Kenny immediately replaced Peter Beardsley with Aldo and we all stepped back to allow him to take the penalty which he unerringly despatched past Perry Suckling. It was Kenny's farewell present to Aldo and when the ball hit the back of the net the Kop went wild. At the end of the game, Aldo ran up to the cheering Kop and threw his shirt, boots and socks to our fans. It was an emotional farewell for all concerned, though I should imagine that if such a thing occurred today, the player concerned would be fined for bringing the game into disrepute and his club charged with not keeping their players in order.

Two weeks later I scored twice in a 3–1 win over Everton at

Goodison Park, our other goal coming from John Barnes who had been in scintillating form from the start of the season. Victory over Everton saw us move to the top of Division One, ahead of second-placed Millwall.

Millwall soon lost their early momentum and were eventually relegated. For much of the season the race for the title was contested by Liverpool, Graham Taylor's Aston Villa, Arsenal and Bobby Campbell's Chelsea. It's worth noting that for much of the campaign Manchester United wandered up and down mid-table like a dog that had lost the scent. Alex Ferguson's side eventually finished thirteenth and there was a period when his job appeared to be hanging by a thread. However, a fine run in the FA Cup, which United won, served to quell his critics and offered evidence that positive things were stirring at Old Trafford.

Following a 2–0 defeat at Sheffield Wednesday on 29 November we then embarked upon a fantastic run that saw us lose just one of twenty-three League matches. Earlier in the season, Kenny had taken Israeli International, Ronnie Rosenthal, on loan from Belgian side Standard Liège. Other than two appearances as a substitute, Ronnie had failed to make it into the side, which was understandable given our terrific form. With seven games remaining, Kenny was loathe to make changes to the team. Ray Houghton, however, suffered an injury in a 2–1 win over Wimbledon and with Peter Beardsley also sidelined, Kenny called up Ronnie for a game against Charlton Athletic.

I might be wrong, but I gained the impression Kenny had made up his mind not to sign Ronnie. However, that day Ronnie was on fire and scored a hat-trick in a 4–0 victory. I suppose he felt he had proved to Kenny that he could do a job for Liverpool. Certainly his agent seemed to think this. Believing he had misjudged Ronnie,

Kenny contacted Ronnie Rosenthal's agent and Standard Liège with a view to signing him on a permanent basis, and was told the fee had increased from £250,000 to £500,000.

That's what one terrific performance was starting to do for a player's worth in the transfer market.

'How many hat-tricks have you scored for this club?' asked Ronnie Whelan, a day or so later.

'I dunno, fifteen, sixteen?'

I suddenly twigged what Ronnie Whelan was impishly alluding to.

'Doesn't work that way,' I said.

'It's beginning to,' he replied.

On 28 April I opened our account against Queens Park Rangers and, though Roy Wegerle equalised, a second-half penalty from John Barnes was enough to give us a 2–1 victory and the three points that secured Liverpool's eighteenth League Championship. It was a Football League record; the club's eleventh Championship in eighteen years, my fifth with Liverpool and none the less sweet for that. I never thought it would be, to date, Liverpool's last Championship success.

Given we had exited the League Cup at the hands of Arsenal, the one big disappointment for me was defeat in the FA Cup semi-finals to Crystal Palace. To accommodate television, the kick-off times of the two matches were staggered (Manchester United were playing Second Division Oldham Athletic) and, as a foretaste of the excessive hype that now surrounds the game, the day was billed as 'Super Sunday'.

We were the Cup holders and riding high in the First Division. Palace were haunted by the possibility of relegation. Once more we had the 'double' in our sights and I really felt we were capable of achieving it. But in the event it proved to be anything but 'super' for me and Liverpool.

All seemed to be going well at Villa Park when I latched on to a great pass from Steve McMahon to glide the ball past Nigel Martyn. Minutes later I challenged for a high ball and took a whack. I felt as if someone had hit me with a fridge-freezer swung from the jib of crane. The pain was excruciating and it didn't go away. The last thing I wanted was to come off, but the rib injury was so painful I had no option but to give way to Steve Staunton. John Barnes switched to striker. Then Gary Gillespie went down with a groin strain and was replaced by Barry Venison, which necessitated another re-shuffle.

Almost from the kick-off Palace drew level through Mark Bright. Even so there was no hint of the goal rush and drama that was to come. We looked comfortable until the seventieth minute when George O'Reilly gave Palace the lead. Then John Barnes and Steve McMahon scored for us. I thought we were Wembley-bound, but credit to Palace, they kept coming at us and, with only two minutes remaining, made it 3–3 when Andy Gray headed in, with our normally solid defence in some disarray.

Four minutes into extra time, Palace again showed how effective they were from set-pieces when Andy Thorn flicked on a near post corner and Alan Pardew destroyed our hopes of a possible 'double'.

Having beaten Palace 9–0 at Anfield and 2–0 at Selhurst Park it was a real blow to succumb to them in the semi-finals but Steve Coppell and his players never gave up and their work on set-pieces had exposed us. It was the highest scoring FA Cup semi-final since Manchester United had beaten Fulham 5–3 thirty-two years previously and, of course, it made for great television, as did the United–Oldham tie which ended 3–3. United overcame Joe Royle's side 2–1 in the replay and the final also went to a replay. After a pulsating 3–3 draw at Wembley, a lone goal from Lee Martin in the replay gave Alex Ferguson his first trophy as manager of Manchester United and, some maintain, kept him in the job.

The rib injury apart, I was delighted to have played throughout the season and to have scored twenty-six goals, which proved, I felt, that my ailments had not resulted in any loss of sharpness. For once I did not end up as the club's leading goal-scorer. That honour went to John Barnes, who had what I believe was his best season in a Liverpool shirt. John scored twenty-two goals in the League, though I did remind him that five of those had come from the penalty spot. I was only jigging him. The sweetest sound to a striker's ears is the hiss of the rigging, and that 'tune' plays the same from whatever source.

A season that started with muted applause ended with English football having regained some stature and credibility. I would like to think the way Liverpool played throughout the season contributed in some way to this. Replays apart, the two televised FA Cup semi-finals produced breathtaking and dramatic football and a total of thirteen goals. The final itself produced six. By finishing fourth in an uninspiring World Cup in Italy, England too restored some prestige.

Generally speaking, the standard of football and entertainment was very good and this was reflected in another rise in attendances. Just under 20 million spectators attended League matches, and this in a season when many grounds had had their capacity severely restricted. Attendances experienced a year-on-year rise for a fourth successive season. The sheer number of games being shown on television helped regenerate interest, and large companies, attracted by the exposure the game was beginning to receive, started to see football as a way of promotion. Money was coming into the game and, as everyone knows, money attracts the money of those who are out to make money.

The following season, 1990–1, began well. I was pleased with my pre-season and raring to go, Kenny seemed content, and the supporters were happy that the League Championship was back in the trophy room with every hope of it staying there. UEFA had even given a hint that our European ban might be lifted in the near future. This feeling of optimism showed in our early season form. I opened my goal-scoring account in our first game of the season, a 3–1 win at Sheffield United, and we proceeded to set a blistering pace in our quest to retain the title. We won our first eight League matches and did not suffer a defeat until December (0–3 at Arsenal). Up to that point we had gone fourteen League games unbeaten. I managed nine goals and Peter Beardsley eleven. On New Year's Day I scored in our 3–0 win over Leeds at Anfield which further cemented our position at the head of the table.

Kenny was pleased with our progress, though he had not been enjoying the best of health, having suffered from, amongst other things, a bad bout of shingles. In mid-February we had still had only lost twice in the League and there was little daylight between ourselves and the chasing pack, which comprised Arsenal, Crystal Palace and Leeds. We were also involved in the FA Cup and had been drawn at home to Everton in round five.

The tie finished goalless, which meant a replay at Goodison on 22 February. It turned out to be one of the most dramatic and closely contested of all Merseyside derbies. We held the lead on no less than four occasions but could not finish Everton off, the game ending 4–4 after extra time. I had scored our third goal and, though we were naturally disappointed not to have held any of the leads, such had been the drama of the night that there was still a detectable excitement in the dressing-room after the game. Kenny didn't say much. I knew he was upset that we had squandered the lead four times, but I can't recall him being particularly downcast.

The following Friday we trained at Melwood, ready to head off afterwards for Luton, where we were playing the following afternoon. I heard the board had called a press conference, and television crews and press reporters were milling about in their droves, which led me to believe Kenny had made a major signing.

I was in the dressing-room with the rest of the lads when Kenny suddenly appeared wearing his best suit and accompanied by our chairman, Noel White. The room suddenly fell silent.

'I'm come to see you, boys, because I want you to know before the rest of the world finds out. I've resigned as manager,' said Kenny.

I was so shocked I felt my forehead prickle as the adrenalin rushed about my head. It was evident from the looks on everyone's faces that they too were completely taken aback by this news.

'Thanks for all you have given, all of you. We've been through a lot together. More than any manager or team should have to endure, but we got through it – together. I just want to say thanks, wish you all the best and . . . '

He didn't say any more. His eyes welled with tears. He glanced about the room as if to take it all in for one last time, then turned to leave, managing a croaky 'thanks' as he passed through the door and into legend at Liverpool football club.

I didn't get over the shock of Kenny's departure for some weeks. I can only assume the pressure finally got to him and, thinking of the well-being of his family, he decided enough was enough. He had totally immersed himself in time, energy and emotion towards trying to ease the trauma of Hillsborough while at the same time maintaining the club's position at the top of English football. I have no doubt whatsoever that he loved Liverpool but maybe to continue his connection with the club was an all-too-painful reminder of what had gone before. As a manager he always protected his players from the pressure of the outside world – he wanted our minds to be concentrated purely on football – but I think the pressure of trying not to display the growing strain he was feeling proved too much in the end.

Kenny always had complete faith in his own judgement, seeming to make decisions without too much deliberation. Now he seemed to agonise over everything. He later said that before the Everton replay he lay on his hotel bed and made one final decision. He had to get out. 'The alternative', he believed, 'was to go mad.'

In times of tragedy and confusion, those with the greatest minds and the biggest hearts come to the fore. Kenny is one of those people. I can't pay him a bigger compliment than that.

Ronnie Moran was placed in temporary charge of team affairs and raised the battle cry even before we left Anfield for Luton.

'We'll all miss Kenny, but these things happen in life,' he reminded us. 'The only thing that matters now is beating Luton and going from there.'

We didn't beat Luton. We lost 3–1 to a team which, under different circumstances, we would have beaten out of sight. We then went on to lose a crucial League game against Arsenal and the FA Cup replay against Everton. I'm at pains to point out these defeats had nothing at all to do with Ronnie in his capacity of caretaker boss. It was all down to us players. The spark that had been so evident in our play had been dimmed.

Defeat against Arsenal saw the Gunners overhaul us at the top, but we galvanised and soon resumed pole position courtesy of a 2–1 victory over Sunderland and an emphatic 7–1 win over Derby

County. Having hammered Derby County no one envisaged any problems when Queens Park Rangers arrived at Anfield, but we were dreadful that day and Rangers inflicted a 3–1 defeat upon us.

A single goal defeat at Southampton was followed by a goalless draw against Coventry City. Arsenal were on a terrific run, however, and a season that had once promised so much was now fraught with uncertainty.

On 16 April we were given another surprise when told Graeme Souness was returning to the club as our new manager. Ronnie had made it clear he didn't want the job and I was delighted to see Graeme return, as I believed if anyone had the qualities to keep Liverpool at the top it was him. Graeme knew how the club operated, and had proved himself a highly successful manager at Rangers. It had been seven years since Graeme had last set foot in Anfield and many of the players didn't know him. 'Don't worry, he'll be perfect,' I told them, 'He's right for the job. Graeme will carry on the traditions of this club, keep us at the top.' Famous last words and all that.

Graeme's first two games in charge resulted in 3–0 victories over both Norwich City and Crystal Palace. We were still in with a shout for the title, but such a shout was severely muted when we then lost 4–2 at Chelsea. To have any chance of overtaking Arsenal at the top we had to beat Nottingham Forest at the City Ground. Graeme brought in Ronnie Rosenthal for Peter Beardsley and continued with David Speedie (who had been Kenny's last signing from Coventry City). Ronnie couldn't reproduce his 'Charlton form' and was substituted, though few of us played to form that day. Forest won 2–1 to end what hopes we had of the title, which was Highbury-bound for the tenth time.

I scored in our final game of the season, a 2–0 win over Spurs. The victory cemented our position as runners-up but I can't say I took any consolation from that fact. Again I finished a season with twenty-six goals to my name. I was joint-leading scorer in the League, John Barnes and I netting sixteen apiece, in addition to which I scored five in both the FA and League Cups. I was pleased with my goal return. I had now been amongst the leading goal-scorers in the First Division for eight of the past nine seasons. I felt fit, sharp and strong and had every reason to believe there were a lot more goals to come.

Graeme's first season in charge was important in more ways than one because we had finally been allowed back into Europe after a six-year ban. As runners-up in the First Division we were to compete in the UEFA Cup and I was really looking forward to playing in Europe again. The ban had affected Liverpool – and the other clubs who had been subjected to it. If you have anything about you, you learn from every game you play, but there is always something to be learned from playing against top Continental opposition that cannot be derived from playing domestic football week in and week out. Here I am talking of technique, technical ability, gameplans and so on. English football had experienced a period of not-so-splendid isolation and I for one relished the thought of playing in Europe again. Football is always in a state of flux as new ideas and methods are introduced. I felt the ban had had a detrimental effect on top players in that we had not been exposed to these new ideas, nor had we been afforded the opportunity to test what we had developed against the best in Europe.

Graeme wasted little time in adding to the squad. During the summer he bought my striking partner with Wales, Dean Saunders, and England centre-back, Mark Wright, from Derby County. Knowing Graeme, I felt he was going to stamp his own impression upon the club, but I never appreciated how different this would prove to be.

The first inkling I had was when we reported for pre-season training. We did a lot of running and followed that with more running and, by way of a change, some running that was longer and harder. I'd just come back from holiday and my limbs and muscles weren't up to such strenuous work at such an early stage. I wasn't alone in thinking this.

Players began to succumb to injuries before a ball was kicked and, to my chagrin, I was one of them. I suffered an Achilles tendon injury and the prognosis was not good. My leg was put in plaster and the specialist told me that not only would I miss the start of the season, it would be some months before I would be fit enough to play again. Barry Venison and Jimmy Carter, whom Kenny had signed from Millwall, suffered identical injuries, so I can only assume it was all down to the training we were being asked to do.

Graeme was still superbly fit and, to be fair, never asked us to do anything he did not do himself. He was always at the front when we did a long power-run and because he managed the training without any discernible discomfort, I think he was at a loss as to why some players could not match him. But long runs were of little benefit to me. My game was all about speed off the mark and I needed short, sharp sprints, not seven-mile runs.

I didn't return to first team action until late September by which time results had been mixed and Liverpool were third in the table. In keeping with other players on the road to recovery I had been told to report back for extra training in the afternoons. The extra training was gruelling. I did wonder if I was doing too much too soon and was worried the Achilles tendon would be aggravated by too much stress.

Graeme introduced a lot of changes. He put an end to the long-established routine of players reporting to Anfield and then travelling to Melwood for training and returning to the ground to shower. He also changed our diet. Under Kenny we often enjoyed 'snack' type meals at Melwood – beans on toast, cheese omelette, that sort of thing. Graeme introduced a new menu which largely consisted of boiled fish and chicken, pasta and salads. When he informed us of the change I mildly took him to task.

'But we won the "double" on egg and chips,' I quipped.

Graeme said nothing, but gave me a long stare, which I took to mean he would not have his authority questioned, even in a humorous way.

But Graeme was ahead of his time. He had learned a lot from his time in Italy and was introducing ideas and methods that just about every manager has since adopted. For a guy who, when he had first joined the club, enjoyed a drink and burned the candle at both ends, I got the impression that he had had a 'road to Damascus' moment in Italy. Our lifestyles were monitored and if a player did things of which Graeme disapproved, he had to change. Being married this didn't affect me, as I was never one for clubbing and leaving Tracy at home, but some of the younger players found their social life suddenly curtailed. It made me think of a cartoon I once saw in a newspaper, depicting Moses coming down from the Mount clutching the stone tablets containing the Ten Commandments. 'It's only a rough draft,' Moses tells the people of Israel, 'but I don't think we're going to get away with very much.'

Graeme shook the club up from top to bottom. Players adapted to the new regime but results did not go particularly well. When a manager takes over at a club and changes the training, preparation and style, he is, in effect, changing the culture of the club. When

Arsène Wenger took over at Arsenal in September 1996 he changed the training, the diet of the players and their lifestyle. But what he didn't do initially was drastically overhaul the Arsenal team. Arsenal won the 'double' in 1997–8, Wenger's first full season in charge, but they achieved this largely with the players he had inherited: David Seaman, Lee Dixon, Steve Bould, Tony Adams, Nigel Winterburn, Ray Parlour, Ian Wright, Denis Bergkamp and David Platt. Because results were good, nobody saw fit to criticise Wenger's methods. On the contrary, just about every manager and coach saw them as a template for the way a modern football club should be run.

In Graeme's first season in charge results were not bad but, by Liverpool's previously high standards, not particularly good either, which resulted in Graeme coming in for a lot of criticism. People felt Graeme had run roughshod over methods that had served the club so well for thirty years and more. Many felt 'the Liverpool way' had been confined the dustbin, and they didn't take too kindly to that.

I don't think Graeme was wrong in what he did. The changes he implemented are now standard at most clubs. I do feel, however, that he made too many changes too soon. Unlike Wenger, Graeme made a lot of changes to personnel in his first full season as manager. For three decades successive Liverpool teams had run off the tongue like a well-known nursery rhyme, not any more. Graeme called upon the services of almost thirty players. Given the increase in the number of substitutes a manager could use in a game, it was still a lot of players. Youngsters such as Steve McManaman and Jamie Redknapp were given a chance and not found wanting. In addition to Dean Saunders and Mark Wright, Michael Thomas arrived from Arsenal, Mark Walters from Rangers, Steve Harkness from Carlisle United, Rob Jones from

Crewe, Istvan Kozma from Bordeaux, Nicky Tanner from Bristol Rovers and Don Hutchinson from Hartlepool United. It seemed every time I entered the dressing-room there was a new face.

I had six games under my belt when I felt a searing pain in my knee playing at West Ham United, Liverpool's fourteenth League game of the season (of which we had won only five). The problem was diagnosed as cartilage trouble and, to my frustration and anger, I was told I would have to undergo an operation. Having not long since returned to first-team action, I was bitterly disappointed to be sidelined yet again.

I returned to training in January, but it was too soon. The problem recurred and I broke down again. There was nothing else for it, I was told, but for me to return to hospital for a second cartilage operation.

It wasn't until mid-March that I was passed fit again and named as a substitute in what turned out to be a one-goal defeat at Crystal Palace. Liverpool were now fifth in the table, but Leeds United, a resurgent Manchester United, Sheffield Wednesday and Arsenal had too much of a lead for me to think we had any chance of overhauling them.

In the event results did not go well. We mustered just three victories from our remaining ten matches to finish in sixth place, eighteen points behind Leeds United, the last winners of the Football League Championship in its old format.

To compound our disappointment, in March we were knocked out of the UEFA Cup at the quarter-final stage by Genoa. I missed the first leg in Italy, which Liverpool lost 2–0, but was pronounced fit for the return at Anfield a fortnight later. We honestly believed we could turn the tie around, but when Aguilera gave Genoa a first-half lead, such belief seemed to drain from our pores. I managed to equalise but, as we threw men forward in the hope of salvaging the tie, Genoa broke, Aguilera added a second, and it was *arrivederci* to the UEFA Cup.

Kenny had seemingly overcome his problems as he had taken over Second Division Blackburn Rovers in October. Graeme, however, seemed to be feeling the pressure and the strain showed on his face. I had desperately wanted Graeme to be successful and enjoy his first full season in charge of the club. The one saving grace was that we had made good progress in the FA Cup and reached the semi-finals. We were drawn against Second Division Portsmouth at Highbury, but if our fans thought we would easily dispense with Jim Smith's side they were in for a rude awakening.

Portsmouth battled from the start and, but for some smart saves from Grob, would have blown our season apart. There was one amazing moment when Grob came to collect a through-ball and did so, only then to spill the ball. Alan McLoughlin hooked the loose ball goalwards only for Grob to arch backwards through the air and tip the ball over the bar. Minutes later a corner caused panic in our penalty area, McLaughlin back-heeled the ball goalwards only for Ray Houghton to clear off the line. Ray's clearance only went as far as Colin Clarke who fired low, and there was Grob again to save our bacon with a magnificent one-handed save.

Having survived this we took the game to Portsmouth. Steve McManaman played a great through-ball, I was on to it like a flash, but Alan Knight came sliding out and we connected with the ball simultaneously. For a split second I thought Alan had the ball in his hands but his momentum carried him forward and he lost control. I regained my footing and stabbed the loose ball home, only for the referee to adjudge I had fouled Alan in the process. I couldn't see that one, and from the look of relief on Alan's face he had obviously thought it was a goal was well.

In the second half I rattled the Portsmouth bar after more good work from Steve McManaman, but that was as close as either side came to breaking the deadlock.

In extra time both sides picked up the same script. It was end-to-end stuff with neither side giving any quarter. Then Darren Anderton latched on to a long downfield ball to run clear. Grob got a hand to Anderton's shot but couldn't prevent the ball from sneaking in at his left-hand post. My heart sank.

When you're chasing a game time seems to whiz by. We bombarded the Pompey goal but their defence remained resolute. There were only two minutes remaining when John Barnes fired a free-kick against the post. Ronnie Whelan was first to react and gleefully side-footed the ball home. A wave of relief immediately swept through my body. I glanced over to the touchline and saw Graeme on his knees. It was almost as if he was offering a prayer of thanks.

Portsmouth had given us a shock but it was nothing compared to the shock that awaited us back in the dressing-room. Graeme didn't say much about the game other than we had done well to keep battling and earn a replay after being a goal down. Then he dropped a bombshell. He told us he was going into hospital the next morning to undergo a triple heart by-pass operation.

His news stunned me. I had detected Graeme was under strain but never had I thought there might be a problem with his heart.

Happily Graeme's operation was a success, but he had to remain in hospital as part of his recuperation, so Ronnie assumed temporary charge for the replay against Portsmouth at Villa Park.

The replay was another war of attrition. Once again Darren Anderton proved a real handful and again it was Grob who denied him. We had a let-off when Alan McLaughlin's rising drive left our crossbar reverberating like a tuning fork, while at the other end I had an effort cleared off the line by John Beresford. The tie went to extra time but still we couldn't be separated, which meant a penalty shoot-out.

John Barnes, Dean Saunders and I scored to settle some nerves, but it was nerves that seemed to get the better of the Portsmouth lads. Having scored one but missed two and with us leading 3–1, it fell to John Beresford to keep his side in the tie. His effort sailed wide of Grob's left-hand post and poor John fell to his knees in despair, his mood in sharp contrast to ours as we celebrated being Wembley-bound.

Our opponents in the final were another Second Division side, Sunderland, who, under caretaker manager Malcolm Crosby, had seen off First Division opposition in West Ham, Chelsea and Norwich.

I managed to speak to Graeme a few days after his operation. He was adamant he would be there for us at Wembley.

'I'll be there as long as the doctors say it's all right,' he told me, only to then characteristically add, 'and maybe even if they don't.'

I felt I was beginning to play at my best and was only sorry that the season was almost over rather than just starting. Before the Cup final we played our final two League games of the season, at home to Manchester United and away at Sheffield Wednesday. The United game resulted in a 2–0 victory but was something of a watershed for me. Friendly games apart, I had never scored against United in the twenty-three games I'd played against them. The newspapers had made much of this but it was just one of those things. It was far from a fag-end game, as United were locked in a battle for the title with Leeds, and as I took to the field at Anfield I felt my luck was about to change against United. I just knew this would be the game when I finally scored against Manchester United and it took just eleven minutes for that to happen. John Barnes and Jan Molby carved the opening for me and when the ball hit the net, I felt a warm glow of satisfaction. Seven minutes later, however, Steve Bruce, with the toe of his boot, tested the resilience of my knee, which had been subjected to the cartilage operation. As I limped off the field I had cause to question my supposed luck against United. In my absence Mark Walters added a second to ensure the title went to Leeds.

Fortunately the knee was fine and I was fit for our next game against Sheffield Wednesday (which ended goalless) but, more importantly, also fit for Wembley. Others were not so fortunate. Both John Barnes and Ronnie Whelan were ruled out, and although Graeme had recovered sufficiently from his op, in the days leading up to the final he sensibly kept away from Melwood and left everything to Ronnie and Roy Evans.

Before the final we stayed at Sopwell House near St Albans. Graeme joined us on the Friday afternoon and we were all delighted to see him, but more delighted that he appeared to be looking well. This was my third FA Cup final in six years and I remember looking around the tables at our evening meal and realising how few players remained from my first final against Everton. In a squad of seventeen players, only Grob, Stevie Nicol, Jan Molby and myself remained from six years ago.

We had ridden our luck in the competition, and had a let-off in the first half against Sunderland. Just before the interval, John Byrne, who had scored in every round that season, was presented with possibly his easiest chance. Byrne was just outside our six-yard box with no Liverpool player near him when the ball arrived at his feet. I thought it a certain goal. Grob scampered across his line but, to my relief, Byrne leaned back, rushed his effort, and the ball sailed over our bar.

Up to that point Sunderland hadn't created any openings. I sensed their players felt they had missed their opportunity as we would not present them with such a gilt-edged chance again.

In the second half our class exerted itself on the game. Steve McManaman was having the game of his life, and created the opening for Michael Thomas to put us ahead. From that point, for all Sunderland battled, I never thought the result would be in doubt. After seventy minutes, Michael combined with Dean Saunders, the ball was fed to me and I slipped it past Tony Norman. It was my fifth goal in FA Cup finals, a record for the competition.

When the final whistle sounded we all headed for Graeme. I was delighted he had a trophy in his first full season as manager. It had been arduous season, particularly for him, and though winning the FA Cup was a crowning moment, the fact he was returning to health pleased me more than anything.

A few days later I went to see club secretary Peter Robinson. I was out of contract and unsure what the future held. Peter told me he'd had a chat with Graeme and they were offering me a three-year deal. I was thirty-one years of age. I knew I had a few more years at the top and saw myself finishing my career at Anfield. I couldn't envisage ever playing for another club, but one of the fascinations of football is its unpredictability.

CHAPTER THIRTEEN

Definitely Maybe

The season of 1992–3 was a watershed for English football, as the Premier League came into being. At the time, the idea was 'sold' to players and supporters alike as being for the benefit of the England team. Clubs in the newly-formed top flight would be playing fewer games, which, we were told, would result in players being 'fresher' when called upon for international duty. The Premiership would also be more accommodating with regard to the release of players for England matches and 'get-togethers' and would prosper home-grown talent. Well, that was what we were told.

It seems amazing now that this was how the idea of the Premier League was sold to people, though I was far from alone in thinking it had been formed for the financial benefit of top-flight clubs and to the detriment of those that would now constitute the Football League.

The chairmen of what were then the First Division clubs had convinced the Football Association that the Premiership was not only a good idea, but seemingly their idea. Initially the very notion had resulted in a lot of disagreement between the FA and the Football League. Bob Kenyon, then a director of Second

Division Stoke City, said the FA was behaving like 'a fox in the hen coop', but the wily First Division chairmen were not innocent of this charge.

The season began with the sort of hyperbole we have since become so accustomed to, but at this embryonic stage I remember thinking little had changed. The same teams played each other. It appeared to be just like the Football League but under a different name. Yet the seeds of change had been planted.

BSkyB was set to become a major influence, particularly regarding the scheduling of fixtures. In this inaugural season live matches were broadcast on Sunday afternoons and Monday evenings. I can recall the Liverpool players discussing the newly formed Premiership and the number of televised games. 'It's the tip of the iceberg,' John Barnes said. I agreed but added, 'Before we know it they'll showing four or five live games a week.' Little did I realise that this too would prove to be 'just the tip of the iceberg'.

For most of the 1990s I played at grounds where building work necessitated the closure of at least one part of stadium. I remember Liverpool playing Arsenal at Highbury in the first season of the Premiership. The North Bank terrace was closed due to redevelopment, and to block the building work from view they'd constructed a huge mural of painted spectators seated in what would be the new stand. It was surreal. I'd receive the ball, see through my peripheral vision what seemed to be a bank of spectators, fire off a shot, only to hear no reaction from that end of the ground. I suppose it was better than being confronted with a building site, though I remember Arsenal coming in for criticism from PC zealots who thought it 'ethnically unrepresentative' of the club's support.

The actual football of the newly formed Premiership was no different to that of the previous season but for one exception, this being a new law forbidding goalkeepers to handle the ball when receiving a back-pass, unless the pass was headed or chested back to the keeper.

The new law did affect the way Liverpool played at the back. On occasions Grob or new signing David James took to acting as an additional sweeper. This led to both goalkeepers having their talent questioned when they got into a tangle with an onrushing striker and lost possession of the ball. The fact all matches were now seen on television, if not live then in the form of edited highlights, ensured any mistake was magnified. It was a far cry from the 1960s when top goalkeepers, such as Gordon Banks or Ron Springett, might make an error which few people saw.

Grob sometimes found himself referred to a 'clown' whereas David, though only young, was afforded the epithet of 'Calamity James'. I felt this was really unfair. Both were excellent goalkeepers and much of the criticism directed their way was the result of them, like every other goalkeeper of the day, having to adapt to a new ruling that contrived to place keepers under additional pressure. Credit to them both, they simply shrugged off the demeaning comments and got on with the job. But the criticism they came in for was a sign of changing times for English football.

Graeme too was coming in for criticism, not only from the press but from certain sections of Liverpool supporters and members of the board. To justify all the changes he had made as manager he needed results to be good. Sadly this wasn't the case. The first season of the Premier League saw Liverpool finish sixth, not good enough to gain entry to the UEFA Cup. We finished twenty-five points behind a Cantona-inspired Manchester United, who pipped Aston Villa to the Championship. The points difference told its own harsh story as to how far off the mark Liverpool now were as genuine contenders in the title race. It had taken Alex Ferguson almost seven years to put United back on top, but the die had been well and truly cast for a new era in English football.

Graeme was not helped by an injury toll that necessitated him changing the team almost from game to game. This led to a very unsettled side with new players not being given much of an opportunity to blend with existing players. Graeme was still very much in control and enjoyed the support of the players, but I knew the team was not playing as well as Liverpool teams of the past. Likewise, the camaraderie in the dressing-room, though good, was not what it had once been. I was still enjoying my football but the thrill of playing in a Liverpool shirt alongside players who were willing to run through a brick wall for one another was missing.

I had a miserable time of it upfront. I wasn't under-performing, just not receiving the service. I have no statistics to back this up, but I knew we were creating nowhere near the number of chances created by past Liverpool teams. We no longer seemed to hold a fear for clubs. Crystal Palace beat us in the League Cup and Second Division Bolton Wanderers knocked us out of the FA Cup. There had been a stage in the season, in February, when it seemed we might even be dragged into the battle to avoid relegation. For Liverpool this was not only unthinkable but totally unacceptable.

Graeme carried on, showing a huge appetite for work and an even greater desire to turn things around. Given he had been so seriously ill, I worried for his well-being. I felt he was trying to do too much. Desperate to find a winning formula, his constant changing of the team was to no avail. Even so, I felt it would only be a matter of time before I was dropped in the continuous reshuffling. However, when it did eventually happen, before a game against Sheffield Wednesday, I was still shocked and not a little hurt. It wasn't a case of a bruised ego. If I had not been playing well or missing chances, I would have accepted my omission from the team. But I wasn't scoring goals because I hadn't been receiving a semblance of decent service.

I sat on the bench against Wednesday, and again for our next match, at home to title-chasing Manchester United. I was called into action during the second half of the game against United and responded by scoring with a thunderous volley. Not archetypal of me but I hoped the stunning nature of the strike helped emphasise a point.

In any case, United went on to win that game 2–1, a result that saw Liverpool slip to sixteenth in the table, a dire position for a team that, until the previous season, had not finished out of the top two for over a decade.

I did return to the side on a regular basis but nothing changed, except the composition of the team. I decided that the only way I could make a point to Graeme, and avoid being dropped again, was to become as selfish in front of goal as I had ever been in my salad days with Liverpool. I scored eleven goals in our last thirteen matches, helping Liverpool to climb to a final placing of sixth, much better than had seemed possible at one stage in the season but, to many, a mark of a club in decline.

I was voted Player of the Year in a poll conducted by the *Liverpool Echo* which, given the barren spell I had endured for three-quarters of the season, may well be seen as indicative of how poorly others had performed throughout the season in the eyes of *Post* readers.

Despite what had happened, there was no falling-out between Graeme and myself. I knew he had a job to do and the decisions he had made were, to his mind, in the best interests of the team and the club. There was, however, an edge to our relationship. I dare say Graeme detected this and I felt he attempted to put things back on an even keel when, before the 1993–4 season, he called me into his office and told me he was appointing me captain.

I considered it an honour and still do. When I thought of all the great players who had captained Liverpool in the past – fantastic players such as Ron Yeats, Tommy Smith, Emlyn Hughes, Phil Thompson, Kenny, Alan Hansen and Graeme himself – I felt very proud to assume such a position within the club. I never saw the captaincy as a nominal position. It carried with it responsibility both on and off the field and, given my experience, I felt I would do a good job.

Delighted as I was, however, I began to think my future might be best served away from Anfield. I was coming up to thirty-two years of age and, though confident I had at least another two years at the top as a player, had begun to think about my long-term future.

For some time, I had become more and more and more interested in management and coaching. I had read every book I could lay my hands on that dealt with coaching and the technical side of the game, and made a point of talking to as many managers as I could with a view to picking up ideas. I had begun to compile files in which I jotted down these ideas, to which I added a considerable number of my own. I didn't, at this stage, possess any coaching qualifications but, as 1992–3 drew to a close, I began to make enquiries about courses that would enable me to gain coaching badges.

In my early days in the first team, I can remember Phil Neal once saying to me, 'You'll never make a manager, you don't think enough about the game.' I think this was Phil's way of telling me to grow up a bit. At such an age I thought all that mattered was the goals I scored for the team but, in time, had come to realise I must contribute a lot more besides.

At the time of my appointment as captain, Robbie Fowler had not long since broken into the first team. I saw a lot of the young me in Robbie. As captain I now found myself repeating Phil Neal's advice, telling Robbie to think beyond scoring goals and more about the team and play in general.

In addition to Robbie, there were other new faces in the dressing-room, including Norway international full-back Stig Bjornebye, Neil Ruddock and Paul Stewart (both from Spurs), Nigel Clough from Nottingham Forest, and Julian Dicks from West Ham United. Jamie Redknapp and Steve McManaman had also established themselves in the side, and Grob had won back the goalkeeper's jersey from David James.

Some of Graeme's signings raised one or two eyebrows amongst our supporters, not least that of Julian Dicks, who arrived with a reputation for being a very physical player and one with a poor disciplinary record. Not your 'typical' Liverpool player at all. As the story went, when Julian made his Liverpool debut at full-back he picked-up the number eight shirt because he saw 'Fowler' written on the back of it. It was just a supporters' gag but it said a lot about our fans' view of the way things were going.

Off the field, too, there were big changes to my life, as Tracy gave birth to our second son, Daniel. We were delighted, and now felt our family to be complete. As with most parents, Tracy and I felt more relaxed in light of the birth of our second child. Having had Jonathan, we were nowhere near as anxious and nervous in the nurturing of Daniel. I am sure all parents who have had more than one child will know what I mean!

The new season started well enough. Our opening three games produced three victories and ten goals scored with only one conceded, then our form dipped once again. September saw us lose five consecutive matches. Thereafter results were, at best, mixed.

Matters were not helped when we exited the League Cup at the hands of Wimbledon and, as the season progressed, we gradually lost ground in the League on Manchester United, Blackburn Rovers, Newcastle, Arsenal and Leeds who had formed a break-away group at the top.

At the end of November we enjoyed a 2–1 win against Aston Villa. I didn't feature on the score-sheet, but felt I played well and had created our opening goal for Robbie Fowler. I expected Graeme to keep with the same eleven for our following game against Sheffield Wednesday but had forgotten the striker's mantra, 'always expect the unexpected'.

I was left out of the starting line-up for that game. In the event we produced a wretched performance and, when Graeme sent me on with just eight minutes remaining, it was too late to for me to make any impact on the 3–1 scoreline.

After the game I told Graeme I was far from happy at being left out, particularly as I felt I had contributed well against Villa. Graeme told me my disappointment was understandable, that he had just wanted to try something different against Wednesday. It hadn't worked and I still had an important role to play.

I returned to the fold for our following game against QPR and scored in a much-needed 3–2 victory. Draws against bottom club Swindon Town (2–2) and Spurs (3-3) preceded a Boxing Day visit to Sheffield United, who were struggling near the bottom of the League. There were ten minutes remaining and the game was goal-less when Graeme substituted me with Ronnie Whelan. I was so pissed off by this that I watched the remainder of the game from the entrance of the tunnel, rather than join Graeme in the dug-out.

If I had not been playing well against Sheffield United I would have understood my substitution but I felt I had been one of our better players. After the game I asked Graeme for an explanation.

He told me that with the game goalless and with only ten minutes remaining, he'd introduced Ronnie Whelan to bolster the defence and ensure we came away with a point. I understood his thinking, but the reason didn't rest easy with me. I was left thinking how different this Liverpool was to the teams I had known. Sheffield United had won just three of their twenty-six league matches. Along with Swindon Town, they were favourites for the drop, yet a Liverpool side had gone to Bramall Lane seemingly content to come away with a goalless draw. Graeme wanted to ensure we didn't lose the game, but I had wanted us to win it and, should I have stayed on, felt there was a chance of that happening. A Liverpool team content to play for a draw against a team struggling at the bottom would have been unthinkable under Paisley, Fagan or Kenny.

I was so down that a few days later I went to see Graeme and told him in no uncertain terms how I felt. I had been granted a testimonial and there was a big game against Celtic planned for the later in the year, but I was so disillusioned that if another club had come in for me then, I would have gone.

'I have never wanted to leave this club,' I concluded, 'but if you don't want me, or feel I can't do you a job, I might as well go.'

'Hey, forget that,' he told me. 'Rest assured, your future's here.'

What I didn't know at the time was that Graeme's future lay elsewhere.

On 4 January we found ourselves 3–0 down at home to Manchester United but rallied magnificently to achieve a 3–3 draw. Having been taken apart by United in the early stages, we galvanised to turn the tables on Alex Ferguson's side and, but for the width of a post, could have achieved a remarkable victory against the champions. The press saw our performance against United as possibly proof that Liverpool were at last starting to turn the corner under Graeme. But this was not the case.

Two weeks after the United game we drew 1–1 against Second Division Bristol City in the third round of the FA Cup. The replay was scheduled to take place at Anfield a week later. A few days before our meeting, Graeme had a run-in with John Barnes.

Graeme was incensed about an interview given to a Sunday newspaper in which John had been critical of his style of management. I like John and respect his opinions, but I felt Graeme was right to haul him over the coals. Graeme was the manager and you can't have players publicly running down the boss. I had been brought up to believe you should never do your dirty washing in public. If a player has a beef with the manager, then he should offer his opinion in the privacy of the manager's office. John hadn't done this so Graeme was right to discipline him. Where I felt Graeme made a mistake, however, was subsequently ordering John to write an apology to him in the match programme for the Bristol City game. This was not so much a reprimand as a humiliation.

The Bristol City match was a disaster. City's Brian Tinnion scored the only goal of the game to ensure we went out of the FA Cup to Second Division opposition for a second successive season. As the players shook hands a section of Bristol City fans began to chant, 'Liverpool, Liverpool, used to be good, used to be good.' Rather than walking, I felt as if I was staggering off the pitch.

Graeme and Liverpool parted company on 31 January. The formal announcement was made by club chairman David Moores.

I was saddened to see Graeme go. We'd had our differences, but the fact we hadn't seen eye to eye on certain issues didn't in any way lessen the respect I held and still hold for him. When I first broke into the team he was forever offering advice and encouragement, always urging me to strive to bigger and better things.

Under his tutorage, and that of Kenny, I had improved as a player in leaps and bounds.

Some newspapers said Graeme left by 'mutual consent', some even implied he had been sacked. Neither was the case. Though, in the end, he didn't enjoy the full support of the board, Graham resigned. He was a winner in every sense of the word and couldn't face up to the fact he had not kept Liverpool at the top. The pressure of trying proved too much. David Moores and Peter Robinson both attempted to persuade Graeme to change his mind, or at least to stay on until the end of the season, but, having made his decision, he stuck to it.

I sensed that not too many Liverpool supporters were sad to see him go. They loved Graeme as a player, but the general feeling was he hadn't cut the mustard as manager. Many fans remained upset over his sale of Peter Beardsley to Everton, and the fact Peter was now doing really well at Goodison only added to their angst. A lot of supporters were not happy with the quality or style of player Graeme had brought to the club. Supporters were also upset he'd made so many changes, which many felt had destroyed the time-honoured 'Liverpool culture'. The treatment of John Barnes also left a sour taste, but the bottom line was that results had been nowhere near good enough. Graeme felt this more than anybody, which is why he resigned.

Roy Evans was appointed caretaker manager and, two days later, was given the job on a permanent basis. The press hailed the appointment, the consensus being the board members were wise to return to the boot room to appoint a manger – except there was no longer a boot room, as Graeme had got rid of it.

Just as I had been with the appointments of Joe, Kenny and Graeme, I was delighted to see Roy take over as manager. He'd been at the club since the 1960s but his playing career had been prematurely ended due to injury, since when he'd fulfilled every role on the backroom staff. Roy had been a brick for me when I'd doubted I had the necessary to make it at the club. He was very knowledgeable about the game, rational, fair-minded and had the respect of all the players. I felt the team was in good hands.

Our remaining results were nothing to shout home about. Only five victories from sixteen games saw Liverpool finish in eighth place, the club's lowest position for twenty-two years. However, the football we played under Roy was fluid and expansive, and there was a certain *joie de vivre* about it which led press and supporters alike to believe that Liverpool was about to embark upon a new, vibrant era.

On a personal note I again finished as the club's leading goalscorer with a total of nineteen goals. Given the sort of season we'd had, I didn't think that shabby at all. I felt confident I would score more goals in the future and told Roy as much.

'Do *Rough Guides* have passports?' he replied.

At the start of the 1994–5 season I believed the club was back on a stable footing. Young players such as David James, Robbie Fowler, Steve McManaman, Jamie Redknapp and Rob Jones were now experienced and producing some level of consistency. Young players are notoriously fickle – on fire one game, virtually anonymous the next. A team can cope with one such player in the side. With five or six young players in a team, performances and results can be seriously affected. Our young signings were now making a positive contribution on a regular basis. The first opponents to feel the full effect of this were Crystal Palace on the opening day of the season.

I felt our young players – talented though they were – had been thrown into the Premiership a little too early. Each one of them had good days – Robbie had once scored all five of our goals in a 5–0 victory over Fulham in the League Cup – but, generally speaking, it had been a steep learning curve for all concerned, with lessons learned in games rather than on the training ground. Now they were hardened by virtue of some fifty games each, which is another reason I felt a great deal of confidence when I led the team out at a sun-kissed Selhurst Park.

It was a hot day and Palace felt the heat. Eric Young, Chris Coleman and Gareth Southgate spent so much time chasing McManaman, Fowler and Redknapp I thought they would end the game with sunburned tongues. Two goals from Steve Mac and me, and one each for Robbie and Jan Molby gave us a 6–1 victory. In our following game Robbie put Arsenal to the sword, netting a hat-trick in a 3–0 win and he was on the score-sheet again when we beat Southampton 2–0.

It was a hell of a start to the season but deep down I knew we lacked the hard, steely edge and single-mindedness you need to win titles. On our day we could beat any team and did. Blackburn Rovers (who won the Premiership that season) were outplayed and beaten at Anfield (2–1) as were runners-up Manchester United (2–0). In full flow we were exhilarating to watch, but perhaps we put too much energy into games when we needed to slow them down. Some of the youngsters got carried away, thinking we could turn on the style every match when some called for the rolling-up of sleeves and a battle. The hallmark of a truly successful team is achieving those single-goal victories when you're not on the top of your game as Manchester United and Chelsea have demonstrated in recent years,. It's the kind of asset a team will only gain through experience – and this particular Liverpool team was still learning.

We were never far away from Blackburn and Manchester

United, but never capable of mounting a consistent run of good results and, for that reason, finished fourth in the Premiership.

I think our supporters understood the situation and if consistency eluded us then there was compensation in the cavalier football we were now displaying. Those supporters also paid me a moving personal tribute I will never forget. Just before Christmas 1994 some 34,000 of them defied incessant rain to give me a rousing salute in my testimonial game against Celtic.

I'm pretty unflappable, and not the type to suffer from nerves, but that night I was like the proverbial cat on a hot tin roof. I had asked Kenny, now forty-three, if he would come along and play in the veterans' game we'd organised before the main event. 'Stuff that, I want to play in the main game,' he told me. You don't argue with Kenny, not least because when he's fired up you can't understand a word he says.

I warned Robbie beforehand, 'If you think I moan at you on the pitch, just wait till Kenny's behind you. It's like playing in front of Les Dawson's idea of a mother-in-law.'

On the night Kenny displayed vintage flashes and ten minutes from time we were 5–0 up. But, to my chagrin, I hadn't marked my special night with a goal. Ten minutes from time Packy Bonner beat-out a shot from Kenny and, to my great relief, I was on hand to sweep the ball home. Even the Celtic fans cheered. It was like the old days when Kenny, his face beaming, ran to congratulate me.

That season I felt we had the sort of team that could lift one of the domestic cups. Having beaten Birmingham City and Burnley in the early stages of the FA Cup, we accounted for Wimbledon in round five winning 2–0. I scored one of our goals that day. It was my forty-first goal in the competition all told, equalling the record as set by Denis Law. I was very disappointed that our FA Cup run ended the very next round when we were beaten 2–1 at home by Tottenham. Spurs' winner came from Jurgen Klinsmann in time added on after it was adjudged he'd been fouled by Rob Jones. As Ronnie Moran quipped after the game, 'Since Klinsmann's been at Spurs even their shares have taken a dive.'

Compensation for us came in the League (now Coca-Cola) Cup. Having beaten Burnley and Stoke City we then received the draw no team wanted: away to Blackburn Rovers. Few gave us any chance of getting a result at Ewood Park but we confounded the pundits – and probably ourselves – by storming to a 3–1 victory. It was a particularly sweet night for me as I scored a hat-trick, my last for Liverpool as things turned out. My first goal was also one of the most spectacular of my career. There didn't seem to be much on when Robbie Fowler pinched the ball from Tim Sherwood but when Robbie moved the ball inside I tried my luck from thirty yards. The ball flew past Tim Flowers' groping right hand and ballooned the back of the net. During Roy's halftime talk he praised us for being one and half goals up, adding, 'And that should be the score, because Ian's goal was a goal and half.' It was good to hear laughter again in a Liverpool dressing-room.

I couldn't have picked a better night for a hat-trick. The Blackburn tie was my 600th game for Liverpool. No one was more pleased for me than Kenny who, though we had dumped his side out of the Cup, was the first person to congratulate me as I walked off the field.

I scored the only goal of the game in the next round to eliminate Arsenal and in the semi-finals we overcame Crystal Palace to reach Wembley. Our opponents were Bolton Wanderers, at the time riding high in the Second Division. In the days leading up to the final I began to get a little twitchy. The majority of the team had never played at Wembley before, but this was my sixteenth visit. I was desperate for us to beat Bolton Wanderers, as it had been three years since Liverpool had appeared in a major Cup final and I didn't want the ignominy of being the first officially appointed captain not to lead Liverpool to a major trophy since Tommy Smith had held aloft the UEFA Cup in 1973. I saw also the League Cup final as being an opportunity to show everyone that Liverpool were back, ready to regain our place at the summit of English football.

I never lost the thrill of playing at the stadium. Football history seemed to seep from every brick. I often thought of the great players who had graced its turf – Stanley Matthews, Tom Finney, Jimmy Greaves, Bobby Moore, Puskas, Maradona and Johan Cruyff to name but a few. I felt I was literally following in their footsteps, and the thought of this never failed to energise and excite me.

Bolton were a division below us but pushing for promotion, and I certainly didn't take them lightly. I was at pains to emphasise to our younger players that there should not be even the slightest hint of complacency. I also told them to take everything in and commit the day to memory, as a Wembley final seems to pass so quickly. 'Remember as much as you can,' I told them. 'These are the good days. When you're too old to play, you'll realise that.'

Steve McManaman did everything in his power to commit the day to his memory – and that of quite a number of us besides. His performance was one of vigorous brilliance, his mazy runs reminiscent of 'the Wizard of Dribble', Stanley Matthews himself, who was present on the day. Before the game much had been made of Bolton's three Scousers, Alan Stubbs, Jason McAteer and Mark Seagraves, but it was the lad whose dad had once played in the same school team as Tommy Smith who wrote himself into Merseyside football folklore with one of the most outstanding Wembley performances I ever had the privilege to be involved with.

Twice, either side of halftime, Steve danced through the Bolton defence to score, his first a sweet, low, right-footed drive from the angle of the six-yard box while fending off the attentions of three Bolton defenders. His second began with a corkscrew dribble that took him past four Bolton players and ended with a sublime finish.

I thought we had the game won but then Alan Thompson scored for Bolton with one of those strikes that lifts teammates and, suddenly, we had a real battle on our hands. The final few minutes were strenuous from our point of view but we dealt with everything that came our way and, when the final whistle sounded, I was consumed by a mixture of relief and joy.

I was presented with the Cup by Sir Stanley Matthews. When I turned to hold it aloft for all our supporters to see I was so excited and emotionally moved I could almost feel the hairs standing on the back of my neck.

I was told it was a terrific game of football to watch, and it hadn't been a bad game to play in, either. Both sets of supporters applauded both teams and each other. I left the pitch with a very good feeling. Not only because we had won and that I had continued the 'tradition' of Liverpool skippers receiving a major trophy, but also because I felt both teams had produced football which offered fulsome evidence that the game was still a beautiful one.

My contract with Liverpool was up on 1 June 1995 which meant I would become a free agent. I had a chat with Roy Evans, who told me he was happy for me to continue at the club. This was good news but I was none the less disappointed when Roy then handed me a one-year contract. I had been hoping it would be for two years. It told me all I needed to know. When the contract expired I would be leaving Anfield.

That summer, Roy signed Stan Colleymore from Nottingham Forest for £8.5 million. With Robbie Fowler having emerged as a striker of real quality a number of people believed my last season at Anfield would be bit-part, though I was confident enough in my fitness and ability to feel I still had it in me to give the young guns and opposing defences a run for their money.

During the close season, Phil Babb arrived from Coventry City, followed by John Scales from Wimbledon and – seemingly, with the mindset of 'if you can't beat 'em, join 'em' – Jason McAteer from Bolton Wanderers. I felt I did well in pre-season games, which involved a creditable goalless draw at Celtic, and seemingly Roy shared my opinion because I received the nod to lead the attack in our opening game against Sheffield Wednesday.

My strike partner on the day was Stan Colleymore, who scored the only goal of the game. We didn't produce a vintage Liverpool performance but everyone was satisfied enough, except for Robbie Fowler who, understandably, was upset at being left on the bench.

We won three and lost one of our first four league matches. Just when I thought all was going well, I picked up a knee injury in our 1–0 victory over QPR. At first it was thought I would only miss our UEFA Cup match in Russia against Spartak Vladikavkaz but the injury proved more problematic than first thought and it was to be a month before I returned to action.

Robbie Fowler had made a tremendous impact at the club but, as I say, was unhappy that Stan and I had formed the main strike force in our opening matches. He was further upset when Roy opted to play Stan upfront with John Barnes in the away leg of the UEFA Cup against Spartak. On the journey back from Russia, he perhaps allowed his disappointment to get the better of him.

During the flight, Robbie had taken off his shoes and fallen asleep. While he was sleeping, someone poured coffee into his shoes. When Robbie came to put them on again, he was not best pleased, to say the least. For some reason he believed Neil Ruddock was the guilty party. As Neil had also removed his shoes, a pair of Guccis which he had bought for some £300, Robbie somehow managed to get his hands on a pair of scissors, crept up to where Neil was sitting and proceeded to cut up his shoes. Neil suddenly awoke and, not having been the perpetrator of the prank, was understandably annoyed. The pair exchanged words and a pushing match ensued. Just when it seemed it might turn a little nasty, some of the lads stepped in to part them and return Robbie to his seat. Roy later had a word with the pair of them, reminding them of their responsibilities, and the incident was buried.

Robbie was a young lad whose performances had earned him headlines and, as was becoming the case with top players, celebrity status in the media. I felt his head had been turned and that he was in danger of making the mistake many young talented footballers make, of believing his own publicity. As the senior pro, I felt it proper to have a quiet word with him.

I told him I understood how disappointed he was at not having secured a regular place in the team, but that he had to earn his place, and not think that past performances (albeit terrific) automatically merited him a place in the side. Credit to him, he listened.

As a young player, I had been fortunate in not believing all the hype written about me. That said, what was written about me as a teenager was nothing compared to what had been written about Robbie – and would later be written of Michael Owen. When I broke into the Liverpool team and started scoring goals on a regular basis it was a year to eighteen months before newspapers started to afford me superlatives – not that I ever believed such things anyway. We were now in an era when one scintillating performance was enough for the media to hail a promising young player as a star. I told Robbie that, rather than have his head filled with newspaper talk, he had to concentrate on working hard at his own game to ensure he was worthy of a regular place. Whether my few words had any effect, I can't say, but Robbie became a real role model for football-mad youngsters.

It is all too easy for people to criticise young players, of whatever era, for the folly of their youth. Having built up a young player, the media are all too quick to jump on any indiscretion. Of course footballers of every age have a responsibility to young people but, by and large, I feel young players do set a good example.

Having been the subject of excessive press hyperbole, Robbie found himself lambasted by certain elements of the press. It was tough for him at times but he learned not to behave impulsively, as he had done on that flight. He matured into a superb player, a great guy, not to mention a most amiable property landlord! On joining Cardiff City he himself imparted sound advice to Dave Jones's emerging young talent such as Wayne Hennessey, Joe Ledley and Lewin Nyatanga who, I take some pride in saying, I coached and helped develop in my current role as Elite Performance Director for the Welsh Football Trust. What goes around comes around.

The season did not turn out quite as I would have hoped. I returned to first-team action in October against Manchester United at Old Trafford, a game marked by the return of Eric Cantona after his enforced eight-month absence from the game. Stan Colleymore was on compassionate leave as his mother was very ill, so I partnered Robbie and we clicked. Robbie had been in fine form, netting four in a 5–2 win over Bolton, and he scored both our goals in a 2–2 draw against United. Though, of course, it was Eric who stole the headlines, scoring United's second goal from the penalty spot. I felt we too should have been awarded a penalty when Gary Pallister tangled with Robbie but wasn't surprised when it wasn't given. As Ronnie Moran said afterwards, 'Referees awarding penalties against United at Old Trafford are as rare as rocking-horse shit.'

We followed a 3–1 win at Southampton with a 6–0 thrashing of Manchester City, a game in which Robbie again scored twice and, much to my delight, so did I. Our next game was Newcastle United and again I managed to score but any joy I felt at that was dulled by the fact my knee flared up again.

Just when I was on a roll I was confined to the sidelines again, this time until March. I was bitterly disappointed to miss the meat of the season, during which we yo-yoed between second and third place. When I was finally pronounced fit I knew I would have to be content with a place on the bench, as Stan and Robbie had seized the day.

Robbie scored a total of thirty-six goals in all competitions that season, including twenty-eight in the League, offering ample evidence of his tremendous talent as a striker. For his part, Stan netted nineteen. With Robbie and Stan hitting it off together as a strike force, I knew my time was up at Liverpool. I wasn't downhearted. Such was my love and devotion to the club I was delighted Robbie and Stan had done so well. I felt I would be leaving the Liverpool strike force in excellent hands.

Having appeared as a substitute the previous week in a 1–1 draw at Everton, I was again on the bench for what would be my last League match at Anfield against Middlesbrough on 27 April. I was due to leave Liverpool on a free transfer and dearly wanted to sign off with a goal for the fans, who had given me so much support and inspiration over the years. But it was not to be.

Before the game a club official collared me as the teams were about to take to the pitch. He told me he wanted to convey his thanks for all my efforts on behalf of Liverpool over the years. I was itching to get out on to the pitch but didn't want to come across as being ungracious or disrespectful, although I was thinking, 'It's not the time or place for this.' Eventually I managed to free myself and hastily made my way along the tunnel to join the rest of the team, only for the true reason for the official's long-winded chat to become immediately apparent.

Both teams had lined up to form a guard of honour for me. I was completely taken aback and not a little humbled as I made my way between the two lines of players to generous applause, not only from the two teams but from all around Anfield. I felt self-conscious and unworthy but, at the same time, also very appreciative of this warm and totally unexpected gesture.

I had 345 goals to my name from my fifteen seasons with the club but just couldn't find the goal I, and everyone present, wanted after replacing Robbie on the hour. Stan Colleymore scored the only goal of the game some ten minutes after I had entered the fray. When Stan scored I was still reeling from the ovation I'd been given when I set foot on the pitch, but that turned out to be nothing compared to the farewell I received after the final whistle.

My teammates urged me to do a circuit of Anfield and I did so to rapturous applause. I just about made it round before the tears came rolling down my cheeks.

When I reached the Kop, I took off my shirt and threw it into the crowd then, still clapping and waving to the fans, I jogged back towards the tunnel where another surprise awaited me.

Then Liverpool players had waited until I had bid my farewells and, as I approached, they formed another guard of honour. It was just too much and my emotions got the better of me as I disappeared down the tunnel for one last time.

After the game I went out to face the press, who asked the impossible: 'How do you feel?' I'm quoted as saying:

It's been a very emotional day but also a fantastic day for me. I had no idea of the reception I was going to get until Roy Evans told me to get stripped as I was going on. The reception I received will live with me for ever. I'm sorry I didn't score – I had a great chance but I caught the ball too well. Sometimes you just try too hard to score.

The fans were willing me to score and, believe me, I wanted that as much as they did. I wanted to stay on the pitch for ever. I didn't want to come off, but I now have to look to the future.

I can't find the right words to describe how I feel just now. Just that I'm sad to be leaving this great club and its fantastic supporters. People often talk about me being able to take an opportunity in front of goal. But the best opportunity I've ever been given was to play for Liverpool football club, and I just want everyone to know I did my utmost to make the best of that.

More questions were fired at me but I couldn't face them. I was too emotional. I thanked the press for their time and their support over the years, and made another tearful exit.

I made another appearance as a substitute in a goalless draw at Arsenal and was named as centre-forward and captain for our final league game of the season at Manchester City on 5 May.

It was a day I finished on a high. I scored our second goal and it was widely considered to be a stylish one. Steve McManaman played a wonderful cross-field pass, weighted and timed to perfection so that I didn't have to break step in rifling the ball past Eike

Immel from twenty-five yards and into the roof of the net. It was my 346th goal for Liverpool, a club record in all competitions, and helped us to a 2–2 draw but sentenced City to Division Two in Alan Ball's first season as manager at Maine Road.

Come the end of the end of the game I again received an emotional farewell from our supporters and, very sportingly given they had just seen their club relegated, from Manchester City fans, too. A gesture which only further emphasised to me that we all belong to the great family of football and, irrespective of how clubs and those who govern football often pay little more than lip service to supporters, they are, without doubt, the lifeblood of the game.

A week later I was back at Wembley for, quite literally, a final farewell in a Liverpool shirt. In round three of the FA Cup I had scored in a 7–0 victory over Rochdale, in so doing passing Denis Law's record of forty-one FA Cup goals. I was thrilled when Denis offered his congratulations to me by way of a press interview in which he described me as the best goal-scorer since Jimmy Greaves. Greavsie had been my hero as a boy, so to be compared to him by another of the game's all-time great goal-scorers made me feel very proud and yet, at the same time, very humble.

I had also appeared as a substitute during our semi-final win over Aston Villa, and though I knew I wouldn't feature in the starting line-up for the final against Manchester United, hoped Roy would include me on the bench, which, to my delight, he did.

The final itself was burdened by excessive hype and expectation which neither team was capable of living up to. Both teams played a cautious game. When I began my career at Liverpool, most teams went out to score goals in order to win a game. Football had changed since then. Rather than attacking opponents and creating opportunities, teams were now often given to playing a possession game in the hope their opponents would make a mistake that would present them with an opening. These days this type of game is seen all too often in the Premiership when the 'heavyweights' confront one another.

Both teams cancelled each other out to such an extent the final was in danger of being remembered mainly for the white suits we had been given to wear. Previous 'Wembley' suits I sometimes wore on other occasions. I knew I would never wear the white suit again. It made me feel a cross between Donny Osmond and John Travolta in *Saturday Night Fever*. It's one thing to play at Wembley and be subjected to a pratfall, but, as far as I was concerned, there was no need to arrive at the stadium looking like a prat.

Such was the mundane nature of the game there was a distinct lack of atmosphere at Wembley that day. Even so I was itching to play some sort of role and, when Roy called me into action in place of Stan Colleymore with fifteen minutes remaining, he'd barely got the words out of his mouth before my tracksuit was off. I had never set foot on Wembley amidst such a low-key atmosphere. It was if as the spectators had been anaesthetised.

I was desperate to give our supporters something to shout about and would have given a king's ransom to have scored in my final bow. It didn't happen. With some four minutes remaining a young player called David Beckham whipped over a corner. David James didn't get enough distance or the correct angle when punching clear and the ball fell just beyond our penalty area to where Eric Cantona was lurking. Eric had just sealed his Lazarus-like resurrection in the eyes of the football nation by being voted the PFA Footballer of the Year and crowned the moment with a crisp right-foot volley that avoided everybody in its path. There was little time left for us to salvage the game and we didn't. United became the first club to achieve the coveted league and Cup 'double' twice, and Eric, shirt collar up, back straight as a board, strode off the pitch, satisfied enough.

The post-final banquet was a low-key affair in more ways than one. Very much hungover by the disappointment of having lost to United, everyone seemed to go through the motions of having a good time. For me the banquet was something of wake, as it was the last time I would be in the company of Liverpool players as teammates. In his speech, chairman David Moores paid tribute to me and the contribution I had made to the club, and wished me well for the future. At this point I wasn't exactly sure what the future held, but I was starting to have a good idea.

CHAPTER FOURTEEN

All These Things That I Have Done

I had received a number of offers, and gave serious consideration to three. Manchester City were very keen, and Peter
Reid wanted me to join him at Sunderland, who had just
won promotion to the Premiership. I liked Peter and respected
him as a manager, but while the thought of moving from one
football hotbed to another was appealing, the third offer I
received was in keeping with what I now wanted to do.

Howard Wilkinson had asked me to move to Leeds United.
What made the offer so appealing was that I would understudy
Howard with a view to succeeding him as manager within two to
three years.

It was an emotional wrench to leave Liverpool, but I was real-
istic about my departure. It was time to move on and the fact a top
club such as Leeds not only wanted me as a player but felt I was
future management material made the leaving of Liverpool easier
for me. I felt Howard and Leeds had seen something in me I felt
was there, but which Liverpool had not recognised or, at least, had
felt was not worthy of retaining in some capacity at Anfield. A part
of me wanted to prove Liverpool were wrong to let me go. As

such, having got over the emotion of the actual leaving, I felt strangely detached from Anfield and a loyalty to Leeds.

I still felt a bond with Liverpool as a club and with its supporters, and still do. That will never leave me. But the game had changed and so too had Liverpool. No more so than the celebrated Kop. The new Kop with its serried seating in uniform plastic was safer, cleaner and more in keeping with the image the club and football wished to project, but much of the magic and spirit of the Kop had gone along with the terracing. The reality of the Kop was always more tacky than the legend, however. The old terrace had exactly one hundred steps and on match days, more often than not, they would be drenched in urine from fans unable, or unwilling, to make their way through the crush to the toilets. Not pretty, but, for me, it had always been a seething, communal culture club that was very much a part of Liverpool's social glue. The fans who gathered on the Kop had been great to me, and I always sensed that for them, just being on the Kop was the next best thing to pulling on the famous red shirt. I would no longer wear that famous red shirt and the Kop had changed, but what disappointment I felt at having left the club was tempered by the sense that the bond I felt with Liverpool supporters would never change, at least, not for me.

To this day Liverpool is still the first result I look for, but the prospect of carving a new career, initially as a player and then in management, with Leeds was exciting. I always knew the day would come when I would no longer experience the joy and thrill of scoring goals and I would miss it, but I wasn't down about it because I knew there would be other things to stimulate me.

My aim was to work towards gaining the UEFA Pro Licence. I felt I would learn a lot under Howard, who was widely respected throughout the game. He'd begun his managerial career with

Notts County but established himself as a manager of note at Sheffield Wednesday, guiding them to promotion to the First Division. Wednesday were still there four years later in 1988 when Howard left to join Leeds United.

Howard had made some very astute signings during his time at Elland Road, one of the first being Gordon Strachan from Manchester United, which set the tone for what was to follow. After Leeds were promoted to Division One in 1989, he continued to make shrewd signings with the likes of John Lukic, Gary McAllister, Lee Chapman and, later, Steve Hodge, Rod Wallace and, of course, Eric Cantona, though some might say his most notable achievement was guiding Vinnie Jones through an entire season during which Vinnie received only three yellow cards.

Under Howard, Leeds won the League Championship in 1992, the last season of the Football League in its old format. He remains the last Englishman to have steered a club to the title. Leeds had been runners-up in the League Cup in the season before I joined but, for me, his greatest achievement was the youth policy he had instigated at Elland Road.

I was looking forward to working with some of the young players who had come up through the ranks under the guidance of Howard, his assistant Mick Hennigan and coach David Williams. Youngsters such as John Butler, Ian Harte, Harry Kewell, Alan Maybury, Paul Robinson and Jonathan Woodgate were all outstanding prospects and, in time, would go on to enjoy highly successful careers in the game.

It was suggested that after Howard's work with the first team I would join him in the afternoons for extra sessions with the youngsters. The idea was for me to begin coaching the young players then, once I gained qualifications and experience, graduate to working with the first-team squad.

I suppose, in many respects, I was Howard's protégé. I liked him. He was nothing like the 'Sergeant Wilko' character he had often been portrayed as by the press. He loved football, cared about the game and his players, and was full of innovative ideas. His enthusiasm and energy was infectious. Senior and junior players alike respected him and hung on to his every word.

His attention to detail was phenomenal. With Jonathan Woodgate, for example, he worked hard on getting him to use his back and neck muscles in tandem to achieve maximum power when heading the ball. He also taught Harry Kewell how and when to make effective runs from deep and enhanced his acceleration. He spent hours working with Ian Harte teaching him when to tackle ('When you are only sure you'll win the ball') and how to bide his time and jockey an opponent into a position whereby he was not a danger.

There was only one problem: a section of Leeds United fans disliked him.

Some supporters have short memories. Leeds United had been a mediocre Second Division outfit when Howard first arrived at Elland Road. In eight years he had guided them back to the top flight, kept them there, won the title, taken them into the European Cup, been to Wembley in the final of the League Cup and produced the best group of talented youngsters the club had seen since the days of Don Revie in the 1960s. In addition, he had exercised financial prudence at the club. Seemingly, this was not enough for some.

On paper I thought Leeds had a decent side. In players such as goalkeeper Nigel Martyn, Gary Kelly, Carlton Palmer, Lucas Redebe, Lee Sharpe, Lee Bowyer, Brian Deane, Rod Wallace and David Weatherall it was obvious the team was not short on talent. I felt we were going to do well and that I was going to continue to score goals.

On the opening day we drew 3–3 at Derby and then won two of our next three League matches, the only reverse being at home to Sheffield Wednesday. I thought this was a decent enough start but the boo-boys on the terraces had it in for Howard. Letters started to appear in the local paper calling for him to go and the disgruntled fans made their feelings known on local radio. I couldn't understand it. We were sixth in the Premiership.

Our next game was, I admit, a poor performance. We were beaten 4–0 at home by Manchester United but were still a respectable ninth in the Premiership and it was still early days.

On the Monday morning following the United game I arrived at the training ground and Howard wasn't there. This was unusual in itself as he was an early riser and was always the first to arrive, attending to mail and paperwork before the players arrived.

Mick Hennigan took the training. Nobody said anything but everybody seemed to sense something was up. Eventually Howard arrived, gathered us together and said he'd come to offer his thanks to us all and say goodbye, as he had been sacked.

'You're fucking joking, boss?' blurted Carlton Palmer.

Howard assured Carlton that he wasn't.

Everyone was shocked and genuinely saddened. The general feeling amongst the players was the Leeds board had bowed to a small section of disgruntled fans who knew, as Brian Deane put it, 'bugger all'.

There was the usual woolly statement from directors in such a circumstance, thanking Howard for all his efforts. The word was the board had just run out of patience – this after only five games of the season, which involved two defeats, two victories and a draw away from home.

I felt that Howard had been a 'dead man walking' for some time. In my opinion, the board were waiting for one bad result which would offer an excuse to get rid of Howard. The board must have done some preparation because in little over twenty-four hours, George Graham turned up and was introduced as our new manager.

I remember Tommy Docherty once telling me, 'In football when one door closes another will slam in your face.' I had joined Leeds with a view of furthering my aim to enter management and coaching. When Howard told us he had been sacked, though I was sad, being human, I also immediately reappraised my own situation at the club.

With Howard gone, my opportunity of serving a managerial apprenticeship at Leeds and one day taking over appeared to have gone with him. However, I've always been one to view the glass as being half-full rather than half-empty. I harboured the slim hope that Howard's successor might continue to offer me managerial tutorage. But when George arrived and announced he was bringing in David O'Leary as his assistant, I knew that hope was dead and buried.

In his first talk of note with the players, George told us that from now on things would be different at Leeds United. Well, he was right about that.

George's first three League games were three defeats. In between we struggled to overcome Darlington in the League Cup, only to exit the competition at the next time of asking when beaten 2–1 at home by Aston Villa. Two goals from Rod Wallace gave us a 2–0 win over Nottingham Forest in our next League match but two consecutive defeats meant we slipped to seventeenth. It was all getting a bit fraught and edgy in the dressing-room.

I didn't get off the mark until I scored in a 2–0 victory over Chelsea at the beginning of December. Results did improve in the New Year, only four defeats from eighteen League matches being testimony to that, but of those other fourteen games, nine were drawn and we finished in eleventh place.

George had almost a full season to assess the playing staff and at the end of the campaign told me, and others, that I was not in his plans. He wanted younger players in the side. This didn't come as any surprise to me. George too was a very good coach and I felt I could learn a lot from him but it was obvious I was not going to be given that opportunity.

I still had twelve months of a two-year contract to fulfil, but as 1997–8 approached I knew my future lay elsewhere. When Leeds went on a pre-season tour and left myself, Carlton Palmer, Tony Yeboah, Tony Dorigo and Tomas Brolin at home, I kind of got the message, as did the other lads.

I didn't want to hang around a club where I wasn't wanted. I was still under contract and made a mental note to speak to George when he returned from the tour, with a view to asking if we could terminate the deal. I couldn't see there being a problem as it would do both the club and me a favour. But I was so keen to get away that I was prepared to buy myself out of the remaining year.

I had applied to do my coaching badges, but had no idea what the immediate future held for me. Then something turned up.

I was at home having dinner with Tracy and the boys when the telephone rang. On answering I heard a familiar voice. It was Kenny, who, in his best impenetrable Glaswegian accent, proceeded to make me an offer I couldn't understand.

It turned out that Alan Shearer had sustained a serious ankle ligament injury which was going to keep him out of the game for six months. Kenny was in the process of overhauling the playing staff at Newcastle. In terms of strikers he had the flamboyant football butterfly Faustino Asprilla, Danish international Jon

Tomasson but needed a more experienced player to lead the line on a stop-gap basis until Shearer recovered. With the Premiership, two domestic cups and the European Cup to contest, Kenny felt he needed to bolster his squad with a striker he could trust to get on with the job. Would I be interested in joining for six or seven months?

My dad wasn't keen for me to enter management. He felt managers were cast aside by impatient clubs before they had a proper chance to show what they could do and, I suppose, he had a point. We discussed the Newcastle opportunity and Dad was all for it, but really I'd already made up my mind that I was going to help Kenny out.

As the deal was of a temporary nature, Newcastle put me up in the Ramside Hotel just outside Durham, deep in the heart of Sunderland territory. I drove to training every day and, when the season got underway, travelled home for a few days after a game on Saturday or Sunday to spend time with Tracy, Jonathan, who was now eight, and Daniel, who was coming up to four.

I made my Newcastle debut in the second match of the season, a 1–0 victory over Aston Villa. I was made to feel very welcome by the players and by those great Geordie fans, which helped me settle in straight away. Newcastle had a decent side. Goalkeeper Shay Given and defender Steve Watson were young players of great promise, while the likes of David Batty, John Beresford, Robert Lee and Keith Gillespie knew how to get through a game at the highest level. At the heart of defence was the Belgian Phillipe Albert, he of the moustache and inscrutable expression. A great guy and a tremendous defender, but not a person noted for his humour. As the saying went, 'If you can make Phillipe laugh, you can knit with sawdust.'

It's a strange feeling when you know you're at a club

temporarily. It's not that you feel insecure, just that there is never a sense of truly belonging. At the back of your mind is the thought: 'What am I going to be doing with my life in six months?'

However, for me, that thought was not particularly disconcerting. Financially I was OK, and I had embarked upon my long-term goal of becoming a fully qualified UEFA coach. Though I only had a short-term contract and was nearing my thirty-sixth birthday I knew I was more fortunate than most players on short-term deals. When I read of much younger players being given twelve- or even six-month contracts at clubs, I do wonder how this affects their mindset. I suppose there is an argument for saying it concentrates the mind, that they have to give their all otherwise they know they'll be out of a job. That said, for a player to be happy and give his best he needs some level of security.

In October I scored in a 2–0 win against Hull City in the League Cup. In the scheme of things, the result and the fact I had managed to score made little in the way of headlines, but the goal was an important milestone in my career. I had equalled Sir Geoff Hurst's all-time individual record of forty-nine League Cup goals. Given top clubs were beginning to field teams of squad players in the League Cup, I felt it might be some time before anyone beat this record, if ever.

I had thought my days of European football were over, but I enjoyed a swansong when chosen to play against PSV Eindhoven in Holland. It wasn't the best of nights for Newcastle, as we lost 1–0. It was extremely disappointing as we had beaten Barcelona 3–2 in the previous group match. That night was marked by a fantastic hat-trick from Faustino Asprilla who, during his time on Tyneside, had been notoriously inconsistent. The following day I offered my congratulations to Faustino, who asked if I had any advice for him.

'Yeah, retire now,' I joked.

In January, with Alan Shearer close to a return, Kenny named me as substitute for Newcastle's third round FA Cup tie at Everton. The game was goalless when he called me into action early in the second half. No sooner did I set foot on the pitch when I was greeted with a chorus of booing from the Everton fans, a reception that was repeated every time I touched the ball. After sixty-seven minutes, Keith Gillespie pulled the ball across goal. Reeling back the years, I made ground to slide the ball past Thomas Myhre. As I watched the ball settle in the back of the net (to near-silence) I couldn't help thinking back to when I was a fifteen-year-old playing for Chester 'A' in the Lancashire League. My response then to overly physical play and threats from seasoned pros was to score against them to show their intimidating tactics had no effect on me. Likewise, my response to the booing I received from certain section of Everton supporters left me thinking that although my career in the game had changed my life and me as a person, in a curious way, I was still the same Ian Rush of my teen years. We all have some salt of our youth in us.

My goal in Newcastle's FA Cup win at Everton proved to be my last goal in top-flight football. I thought it somewhat fitting that my last goal should have been against Everton, fiercest rivals of the club I loved, and against whom I had always done so well.

Later that month, Alan Shearer returned to the Newcastle first team. Such had been the severity of his injury it took him some time to get back into the swing of things. Alan being Alan, he even-tually rediscovered his form and recommenced doing what he was best at – scoring goals.

I warmed to Alan. He's an honest, down-to-earth guy and for me he's up there with the all-time great goal-scorers of English football. In many ways he reminded me of an old-time centre-forward, though such was his talent he was much more besides.

I remember watching him play in the 2–1 defeat of Barnsley. He biffed and banged around the Barnsley penalty area all afternoon. He eventually got a goal and I saw his face immediately light up with the joy and satisfaction of it all. Rather than then take off like a Olympic sprinter, pushing aside teammates who wanted to proffer their congratulations, Alan simply raised an arm, looked down to the ground and smiled with satisfaction, as if he had sated a great inner need. It was a feeling I knew only well, but from now on it would be confined to my memory.

In March 1998 I spent a month on loan at Sheffield United. My old Liverpool team-mate Nigel Spackman was manager, had some injury problems and asked if I would help out for a few weeks, which I was only too pleased to do. I thought my brief sojourn at Bramall Lane would be my final bow, but not quite.

In the summer of 1998 I received a call from former Liverpool full-back and twice European Cup Winner, Joey Jones. Joey was the Wrexham coach and, knowing I was studying to be a coach, asked if I would consider going to Wrexham to help in the development of their young players.

The Wrexham manager was Brian Flynn and his assistant the former Manchester City centre-forward, Kevin Reeves. I got on very well with both of them. I went to Wrexham primarily to gain some practical experience of coaching, but Brian persuaded me to sign as a player in the event of emergency. Clubs such as Wrexham are in a constant state of emergency, however, and I ended up playing eighteen games for the first team. I no longer had the speed I was once possessed, so played the majority of those games in midfield where, I would like to think, the young players about me benefited from my experience.

I enjoyed my year with Wrexham, particularly my work on the coaching side. It was great to work with Joey who, in addition to being a fine coach, is one of football's great characters. He had me laughing every day with stories from his career and of the players he had come up against.

One of the stories Joey told me was of joining a junior side in North Wales when still at school. On entering the dressing-room Joey sat next to the team's goalkeeper, who he described as 'a chubby bastard with unkempt hair and a po-faced expression'.

'Hi, my name's Joey Jones,' said Joey.

'I'm Neville Southall,' replied the keeper.

On another occasion we all turned up for light training on Christmas Day in preparation for a Boxing Day fixture. When I turned-up there was a chorus of 'Merry Christmas' from everyone, except for Joey who, clapping his hands together with glee announced, 'It's a boy!'

I might have stayed a little longer than my twelve months had I not been presented with the opportunity of another irresistible experience.

The top Australian club, Sydney Olympic, had offered me a short-term contract. As Tracy and I did not want to uproot the boys from their schooling, I went out to Australia on my own. I was thirty-eight years old but still fit enough to make a telling contribution to games for Sydney Olympic. The city itself struck me as an energetic, cosmopolitan city with a smalltown, easy-going charm, and the standard of football was decent enough. One of the young players who caught my eye was a lad by the name of Bret Emerton. I enjoyed my time at the club, and loved the Australian experience. Obviously I did miss Tracy and the boys but vowed that one day we would visit the country as a family. While I was in Australia I received a telephone call from Liverpool's Chief Executive, Rick Parry. Rick informed me that following the departure of Phil Thompson and Sammy Lee, Rafael Benitez was looking for someone to assist him with coaching and to help from the bench. Rick asked if I would be interested and I had no hesitation in saying 'Yes'. The thought of returning to Liverpool and working alongside 'Rafa' was my dream job. My elation, though, was to last only a matter of forty-eight hours, when Rick rang to tell me the club had appointed Alex Miller to help Rafa. Needless to say I was very disappointed but I got the impression the door had not been closed and I continue to harbour the hope of returning to Anfield in some capacity one day.

On returning to England I continued to my coaching courses, eventually qualifying for my UEFA Pro Licence which gave me a great sense of achievement.

In 2003 I was offered an opportunity that excited me beyond belief. Liverpool manager Gerard Houllier contacted me and asked if I would return to Anfield to coach his strikers, who included Emile Heskey, Milan Baros, El Hadji Diouf and, of course, Michael Owen.

I rate Gerard as one of the best coaches in the world. He's very astute and cerebral, and is constantly coming up with new ideas. I remember first discussing the job with Gerard and asking what he hoped I would achieve with, for example, Michael Owen. He told me that if I could improve Michael's ability as a striker by, say, half a per cent, then I would have accomplished something special. Some players you can improve a great deal but when dealing with the very best players, even a modicum of improvement in their play can produce remarkable results.

I found my work with the Liverpool strikers challenging but very rewarding. Michael, Emile and co were accomplished, top-class players, but even the best have a capacity to learn and improve.

The actual coaching apart, one of the key elements to working with strikers is to engender confidence. Mistakes tend to have an effect on confidence. I kept telling the lads I was never afraid to miss and that they had to have the same mindset. The striker that doesn't miss a chance doesn't exist, but it is crucial to learn from your mistakes. To examine what it was you did wrong and implement a solution so that you minimise the odds of making that same mistake again.

Working under Gerard Houllier was an education for me. One of the many things he told me was that in the modern game, you must give players the best of everything. The best training techniques, the best coaching, the best facilities, accommodation, diet and so on, so that they have no excuse for not performing to the optimum of their ability.

Training is high tempo because the contemporary game is so intense. That said, you have to be very careful in the composition of a training session, so that what you are asking the players to do does not result in them sustaining an injury. Today, more than ever, I read of players sidelined due to injuries picked up on the training field.

Gerard demonstrated to me that some of the more traditional elements of the British game can produce better results when aligned to the Continental approach to coaching and tactics and a more considered approach to the conditioning and preparation of players. In short, you look to combine physical attributes with excellent technique, skill, pace and athleticism, and that indefinable element, football nous.

In this era of increasingly peripatetic players, Gerard was keen to foster an attitude at Anfield whereby every player felt strongly connected to the 'project' or 'team goal' because the game had changed in such a way clubs lacked the wherewithal to guarantee club loyalty. Money is important, of course, but what was being done at Liverpool to keep players highly motivated was engendering the feeling of being close to achieving real success. To have this philosophy ingrained into the culture of the dressing-room and players' minds will result in the very best players being motivated to give of their best.

I really enjoyed my time working under Gerard but I had to get out there and find more coaching and hopefully management work, and soon an opportunity came my way.

In August 2004 I was appointed manager of Chester City, then, as now, in League Two. It seemed fitting that I should begin my managerial career at the club at which I had begun my playing career. I hadn't applied for the job but had intimated in a press interview that it was of great interest to me. The chairman, Stephen Vaughan, had been made aware of this and he rang to invite me for an interview. I thought I gave a decent account of myself on the day and seemingly the Chester board thought so, too, as Mr Vaughan offered me the job there and then.

The only disappointment was when I heard Mark Lawrenson making disparaging remarks about my potential as manager on television, at one point saying, 'He has no chance'. Mark is entitled to his opinions, of course, but I had not spoken to him, nor seen him, in more than ten years and was saddened to hear such a remark before I had even set foot inside Chester. I spoke to one or two former Liverpool players who were of the mind Mark still thought of me as the callow youth he had known from our early days together at Anfield. Much had changed in that time, not least myself.

In the twenty-five years since I had left Chester much had changed, of course. Not least of which was the fact that the club had a new home, the Saunders Honda stadium, as it was called then, a small, tidy ground situated off Bumpers Lane. The ground, with a retail park and a household waste site as its neighbours, has nothing in the way of charm. It's purely functional and utilitarian. I find this of many of the stadiums built in recent years. They're smarter, safer and have better facilities for supporters, but, like an airport, they never seem to have any character or spirit.

I brought in my old Wales teammate, Mark Aizelwood, as my assistant. I was really excited to have been given my first managerial appointment but had no illusions as to the size of the task I was taking on. I wouldn't be working with players of the quality of Michael Owen and Emile Heskey, of course, but the Chester squad was of decent quality, and I was confident of improving every player and the team as a whole. I didn't feel any great tide of emotion in going back as manager to the club at which I had started my playing career. I was so intent on doing a good job, and had so many ideas and plans I wanted to put into action, that any emotional ties for the club were overshadowed.

I succeeded Mark Wright, who left the club some four weeks into the new season. Chester had already played five league matches without a victory and been knocked out of the League Cup before I took the reins, so I knew I had to hit the ground running. I told every player this was a new start for the club but, more importantly, for them. What had gone before, how they had played, did not matter. From now on I would be assessing the strength of the squad and everyone would have an opportunity to show me what he could do.

The players responded well. I wish I could say I won my first game as a manager but we lost 3–1 at Boston United. However, the game gave me an insight into what was needed. I made three changes for our next game against Macclesfield Town. We played well enough without creating many chances, but just when I thought we would have to settle for a draw, up popped Danny Collins in the dying seconds to give me my first win. This gave me as much satisfaction as any goal I had scored.

Victory over Macclesfield was the beginning of a run that saw Chester remain unbeaten for ten League and Cup matches in which we reached the quarter-finals of the LDV Vans Trophy courtesy of an excellent win at Sheffield Wednesday. In October I even won the League Two manager of the month award. The confidence of the players grew from game to game and they seemed to really enjoy the training and coaching. A lot of the ideas I introduced were new to the players, but they responded in a very positive way and I sensed the general feeling among them was we had a bright future.

Mark and I also spent a lot of time working with the young Chester players. At every possible opportunity we conducted extra coaching sessions in the afternoon. I'd arrive at the ground early to attend to mail and paperwork and discuss arrangements for forthcoming games, work with the players throughout the day, and at night was out and about watching games in the hope of seeing players who could do us a job.

We went to see Liverpool and Everton reserves and the second strings of other League clubs, hoping to see a good player who was surplus to requirements. We picked up Robbie Foy on loan from Liverpool, Dave Bayliss from Luton, Andy Nicholas from Swindon Town and signed Ashley Sestanovich from Sheffield United on a permanent basis. In the main, however, we trawled the grounds of the lower divisions and non-league. Again this bore fruit. Goalkeeper Chris McKenzie joined from Telford United and made the transition from non-league to Football League without too much difficulty.

To accommodate these new signings and keep the wage bill to budget I had to move players on. Andrew Watson went to Forest Green Rovers, Kevin McIntyre to Macclesfield, and I did a nice bit of business in selling Danny Collins to Sunderland for £150,000, Kevin Ellison to Hull City for £100,000 and Daryl Clare to Boston United for £50,000. In the first few months the club generated £300,000 from transfers, with no outlay on new players other than signing-on fees.

Having enjoyed such a good start, results were not as I had wanted in the second half of the season. We did reach the third round of the FA Cup but fate did not provide us with a money-spinning tie to get the city buzzing. Bournemouth away was one of those ties you knew would be tough and not, by any stretch of the imagination, a money-spinner. In event we gave a good account of ourselves but went down to a team who, at the time, were challenging for promotion to the Championship.

At the end of February we were beaten 5–0 at Shrewsbury Town. Shrewsbury is a derby match for Chester and the margin of our defeat incensed a section of our supporters and, seemingly, others. It was at this point that I became aware I did not enjoy the full backing of the board. There were calls for me to resign, but, having been at the club for only six months, there was no way I was going to do that. I carried on.

Towards the end of March we went three games undefeated, beating Notts County 3–2 and Bury 2–1, and drawing 0–0 at Mansfield Town. We then travelled to Darlington and lost by the only goal of the game.

On our return from Darlington, Mark Aizelwood was sacked. That did it for me. Chester were safe from relegation but I felt my position as manager had been compromised by the dismissal of my right-hand man so I went to see the Chester board and tendered my resignation. The chairman, Stephen Vaughan, refused to accept it and tried to persuade me to stay on. In my opinion, however, Mark's dismissal indicated to me that I wasn't being allowed to be my own man, to appoint or dismiss my own staff. Such matters, it appeared, were out of my hands. I listened to what Mr Vaughan had to say but told him I felt my position as manager had become untenable and while I appreciated his attempts to persuade me to continue, felt I had no alternative but to stick by my decision to resign.

Of course it hurt to leave Chester. I was annoyed by their dismissal of Mark, the reasons for which, to this day, I am still not aware. As the manager, I felt the responsibility for the team was mine. What irritated me most, however, was the fact I had just begun to lay down what I believed were strong foundations that would ensure the long-term future of the club.

True, results were not as I had hoped, but Chester were not in danger of relegation and after six months I hadn't expected us to be challenging for promotion. I felt that would happen the following season when the initial work we had done began to bear fruit.

Stephen Vaughan and his directors acted in what they believed were the best interests of the club, as I had. It was sad that we had different ideas on how best this could be achieved. Where football managers and chairmen are concerned, it is ever thus. That said, I would like to thank Stephen Vaughan for the opportunity he gave me of my first managerial appointment; there were no hard feelings on my departure and we have remained good friends.

My experience at Chester didn't put me off management. It hadn't worked out the way I had hoped, far from it, but I had enjoyed this brief spell in the job. I felt I communicated my ideas well to both players and staff and had learned much about man-

management from Bob Paisley and Kenny. I didn't enter into it naively believing all would come good overnight, but I had every confidence in my ability to do a good job at Chester and just hoped I would be given the greatest asset a manager can be given – time.

In every problem there's a gift. Far from putting me off management, my experience at Chester fuelled my enthusiasm to enter management again some day. I enjoy coaching but I would love the day-to-day involvement of making the decisions, working with players and bringing about individual and collective improvement; planning and putting into place a strong and productive youth policy; pitting my wits against those of other manager and coaches.

People often ask me, 'What is the biggest difference between being a coach and a manager?' I can tell you: as a coach you never win so many games of golf against the players in your charge. Joking apart, they are two entirely different roles, but I feel I now have the necessary skills to fulfil either and make a success of whichever path I take.

During my time with Chester I'd been sounded out for the vacant job of manager of Wales. To manage Wales was a dream job for me but I declined an interest as I felt a loyalty to Chester. I had plans for the club and wanted to see them through. Besides which, I felt the possibility of managing Wales, fantastic as it was, had come a little too early. I wanted to gain more experience of coaching.

These days my coaching takes me all over the world, particularly to the Middle East and the Far East. In September 2007, I was appointed Elite Performance Director for the Welsh Football Trust. In essence my role is to help develop young players for the national teams. As a patriot, I was delighted to be offered the opportunity of working with talented young Welsh players.

I now work with young players under the age of sixteen. I love the job and find it very rewarding. Amongst other things I pass on skills and technique that I hope will develop the youngsters into good players and, in some cases, very good players. My work involves not only individual performance but also positional play, tactics and formations, and preparation for games. In essence my job is to improve young players and I like to believe good progress has been made on that score.

I teach the different techniques of how to strike the ball, push pass, driving the ball, volleying, follow-through, chip, use of the heel and toe, and so on. I'm not looking for players to master every one of these techniques – many top pros don't – but the more you are able to execute the better the player you will be. I may be stating the obvious in saying football is a team game but in order to play as a cohesive unit players have to be adept at passing the ball, and so I also spend a lot of time on timing, direction, speed, height and weighting a pass. Other work involves control of the ball, anticipation, creating time and space, shooting, heading and what some might think to be the lost arts of tackling and dribbling.

Regarding shooting I keep repeating: never be afraid to miss. Shooting and goal-scoring are partly instinctive but there are techniques to be learned. Firing off the shot as early as you can, aiming low as it's harder for a goalkeeper to get down and execute a save, when and how to go for passing the ball into the net or for power, using both feet, anticipation and alertness in and around the box.

I often hear people talk about a team playing to a certain formation. But one aspect of a coach's work is to know his players and decide upon the system of play that will utilise their talents to the best advantage. A system or pattern of play that works well against one team might not be appropriate against another side, so you have to be flexible without disrupting the cohesion of your team.

Above all I want football to be fun, particularly for youngsters. For all I took my work very seriously, fun is what I had as a player. If a player feels too restricted he or she won't express themselves on the pitch and the game will be devoid of imagination.

I am fortunate that my role as Elite Performance Director also enables me to coach elsewhere. In addition, as and when, I do media work for Sky and continue to fulfil my commitment to Nike.

I'm often sounded out about vacant management and coaching jobs but, as yet, the right offer (and I don't mean money) hasn't come along. People often ask me why I would ever want to return to management or coach an English club. My reply is always the same: 'If you know you don't have to ask, and if you ask then you will never know.'

Tracy and I and the boys still live in the house we bought on my return from Juventus. Jonathan is now nineteen and studying for a degree in Psychology at university. He's a promising footballer himself but I have never pushed him in that direction. Whatever he decides to do in life then Tracy and I will support him. Daniel is fifteen and coming up to a very important stage in his education. Again, whatever he chooses to do Tracy and I will offer him all the encouragement we can.

I had a great career as a player and achieved far more than I ever thought possible. I loved every minute of it but I love my family most of all and I feel eternally blessed to have them.

Football has changed since I played my last game in 2000. It's a good thing. Without change football would be sterile and predictable, a game without drama, spirit, creativity and imagination.

I am often asked for my opinion of football and the players of today. I think the modern game is fantastic and we are fortunate to have many highly skilled players in the English game. However, not all changes have led to the improvement of the game.

In my early days at Liverpool there were constant calls for football to be run more like business. Well, it's a business now, a multi-million-pound one. I don't have a problem with football driving business, but we should not allow business – especially related business – to drive football. That does concern me.

I'm particularly against the idea of Premiership clubs playing matches abroad to make even more money. It smacks of colonisation to me. Only a handful of our top clubs have a large following abroad. Such an idea runs roughshod over supporters who attend games week in week out. In addition, we are supposedly helping to develop football across the world, particularly in the Far East and Africa, not imposing our game on other countries.

I am also concerned about the number of people who own clubs or have executive positions within clubs or governing bodies who have no history of involvement in the game before they managed to acquire these positions of authority. Such people are attracted to our game for one reason: to make money for themselves. They have little or no idea of about the culture, tradition and fabric of our game, qualities which mean so much to players and supporters alike. They talk of 'brands', the need for 'blue sky thinking', 'B2B variables and consistents'. They have brought the culture of the businesses they were involved in and imposed it upon our beautiful game, in so doing often out-pricing and alienating the bedrock support.

As for branding, perhaps the most ludicrous example is the re-naming of the divisions within the Football League. What was wrong with First, Second and Third Divisions? For me it's a case of the Emperor's new clothes.

The grossly unfair distribution of wealth within our game worries me, too. I started my playing career at Chester and still have great fondness for the club. To me such clubs are as much a part of our game as Manchester United or Liverpool. That it will take a Championship club over thirty years to earn the same amount from TV revenue as the club that finishes bottom of the Premiership earns in a single season can never be right or fair.

Manchester United and Chelsea contesting the European Champions League Final did the hubris of our game no harm, though it is ironic that in a year when two English clubs contested the final of Europe's premier club tournament not one home nation qualified for the finals of Euro 2008.

I tend to think one of the reasons for English clubs doing so well in Europe while our national sides struggle to overcome the likes of Israel and Cyprus – and often don't – is that our players perform better alongside top-quality overseas teammates and, perhaps, under managers and coaches who are more astute.

I think the majority of overseas players who have come into our game have contributed in a very positive way. The same goes for managers and coaches. It is worrying, however, that little over 30 per cent of all starting line-ups on any given weekend in the Premiership are home-grown players. But the dilemma is: do you support and develop your home-grown youngsters or buy fully-formed stars? I would like to believe the answer is a bit of both. Arsenal do this, although it is also true Wenger and his staff comb the world in search of the best available young talent.

To get a successful and productive youth policy up and running can take five years. Many clubs, as I found to my cost, never give a manager that time or anywhere near it – Crewe Alexandra in the case of Dario Gradi being a rare exception – and just think of the dozens of good players Crewe produced over the years, from

David Platt, Rob Jones, Robbie Savage and Neil Lennon to Danny Murphy and Dean Ashton. In developing young talent you have to invest time and expertise as well as money. With many managers given a year or, even less, to show what they can do at a club, it is little wonder that many opt to buy a finished article from abroad.

I'm not one to say football in my day was better than today, only that it was different and this was because the game was different. Football today boasts great players, the majority of which are fine role models for young people. Here I cite Michael Owen, Cristiano Ronaldo, Ryan Giggs, Steven Gerrard and Jamie Carragher, to name but a few. The same can be said of those players who have not scaled the very summits of the game. What better role model for an aspiring young player could there be than Dean Windass?

I don't have any regrets from my playing years. How I could I? I was paid to do what I enjoyed doing most – scoring goals. Whichever team you support or play in, enjoy your football. Every game is an opportunity to create memories, which, with the passing of the years, will be a treasure to you.

Life is good. As such, this is a book with happy ending. I am very optimistic for the future of football and that of my own, for, as I have always believed, happy endings make for good beginnings.

Records and Statistics

SENIOR CLUBS

SEASON	CLUB	APPEARANCES	GOALS
1979–80	Chester City	39	17
1980–7 and 1988–96	Liverpool	616	346
1987–8	Juventus	32	14
1996–7	Leeds United	36	3
1997–8	Newcastle United	11	2
1998	Sheffield United (loan)	4	0
1998–9	Wrexham	18	0
1999–2000	Sydney Olympic	2	1

INTERNATIONAL

1980–96	Wales	73	28

CLUBS MANAGED

2004–5   Chester City

CURRENT

2007–current   Elite Performance Director, Welsh Football Trust

RECORDS

All–time record Liverpool goal-scorer in all competitions with 346 goals. Second top goal-scorer for Liverpool in League football with 229 goals (Roger Hunt, 245 goals).

Record FA Cup final goal-scorer with 5 goals.

Second highest FA Cup goal-scorer of all time and highest in the twentieth century with 44 goals (39 for Liverpool, 4 for Chester City and 1 for Newcastle United).

Joint record League Cup goal-scorer (with Sir Geoff Hurst) with 49 goals.

First player to win 5 League Cup winners' medals.

Record goal-scorer for Wales with 28 goals.

Record goal-scorer in Merseyside derby matches with 25 goals against Everton.

Record transfer fee received by Chester City (£300,000).

HONOURS

First Division (Premiership equivalent) Championship medals: 1981–2, 1982–3, 1983–4, 1985–6, 1989–90

FA Cup winner: 1985–6,1988–9,1991–2

European Cup winner: 1983–4

League Cup winner: 1980–1,1981–2,1982–3,1983–4,1994–5

Charity Shield winner: 1982–3,1985–6,1989–90,1990–1

RUNNER-UP

First Division: 1986–7, 1988–9, 1990–1

FA Cup: 1995–6

League Cup: 1986–7

European Cup: 1984–5

Charity Shield: 1983–4, 1984–5, 1992–3

European Super Cup: 1984–5

InterContinental Cup (World Club Championship): 1984–5

PERSONAL HONOURS

Wales: 73 caps, 1980–96 (also captained Wales)

PFA Young Player of the Year: 1983

PFA Player's Player of the Year: 1984

Football Writers' Association Footballer of the Year: 1984

European Golden Boot Award: 1984

UEFA Goal-scoring Legend Award: 1989

Liverpool AFC captain: 1993–6

MBE (for services to football)

Included in Football League 100 League Legends: 1998

Inducted into the English Football Hall of Fame: 2006

LIVERPOOL CAREER

APPEARANCES

SEASON	LEAGUE	FA CUP	LGE CUP	EUROPE	MISC	TOTAL
1980–1	7	0	1	1	0	9
1981–2	32	3	10	4	0	49
1982–3	34	3	8	5	1	51
1983–4	41	2	12	9	1	65
1984–5	28	6	1	7	2	44
1985–6	40	8	6	0	2	56
1986–7	42	3	9	0	3	57
1988–9	24	2	4	0	2	32
1989–90	36	8	3	0	1	48
1990–1	37	7	3	0	1	48
1991–2	18	5	3	5	0	31
1992–3	32	1	4	4	1	42
1993–4	42	2	5	0	0	49
1994–5	36	7	7	0	0	50
1995–6	20	4	2	3	0	29
MATCH TOTAL	469	61	78	38	14	660

(MISC/Miscellaneous = Charity Shield, InterContinental Cup, Centenary Trophy, European Super Cup etc)

OTHER

Ian played more games against Everton (36) than against any other opposition.

He started 630 games for Liverpool and was substituted on 36 occasions. He was named as a substitute on 52 occasions and was called into action in 30 of these games.

Ian made his international debut for Wales on 21 May 1980 against Scotland.

He holds the UEFA Pro Licence, the highest coaching qualification awarded by European football's governing body.

TRIVIA

When Ian joined Wrexham as a player/coach in 1998–9 his one of his fellow coaches at the club was Cliff Sear, who had been Ian's youth team coach and mentor at his first club Chester City.

From 1980 to 1987 Liverpool never lost a game in which Ian scored – a total of 145 matches. The run ended in the 1987 League Cup final.

In a 2006 poll conducted by thefa.com Ian was voted Number One All–Time FA Cup Hero.

He is one of the few footballers to have a rock band named after him, not Canadian rocksters Rush, but Welsh indie band Ian Rush.

As with George Best (Northern Ireland) and Ryan Giggs (Wales), though he played in the qualifying stages of four World Cups (1982, 1986, 1990 and 1994) and three European Championships (1984, 1988, 1992), he never appeared in the finals of a major international tournament as Wales failed to qualify on each occasion.

INDEX